Jim Emerton

Pigeon
MAN

*Notes, tips and observations from a lifetime
of pigeon rearing and racing*

Jim Emerton

Pigeon
MAN

*Notes, tips and observations from a lifetime
of pigeon rearing and racing*

MEREO
Cirencester

Mereo Books

1A The Wool Market Dyer Street Cirencester Gloucestershire GL7 2PR
An imprint of Memoirs Publishing www.mereobooks.com

Pigeon Man: 978-1-86151-691-6

First published in Great Britain in 2016
by Mereo Books, an imprint of Memoirs Publishing

The address for Memoirs Publishing Group Limited can be found at
www.memoirspublishing.com

The Memoirs Publishing Group Ltd Reg. No. 7834348

The Memoirs Publishing Group supports both The Forest Stewardship Council®
(FSC®) and the PEFC® leading international forest-certification organisations. Our
books carrying both the FSC label and the PEFC® and are printed on FSC®-certified
paper. FSC® is the only forest-certification scheme supported by the leading
environmental organisations including Greenpeace. Our paper procurement policy
can be found at www.memoirspublishing.com/environment

Typeset in 10/14pt Century Schoolbook
by Wiltshire Associates Publisher Services Ltd. Printed and bound in Great Britain
by Printondemand-Worldwide, Peterborough PE2 6XD

My thanks and gratitude go to the influences of Mensa Special Interest Groups eg Green Scene, Elimar Pigeons, The Racing Pigeon magazine, and all the people whose paths have crossed paths with me in a rich and diverse life and who may have enjoyed my writing.

Jim Emerton

CONTENTS

ONE

—

PIGEON RACING FOR BEGINNERS

WATER FOR THE BIRD

All pigeons need access to water; without it they will die. Dorothy and I topped our drinking containers daily. In my opinion it is not necessary to give fresh lots at intervals during the day. We would clean out the biofilm from the 5pt plastic containers with wire wool. My mother did this for us until she was 91. When the water froze we would hit the ice with a hammer or melt it with hot water.

Normally pigeons drink less in colder, wintry weather, ie in temperatures less than 50F. Conversely they will drink more above 70F. I prefer natural rain water but most tap water will do. When racing, birds will drink from gutters, ponds, lakes and rivers and other people's lofts. My birds, living naturally, could drink outside the loft as well, and also from the bath water.

A virus can run through your loft whether you are strict with your hygiene or not. It may help to sterilise the drinkers with, say Milton, once per week. For long distances I liked birds that could live wild especially at marathon distances (over 700 miles). I would advise novices to be scrupulous about cleanliness at first.

TOUGH NUTS

To survive a full racing programme of competition you need to be pretty durable and tough minded. I think many train too hard and find it difficult to last a season. To remedy this, you can specialise and pick your racepoints. For many years I specialised in two or three races per year; all the rest were trainers. There are some wonderful pigeons which fly long or marathon distances against the odds, often sent by the same old stalwart fanciers. I admire Neil Bush for his marathon performances in the NFC Grand National since 1982. A man with pure long-term focus, and a visionary. His sustained record in 700-mile racing is unsurpassed, and the amazing thing is that he seeks no publicity to embellish his ego.

I've had a few marathon tough nuts in my time, eg Oddball, which was only two hours or so behind Brian Denney's Tuffnut in 2002 in Pau, 735 miles. It was a head wind all the way. Another was Dark Enchantment, which flew Barcelona at 879 miles with a wobbly flight. These are pigeons which become your favourites and are often your strain makers. I love breeding around such birds.

I would call the Barcelona man Frank Kay a tough nut with his ruthless marathon approach. However as a friend, I find him a man of profound and deep feelings and convictions.

Keep racing – it will steel you up!

FAVOURITES

We are sentimental beings, and over time we will attach ourselves to our favourites. For children and ladies in particular these can be the pretty, good-looking ones, or those with a distinctive character and personality. Pretty soon afterwards our good breeders and racers will take their place in our affections, since they perform to our desires. If you are kind you will look after and treasure your favourite birds until they pass away – this tells a lot about you as a person.

My favourites have been well described, yet I will mention the 'Iron Hen' who would fly down the garden, land and sit on my head. Some wonderful, quiet, tame (like me) birds have come down from her. You should keep your birds nice and relaxed and tame – this will reward you, especially in races over 500 miles.

One great beauty was Dancing Boy. A very vital, gay pied young cock – he jumped up and down off the floor when I went into the loft. Someone down south bought him and should let me know. Personally I like all birds, yet I persist with my favourites.

Peter Fannan, a well-known top York fancier, will have four young birds for a young, local fancier (York area) free of charge. The results of the birds racing and breeding, and the fancier, can feature in 'Squeakers' Corner'.

JUDGEMENT

It is easy to cast an opinion on a pigeon as to its suitability for breeding or racing, both in the loft and in the show pen. In reality many nice handling birds with good bodies, silky feathering and all the external attributes are useless for racing or breeding. Cast aside your subjective opinions and send the racers to the racepoints, as far as you can. Good pigeons score well in the races and good breeders breed good pigeons. It's amazing how well they seem to look and handle when they have won – judgement is a personal, individual opinion which may be right or wrong. With maturity may come wisdom when you can discern the true nature of things.

We are bombarded by hype and clichés in pigeon advertising. Example, what does 'many winners' mean? How far is distance? What does 'world's best' mean? What does 'champion' mean? What are the reasons for parting with such apparently good birds?

You see, money is behind a whole set of sales tricks. Learn who seems genuine and who not, who is overcharging and who isn't. After a while you may develop a shrewd eye of intuition, then, my friends, you will know. There are very few birds in the UK which will compete at over 800 miles from Barcelona International. Most birds from most sources will fail when put to the test. Can you tell the real nature of things?

EXCUSES

I think we all have, or will have made, excuses: why we have not won races or done well, or had a bad day. It is only human to make these ego-defence mechanisms work. No matter who we are, we are all in it to do well, to achieve, to accomplish. There is an endless variety of excuses from the mundane to the highly creative. Here are some of the many excuses:

It was only a yearling.
It flew round and round and round!
It went up the coast.
A chainsaw started up next door.
I was in the toilet.
A hawk flew over.
It landed on the house.
It went back to the old loft.
The neighbour had some washing out.
I had gone in the house for tea.
It got infected in the transporter.
The convoyer should not have let them go.

Any reason, yes – other than looking at ourselves when insight yields the truth!

WINGS

'O for the wings, the wings of a dove.' Most pigeons are born to fly. There are many wing theories, and that's what they are – theories. The physical aspects of the feathers and bones are pondered over.

Pigeons may have, in relative terms, broad flights, narrow flights, a small or large backwing and various degrees of steps in the flight patterns. People theorise on the aerodynamics of these structures.

Underpinning all the theories is an essential fact, and that is that good winning birds at your chosen distance, from say 30–1000 miles, by definition, have wings that are good enough for the task in hand. It is probably more useful to examine the wings of the good and champion birds, since all wings are different and individual to that particular bird.

Wings are just one aspect of the overall qualities and characteristics of a bird, and should be viewed as part of the whole. I do like to see nice clean flights, free of pests and fret marks.

Birds will recover from minor wing muscle injuries, but not normally from broken bones and tendons. A hen of mine flew Barcelona with top-sided flight, due I think to damaged tendons.

To test, and in reality to prove the wings of your birds, then fly them at your distances. Racing proves everything, rightly or wrongly, about theory.

COLOUR

A fit pigeon has a rainbow of colours; it is a creature of great beauty. Have you noticed how closely-bred families tend to be dominated by a single colour? A variety of colours often indicates cross and outbreeding.

For many years my colony of birds were blue chequers, dark chequers and dark velvets. This was due to related genes and the fact that I could perceive condition on a dark chequer. They were peas in a pod, yet each one was an individual. Now racing pigeons will win in any colour you can think of, yet many fanciers prefer the blues and chequers. I notice the modern trends, disseminating from Louella Pigeon World, notably the grizzle Roland Janssens and the new black birds of the Severi family. With shrewd publicity these attract the eye and will sell well.

I think in practicality you tend to favour the colour of the birds that do well for you, although colour becomes linked with a stream of family.

Some fanciers try to reproduce the colour of a champion,

but a bird of the same colour is not necessarily a good racer. Beauty is in the eye of the beholder.

In the show world, the opals are the magnificent!

RULES

Rules are designed to bring the correct stability and order to racing organisations. They can bring honesty and integrity to pigeon racing, but in practice they are often used and abused and interpreted for the purposes of personal advantage and political power. Rules have a series of words which can be scanned for loopholes or double meanings. Beware of control freaks, who always quote rules – these people will want to dominate the club. Sometimes they cannot fly a kite!

I confess that I don't know to mind any of say the RPRA rules. If you have a good moral sense of right and wrong, you will fall inside the rules. A rule that is often abused is the one referring to 'ungentlemanly conduct' – very many would violate this one. I have seen some hideous battles using rules in an attempt to prove a point or settle a scene, some of which have gone as far as full RPRA Council. They usually leave scars in the form of grudges and chips on shoulders. My advice is to do your own thing and keep clear of jealous disputes that become personal. Use your mind to plough a free furrow for yourself – be a free spirit, be unique!

READING

It is my feeling that many fanciers do not read enough. Everything you need to know is in books, magazines like the BHW and on the net. You really need to read the work of the experts like Zsolt Talaber (vet) and the reports on top fliers like Mark Gilbert and Neil Bush. Check out who is at the top of the world of pigeon racing (not just the UK) and learn how they got there. Any fool can have a website!

Try and look at the material of fanciers who have been selected by others for their contribution to the sport. Look at Elimar, Prestige Pigeons, IPRR and ask.com Pigeon Encyclopaedia for expert input. As for videos and DVDs, which are largely visual rather than verbal, I recommend the series by the renowned John Halstead, who is a bright lad and a great flier.

In terms of books I enjoyed *Roads to Rome* by Camons Stansfield (ask him for a copy) and *Healthy Pigeons* by Shraag. Place copious amounts of salt on a lot of what you hear at the club. For starters take out a subscription with the BHW for a Thursday delivery.

As an offshoot to reading, can you use your invitation to read behind the lines; can you read the weather and are you a good reader of human character? If so you will be wise! Make sure you absorb the best of reading.

Most of the outstanding fanciers, those who become household names, are specialists with pigeons. Trying to compete at every race often weakens your overall position, with some exceptions to this rule of thumb. For many years I entered in two races only at 466 miles and then either at 687, 735, 737 or 879 miles. The 466-mile race was to condition the birds for my desired race point. All other races were training only. Having said this, I started off with club racing and was a young bird specialist. I see racing as a journey from club to international racing. After a while and with success you learn to target the important and prestigious races, after due consideration of the old saying 'small fish are sweet'. We know that many people will always be content with club racing and this will always be the case. The key element of course is to enjoy what you do!

Good examples of excellent specialists in the UK and Ireland are Ronnie Williamson of Ireland at middle distance, Neil Bush at marathon 700-mile plus racing and now Frank Kay at 869 miles Barcelona International. All of these men have reaped and will continue to reap the benefits of all the eggs in the basket, out and out focus and dedication to set goals. My advice from experience is aim for the top and specialise and specialise.

Note: My trophy in the Single Bird Club for Barcelona over 800 miles is yet to be won...

INFLUENCES

As near beginners you will be influenced by what you read, see and hear. We may think we know it all or are the best; yet we are influenced by articles in books, on the web and in magazines. I think it is important to realise the sort of racing we want to excel at and learn all we can from the top people. The articles written by scientists like Zsolt Talaber are excellent and well researched. Scribes often interview some of the top flyers like Mark Gilbery and Ronnie Williamson. Look for the well written and deep answers. There is so much information out there, and some of it is good and factual and can be put into practice.

Before you take on board what people say, check the credentials of the person carefully – how good are they? It is likely that this stage your biggest influence about pigeons will come from your parents, grandparents and friends. Eventually and with patience you will reach your level of success and individual judgement. Some useful websites are: Prestige Pigeons, Elimar, IPRR and ask.com Pigeon Encyclopaedia. I trust I have used my 'influence' to good effect!

WHAT IS DISTANCE?

In strict terms distance refers to the space between two points or things. With pigeons it is a vague term, often to denote a long way. Its use is often random and arbitrary with no close definition. Attempting to bring more accurate meaning to the term, I will divide distance into sprint, middle, long and marathon. My favourite of course is marathon, yet I have enjoyed races at all levels up to this. Sprint racing would be up to 250 miles, middle 250 to 500 miles, long distance 500-700 miles and marathon over 700 miles.

I regularly clocked at 466 miles but never called it long-distance and it always left me wanting. However it is ideal for preparing marathon candidates. At York we are placed beautifully for races up to over 800 miles, whereas the south coast flyers have to go to Barcelona for near marathon or 700 miles for that extra distance. I think the secret is to fly as far as you can to test and improve your birds, although what I say has bias towards the extra long distance. With good management there are many birds capable of huge distances and 800-mile racing is not out of the question. It is relative and 100 miles on a tough day seems a long way, does it not?

HOURS OF DARKNESS

Pigeons often don't worry about darkness. They will fly, depending on the conditions, any time of the day or night. Sometimes, and perhaps helped by street lights and starlight, racers will keep going into the night and the small hours.

Organisations make rules and try and make racing fair. Captain Cutcliffe formulated an hours-of-darkness model, later taken up by the RPRA. The times vary with the time of year and times are different for the international races into the UK.

In reality a pigeon arrives when it arrives and often in the so-called hours of darkness, eg 10 pm to 5 am next morning. Really the time a pigeon takes to home is just that and we do not know of a two-day race or longer when they actually roost. A lot of us guess, and that's all it is.

The earliest bird I know in 2010 and in Yorkshire was clocked at 4.05 am, second day after a Channel race.

We do the best we can and try to work within the rules, yet hours of darkness are purely a human intervention. There is normally a lot of debate and controversy around the fairness of hours of darkness.

WHITE PIGEONS

White birds are lovely to look at and especially appeal to the children and ladies. There are some good white racers about, yet most fanciers don't keep them.

I see white Logans advertised, yet Logan passed away donkeys' years ago! Many a loft has some white garden fantails and these make superb drop or decay birds for your racers. Just have the dropper ready in a basket and let it flutter to the loft and observe the response in your racer, especially young birds. Now the white colour acts as a super-stimulus to the brain of your racer. Racers, being flock creatures, will respond strongly to the movement of the white colour.

I used white birds for years, a white racer (Snowball) for 15 years and a garden fantail for 13 years. The latter I caught in Rowntree Park, York from the collection there. They served me well.

Just watch the impact of your racers if locked up with white birds. Two of my hens excelled when paired to the white drop cocks. Try it – the added motivation can work wonders.

I am pleased to say that at Barry's dovecote in York, both white garden fantails have settled. We kept them in for a while and Barry built a veranda for 360-degree vision. It worked a treat, and the witty and droll Barry and I have derived much amusement from the two 'Doves of Peace'.

YOUR GOOD NAME

You may develop a reputation as a good flyer or for your impact on the sport. You will never be universally popular, since there are individuals where criticism is a speciality. This is often fuelled by jealousy and negative thinking. It can be important for people on a face-to-face level to treat you well and with some respect. This is probably a basic human requirement, yet you cannot please all the people all of the time.

In the early stages at your local club level, it is important to turn up and help in a conscientious manner with the many tasks. It is important to handle others' birds calmly and with quiet hands – this will go a long way.

It is very nice to have people who you perhaps look up to, and this goes right through the sport. At the end of the day the chief impulse should be to do well or excel in the races of your choice, and it is very easy to be popular if you are bottom of the list. However there are many who rarely win yet achieve a lot of pleasure in the sport, and these are the backbone of the fancy; long may they continue.

Perhaps one day you may be like the image of Ronnie Williamson, which travels far and wide, and his results are difficult to criticise.

RACING YOUR HENS

I was a hens specialist with success from 71 to 879 miles from related pigeons from the same family and all bred by myself. Now I will assert that you cocks-only people are wasting your hens. Good hens, well managed, will win and do win right through to international level. I absolutely love hens, either on widowhood, semi-widowhood or in combinations with natural flying. For nest conditions, I like them deprived of nest (ie separate from the cocks) and then paired to be on the first squeaker of the year prior to basketing.

I warmed mine up at 466 miles in NFC and then as 2ys to 735, 737, 687 and 879 miles. Here good keen, hard hens (usually small to medium) will come through in good condition. The hens from my family of related pigeons also won the Young Bird Open races from 71 miles and topped the Yorkshire Middle Route Federation, eg 1st, 3rd, 14th of 6,066 pigeons.

That's enough boasting. I am trying to get you to race your hens on any system as far as you want. All my good hard hens have left lines of good pigeons up to Barcelona, eg Mystical Queen, Deltalady, Dedication, Sister Damien, Dot's Delight. One of the top key ones is Dark Enchantment, perhaps my favourite. My advice is sprint them and change your methods to get more and more distance up to Barcelona.

To conclude, I advise all beginners to race hens.

HELPING OUT

In the final analysis you should help yourself, as pigeon racing is largely a selfish pursuit. However, a wise old man at Holtby called Herbert Marriner said to me, 'We are on the earth to help one another'. I can see the beauty and kindness of this statement.

On your journey into pigeons, it will be sensible to help out at the club with the available tasks. This may help with your popularity, and believe me you will need some good will if you become successful in the races, as the tide will turn.

You should decide though on your priority which it is: to become an outstanding club man or woman or known as an excellent racer of birds. It is possible to be both and you will find your way. A shrewd move would be to help the top fancier in your area, as if you are lucky he may take you under his wing and help you with advice, and birds. The keener you are as a beginner, the more likely you are to be a future success. I spend my retirement helping the sport and I like doing it, especially promoting the sport.

WRITING FOR THE BHW

This is a creditable thing to do and a good pastime. Try and think of a topic that you know about and express it as clearly as possible using as few words as possible. The 'long' articles make the readers eyes glaze over or they tend to scan the article.

As new starters you could become well known or even 'expert' in your field with time. See if you can get an article accepted for the Stud Book. I am sure the BHW staff will be most helpful. Of course it helps with your process if you have some decent race results to back you up.

Articles hold power and influence and many a household name has been launched by some generous journalist. A writer who has helped to make famous many a fancier is Les J Parkinson. The fancy owes him a debt of gratitude just for this one element. One of the cleverest and most loft journalists has been Liam O'Comain. As for me, I have thoughts on any topic in pigeon racing and find writing a cathartic experience. So pick up a pen and create!

PIGEON COMFORT

It's a hard life being a racing pigeon, being sent from home to foreign lands. A good fancier makes the birds as comfortable and relaxed as possible. A warm, dry and airy loft is essential. Many lofts are too crowded and too hot in summer, with stale air. Have lots of space for your birds and bed them down on shavings and Easibed or similar. When you basket your birds, do it quietly and line the basket – they are living creatures. Caring for your birds will repay you tenfold. They should be tame and happy with you.

A lot of transporters do not meet the needs of birds over many days – the NFC ones are good, with controlled air quality. Much needs to be done. I do not like to see any cruelty to birds. When breeding give plenty of food and nest box space. Overtraining your birds will make them too light and stressed.

HYGIENE

There are two schools of thought here: maximum or minimum hygiene in the lofts. At one time I attempted to keep bugs and viruses down using Virkon or Vykil. I do not in retrospect favour a sterile environment. Young pigeons will come into contact with many diseases and pests in the baskets. The secret, surely, is to build up the immune resistance of the birds.

On the contrary I like scraped perches and nest boxes, on a daily basis for the birds. In my opinion the rest of the loft can be a floor of Easibed Shavings litter. 'Good' bugs will breed in this and give the birds a dose of probiotics.

In the last analysis, it depends on the predilections of the fancier. No matter how careful you are, sooner or later you will get diseases in your loft, whether you know it or not. Antibiotics are expensive and perhaps will not work – keep your birds content, calm and happy. The key factor in disease is stress – too much basket for these YBs – better a good long toss say 50-60 miles. Birds should have access to a bath, with salts twice per week; some stock birds never get one, a cruel practice. Keep 'em calm, keep 'em happy.

KEEPING RECORDS

Many fanciers do not know to mind the parents and grandparents in their lofts – they may have a clue if they look up the ring number. In the BHW Stud Book you will find pages devoted to pairs, and I recommend you put your stock pairs in this book and keep them. When you build up a family or strain you will need ready access to the history of your birds.

Some years ago I sold pigeons (I now give them away or exchange them with no money involved – this is a more sporting thing to do). Eventually when I made my name in racing I gave details of the parents only, it having been wildly documented that my birds were from seven foundation birds. I found it sufficient to say that the birds were bred by me as Busschaert did!

It is not enough to say a bird is a van Reet if it wasn't bred by him – van Reets are birds bred by van Reet only. This applies to any family or strain. A lot of fanciers do not know this. That means, for example, that all the Stichelbauts are now dead, as the man died in the 1940s.

The object lesson is to try and keep track of your birds, although it is not always possible to be accurate unless you have individual stock pairs in isolation.

PERSONAL QUALITIES

It's simple: when you succeed at your racing, whatever the distance, then you have the attributes required. As birds are under your management control – they do not have a place or home without you – you are the most important part of the equation. The onus is on you. Good fanciers breed or obtain good pigeons and due to the fancier, get good results. The fancier is king at any distance, as the bird responds to what he does. No fancier, no pigeon – simple. You will need to be tough, gentle, patient, persistent, calm and full of ambition from Club to International level. John Halstead, who has recently won from Barcelona into the UK, is a model fancier, being patient, fastidious and methodical. His bird is the long-distance performer of the year into the UK and deserves plaudits and awards. Look out for John's excellent educational videos. Above all persevere, keep at it.

HONESTY

I do not believe that a human can spend his or her entire life being honest and true. What we can say is that some fanciers are more honest than others. If they are exceptional flyers, these are the ones to obtain birds from. A more-honest-than-the-norm man is Jim Donaldson of Peterhead – he is noted for it.

On the other side of the coin, aren't there some rogues in the pigeon sport? Watch the advertisements – they are outstandingly good at verbal tricks. As new starters you will learn, it is hoped, to spot the real people around.

However, honesty can be linked to conscience and I say be careful who you bare your soul to! The sharks bite in the pigeon waters. When buying anything, look for the genuine small-team man who wants to help the novice; usually these are the older people who perhaps already have a penny or two. On the other hand, we go our own way and learn our own lessons – mine the hard way.

BIRDS OF PREY

It is very hard to bear when sparrowhawks, peregrine falcons and goshawks kill, eat and scare your bids. At Sycamore Cottage, Holtby in winter and early spring I would normally lose 5-10 birds to hen sparrowhawks. When fattening up for resting and especially when the fieldfares and redwings have migrated to Russia and Scandinavia, they get to be determined killers of your birds. They will knock your birds down at your feet. It is hard, yet I let my birds run the gauntlet and it is amazing how acute the instincts of your racers become. After all, they will have to evade predators when nighting out on the big races.

The pigeon is the staple diet of the peregrine, which is a falcon, not a hawk, and many are troubled by these aerial killers, especially near quarries and cliffs. The exact number of birds and kills are not known. The goshawk is normally an ambush predator from its haunts in wooded areas.

I would say that hen sparrowhawks account for more pigeon kills in the UK than other birds. If you can keep racing, then after April pigeon kills by sparrowhawks seem to be less frequent. My philosophy was always to hope that they didn't kill your main candidate. Pigeons kept in all winter are easy meat for sparrowhawks. Ironically, I see lots of small birds every day on my country walks and love the dawn chorus.

FOOD SUPPLEMENTS

There's no doubt about it, pigeons will fly on mixed corn and a variety of grains. However, in an attempt for more speed and stamina, most fanciers today give one or more supplements on the food. The best known is Hormoform – cut cereals with yeast, multivits and oils and this probably proves to be of benefit to the birds.

It is well known that I mixed brewer's yeast, peanuts and condition seed (eg Red Band) into my corn mixes. My layers' pellets were fed as a staple food, not as a supplement. By giving these supplements we try and boost the birds with fats, proteins, carbohydrates, vitamins, minerals and trace elements. They are considered beneficial by some of the top pigeon men and women. Having said this, I would like to see the results of some scientific research, using different supplements and the results with no supplements. This would be very difficult in practice, since so many things can influence the outcome of a race. Yet we see the same pigeon fanciers at the top or near the top time and time again. You see the most important 'supplement' is the pigeon fancier, because they breed and gather good birds around themselves and also get the ways to feed corns and supplements right. All in all I prefer to give specialist feed supplements. NB: I have also used Tovo. Once again, if it works for you it's right.

WATER SUPPLEMENTS

There are very many things that we can add to the water of our birds in an attempt to improve overall health and condition for the best racing potential. Many people add to the water, whether the additive is proven by good scientific methods or not. I tend to favour substances with an apparent proven research background. I am thinking of Rohnfried products and Chevita, both from Germany. My method was Bovril with a probiotic such as Prolyte or E Plus (Aviform) on Wednesday and Aviform Ultimate on Thursday and Friday. Before basketing for 500-879-mile racing I gave Mycosan-T on Friday and Saturday, Vydex Super Six on Sunday and Mycosan-T with Chlortetracycline + on Monday/Tuesday. This was an attempt to flush the birds with vitamins, sugars, carbohydrates, amino acids, trace elements etc before racing. It would appear to have worked for me, yet I have done no proper scientific testing.

In pigeons a lot of what we do is psychological, with trial and error and guesswork. Top men today are using Mycosan-T CCS (Chevita GmbH) fresh, plain water and then experiment with water supplements which can be likened to liquid feeding. Check out the BHW and Gem supplements for information.

MIND OR MAGIC

With a million pounds and the best birds in the world, you will not reach the top in pigeon racing without plenty of substance between the eyes, ie 'mind'. A good mind enables you to plan, focus and dedicate yourself to the tasks in hand to be a champion flyer. I have cultivated my mind to the best of my ability and within my limits. It has helped me greatly with my overall pigeon career from beginning to end. An enquiring, vigorous mind means you learn the essentials for racing from sprint to International level. Set yourself personal achievement targets, visualise the future. All the top fanciers have good pigeon brains; the success is the result of their inner selves.

The mind can be very powerful. In the 1980s I foresaw my future with my strain. I made it happen and my strain is still a great success today. You can sometimes visualise and see in your mind's eye which birds will come in the races. This comes from a deep empathy with individual birds. My advice is to develop your mind, as it is the most important entity in racing. Perhaps the key element is intuition (crystal ball brain) – I love it!

CLUB MEETINGS

To train and race your birds, you should join a club. From time to time there will be meetings with the Secretary, Chairman, President and other officials. In theory, the meetings should be run in a fair and controlled manner, observing rules and facts. However, they are often disorderly, with dominant individuals seeking power over others. My advice is to make your birds competitive and keep out of these largely petty club politics. If necessary, go out on a limb and train and send our birds in the Nationals. It is not necessary to be embroiled in aggressive club verbal boxing matches. Do your own thing and set your own target racepoints.

If you become an official, keep to the rules and facts and keep accurate minutes, as you may be called up to represent the club at a hearing. If you have not dotted the i's and crossed the t's, then clever men will prove you wrong. I have yet to see a really happily-run local club, as most consist of different people after different things.

You could hear all, see all and say nowt, but even then you will be sensitive to bad thoughts at clubs. For many years I sent birds as trainers and then concentrated around Nationals and Internationals, although I was asked to be secretary of Strensall PRS. Believe me, to get to the top you have to be a lone wolf.

WHAT YOU NEED TO KNOW

There are certain essential truths you need to learn in pigeon racing. One of these is that a good fancier or pigeon manager and flyer will seek, breed and obtain some good pigeons that will fly satisfactorily. A good fancier with knowledge and application will be successful.

Having said that, most pigeons you breed, of any family or strain name, will fail when the flying conditions are tough, and if you send them often enough, far enough and long enough they will all fail. Pigeons that will race over 800 miles into the UK are rare, whether sent in fantastic conditions or not.

Most birds are sold at inflated prices, when good birds can be given or exchanged. Do not be lured by skilful and tricky chat or advertising. I have given away birds that are performing at a high level today in National racing for National flyers. My reward is not money; it is the satisfaction I derive from the process.

It is nice to be liked and popular, but watch how things can change when you start to dominate your club. Now you will realise how personal and competitive pigeon racing is. In the final countdown you should make your own way, in your own fashion and at your own level.

FAME

Most people want a slice of the 'fame cake' Our society thrives on it, but it does not suit everyone. Many are happy as relative unknowns and they may be equally good or talented. As new beginners, some will become famous in pigeons, and not just as names on the net, which is easy. You may be a writer, racer/breeder, seller, auctioneer, in sales or pigeon politics. You will hopefully be good or excellent at what you do.

The whole world is open to you for publication on the net, books or magazines, or other media. In pigeon racing a well-known writer may review or interview you and this, especially if repeated, will bring you into the spotlight. Naturally, outstanding results in racing will make you a household name.

In our sport there are many famous names, but few can be called 'great'. The most famous race is the European Barcelona International, and this is the ultimate race for the purist distance and marathon fancier. When you are well known, I believe you have a responsibility to promote others and all aspects of the sport. This can become your legacy and your personal contribution.

Pigeon racers tend to be in the minority – let's see if we can bring them into the mainstream.

THE SOCIAL ASPECT

Depending on your personality, you can make many friends and contacts in pigeon racing. One or two may become good close friends if you are lucky. Note that people at your local club will tend, in fact to be your rivals, so be careful with these.

There is often much gossip between club people and if you are any good at the racing side, you will be talked about. I advise you to take it all with a pinch of salt and continue with your aims and targets in the sport. People come and go, yet some of your achievements may remain on historical record.

I receive some letters and calls from people, most of which are friendly enquiries about my birds or my writing work. Beware of timewasters who want to sound off and use you. I do not attend any pigeon functions, since they are often full of competitive tension and rivalry. However, each to his own, and if you want to dress up and show off, then so be it.

One good aspect of the social side is that you will become friends with some top fanciers where you can exchange 'good' birds. But my idea of a good party is watch the birds in the garden. In the last analysis your best friends may be your mother and yourself!

FOR THE YOUNG 'GROWING UP'

I hope you will have your house and pigeon lofts where you can enjoy your pigeons and racing. I believe it is best to have your birds in a detached house in the country. Many of the greats fly from the countryside without potential neighbour problems and with some open loft.

You may be involved later with the sale of pigeon products and/or pigeons – there are many people making plenty of money out of birds. Or you may become a vet like Zsolt Talaber, or even a writer for the BHW. If you concentrate and are talented you could make a large impact in the pigeon racing world.

At the end of the day, the eternal secret is to enjoy your

life in pigeons and put plenty back into the sport. I enjoy my life in pigeons after all the years of hard work and study and do what I can for the hobby.

JEALOUSY

Jealousy and other negative emotions are the scourge of modern pigeon racing. When you race your birds you try to succeed, to feel good and rewarded. Everyone is trying to do the same, and if you succeed and they don't they will probably feel bad and perhaps jealous of you. This may show itself as verbal insults, mutterings, bullying and other ungentlemanly behaviour. My advice is to treat it all as a form of flattery and accept the compliment; it shows you have affected them with your results or success.

This is, of course, part of being human, and I suggest you try even harder when things are tough and keep focused on your goals in racing and breeding, and all aspects of the sport. Many a club has broken down because it did not accept the performances of outstanding flyers. I do not like this aspect of the sport – it really spoils it for all, and yet it is so widespread.

WHAT IS NATIONAL RACING?

To qualify as a National the club must have a radius and catchment area for membership which covers the whole nation or country. There are true National clubs in England, Scotland, Ireland and Wales. Three true English Nationals are the NFC, BBC and BICC. Good racing is to be had in true Nationals and it is very good training for International racing, which is as difficult as it can get, especially if you go for Barcelona.

There are many good birds and fanciers in the Nationals and I was very thrilled when I clocked my first-ever bird at the old Nantes to be 7th Section K. It was a lovely point to test yearlings on the day for future big races out of Pau, San Sebastian and Barcelona. I can understand the many financial and other reasons why the NFC has dropped International racing, yet I feel we should be taking on the rest of Europe and take the races as they come, hard or very hard. The International races into the UK are nearly always difficult – that's the essence of the game. I like to see a few real quality tested pigeons in a loft. However as long as we enjoy what we do, as you can go on raising the bar for ever, eg what comes after Rome?

I do hope the BBC go to Barcelona International again as the BICC will do. The best of our fliers can stand up against the best in the world, yet I do like 800 miles second-day birds, don't you? Some of you beginners will be the greats of the future, you are our legacy!

LEGACY

We are on the earth to help one another. When we are young we want to win and win, living a selfish life, even in pigeon racing. I am at the stage now where I tell the fancy virtually all I know about the sport. My articles are whizzing around the world as I speak. The fact that I have the only interview on pigeon keeping in Ask Jeeves and Ask.com makes me proud.

My strain of birds has scored from 31 to 879 miles, all bred down from the No 1 pair, and this makes them unique to the UK.

It softens my heart to see the development of the Squeakers' Corner in the BHW and I contribute where I can.

Of special importance to me is that I mentor other fanciers, here in the UK. I take a special interest in the York area with Booth and Shipley having 10 pairs of the Emerton strain. As usual I am willing to help any reasonable fancier with my knowledge.

In conclusion, it is not so much what you take out but what you give back in return. This sounds like an epistle, does it not?

POWER

Good birds demonstrate their power as producers or racers. There are many stocky, strong-looking sprint/middle distance birds with multiple firsts, and these exude power. I like birds which will fly over 500 miles on the day, or over 700 miles by the second day, all against the wind, especially north east.

Stock birds which leave a dynasty of good racers have genetic and producing power. You can build a strain with these. My No 1 pair have left a line of 879 miles and counting. Some racers are very bossy and dominant in the loft; and there is a hierarchy of power structure in your loft.

TARGET RACEPOINTS

I think it is correct to say that many people aim to beat others in pigeon racing. When you are a beginner you may aim to be the top prize winner in your local club or Federation. This is the way many people cut the ice. You will have well-known fanciers in your area who you try to emulate; I know I did. In fact, one of the best fanciers of all time come from the York area is Brian Denney and we have been friends and rivals. Extremely dedicated, he has emerged as one of the best fanciers in the world, never to be forgotten.

I cut my teeth in St Lawrence Working Men's Club, Strensall Pigeon Racing Society and Four Alls Pigeon Racing Society, flying in my favourite Yorkshire.

FAIR-WEATHER FLYERS

To be brutally honest, many people leave their birds at home when the going gets tough or there is a bad forecast. Often this is to try to gain points and wins in seemingly better flying conditions. Fanciers don't want to risk not being their club's top prize or points winner. To me, this proves nothing other than a little local prestige and dominance. I can honestly say that in my many years of racing, I never kept back birds due to a bad forecast. You see, hard, long races against the wind and elements prove the real stamina, endurance and strain-making value of your birds. A loft full of nice looking birds at the end of the year usually shows me that the racing was not hard enough. The Tarbes International in 2010 was a good test and birds returning in good time will have some quality.

As a young wildfowler I remember sitting out in a creek on the Wash marshes in ice and snow with fingers nearly frozen to the gun barrels.

Really, the way forward is international racing since this tends to be as tough as it gets, with much bigger birdage and competition. To balance my ideas, I think it would be safer and less heart-breaking for beginners to start off carefully and gently with the birds.

NAMING PIGEONS

Any good and treasured pigeon should be given a name. With a little imagination you can think of one which suits you and your bird. I think it unimaginative to use numerals or numbers off the ring, unless they have significance, like 666. Having studied the occult, two of my favourite names are Diabolos and Mystical Queen. To me they sound powerful and mysterious. I have yet to see another pigeon in the world called Diabolos, so it must be pretty original.

The studs of course normally name their birds, as it smacks a little of professionalism, sophistication and commercialism. I find that names say in an expressive way a lot about you as a fancier, eg I called one of mine Dark Dedication and another Dark Expected. One of my favourites was Oddball, since she had odd-coloured eyes and a ball of a white head. Two of my favourites have been Lancashire Rose, a poetic name for the great Pau winning hen, and Millennium Superstar. As a squeaker myself I was inspired by the great Storm Queen and Woodsider. However I confess my bias, since I love words. Next time you get a good bird, think and name it, even if it's Lady Gaga!

YOU'VE GOT TO SEND THEM!

I can say, honestly, that I always sent my birds, and my best ones, to the most demanding and difficult races. Many people shy away and avoid the tough races when the weather is poor. This proves nothing and does not test your birds. A way to really test your bird or family of birds is to keep on sending them until your goal is achieved. Normally, the hardest and most challenging race into the UK is the Barcelona International – now this is as good as it gets.

Birds that do well and even up to 700 miles will often fail at Barcelona.

May I draw your attention to Frank Kay of Bolton, Lancs. Now, he sends all his 2ys and upwards to Barcelona, 869 miles. This is a very individual thing to do and Frank will become unique – a one-off. This example is how greatness is realised!

You will never know what your birds and you can do unless you send 'em. This is probably the wisest thing I can advise you to do; let the basket be the judge of you and your birds. Go where many fear to go: go to Barcelona.

Naturally it is your job to send the birds in the best possible condition; this comes with experience. I recommend that you send your young birds in the year of their birth – they will gain invaluable experience.

LATEBREDS

In my definition these are birds bred July onwards in the UK, and do not complete the moult in the year of birth. To my mind April to June hatches are NOT latebreds.

You know my policy – always take latebreds from your top birds of the season, every year. Then you can pair these together to keep your family or strain (birds of a distinct hereditary character). A strain can be made a reality, not just an abstract theory.

Feed your latebreds on a high protein mixture. Hormoform, yeast, Red Band, peanuts and Green Matrix or equivalent. Let them grow and grow, and if for stock, they need an aviary with open top for sun and rain. I love latebreds for stock and so do many serious-minded fanciers. Purely my preference, but I do not like latebreds for racing, although there are exceptions. My No 1 and 2 stock cocks were bred in September. I am pleased to report that birds of my origin have now had success from 35 to 879 miles. Latebreds for racing need gentle training in the year of their birth and losses can be great.

TALE OF TWO FANTAILS

Much to my delight, a gentleman called Barry moved into my area and made a white dovecote. Overcome by curiosity, I introduced myself and said I was charmed by the two fantails which adorned the cote. These were bought at an auction in Selby as a pair but turned out to be two cocks. Barry could not resist giving them their freedom and let them out daily.

Eventually one homed and a neighbour alerted me to the presence of the second bird, which was in a garden. With feline stealth I pounced and caught it. For a while the two birds lived and added glamour to our neighbourhood, eventually dispersing into the wild.

As a dove lover, Barry took me to the auction in his Jag. Now that was a revelation, observing the motley crew of rogues, characters and conmen. We all stood in fear with our hands in our pockets as everything from a goose to a canary was put under the hammer. Our patience was rewarded by two young fantails with huge tails for £5. I advised Barry what to do with them and after some days they were liberated from the cote. They said 'bye bye' and flew from rooftop to rooftop, seemingly never to return. To the collective amusement of the area they went from bungalow to bungalow.

A sad ending for one of the creatures was death by sparrowhawk. Now, amazingly, a stray hen fantail joined the other. Amusingly, Barry went to catch them with his fishing net – that was a laugh a minute. Eventually my predatory instincts took over and, like an old hunting fox, I caught them both by hand. The consequence is that they are a matched pair and back in the safety of the cote.

White fantails make lovely decoy or drop birds for your racers and act as a super-stimulus for your racers. Try a few.

YOUR PARENTS (AND GRANDAD)

As a new starter to pigeon racing, you will probably be supported both financially and in other ways by your parents. Many of you will be mentored by a kindly grandfather. With the passage of time you should gain in appreciation and gratitude for what your relatives do for you. Your parents may be 'champion' fliers in their own right and encourage you to be the same. My mother was very pushy, yet I would not have managed in the world of pigeon racing without her. You may well finish up flying in partnership with your relatives.

I notice how many of the Up North Combine fliers are in partnerships – all very well if you get on, yes? Naturally, on a biological level the genes from your parents will greatly dictate who you are and who you become. If you have what it takes, then you can do well with your birds in life. Look after your relatives well – they are on the earth for only a short period! Listen, watch and learn. As my mother said, 'It's later than you think!'

THE SINGLE BIRD NFC

The greater distance Single Bird NFC is an elitist, singular and prestigious club. You nominate one bird in the blue riband proper national races of the NFC, BICC and BBC. It certainly is a great test of your selection and management skill.

The club will welcome all new people who want to pitch their skills against some of the top fliers we have known. There is no hiding place in this club and no mob flying, as you put out just one bird from your team. Naturally, you can send as many as you like from the parent national organisations.

My record from four races into York is as follows 3rd Open Pau, 735 miles with Oddball in 2002 when it was hard; 1st section B, 4th Open Dax in 2004, to record Dax My Girl as the longest flying pigeon in the International result at 687 miles; 10th Open San Sebastian, 737 miles in the club. These three hens with the NFC are leaving their winning lines now. Come on then, have a go and join the club for specialist pleasure, it's another arrow in your bow.

THE FUTURE

For dedicated fliers in the UK, the future is rosy. We are faced with declining numbers, yet the quality continues to rise with modern management techniques.

I am delighted to see a new wave of International racing, and the NFC joining in at Tarbes for 2010. I have been banging this drum for many years. This is racing at the top (especially Barcelona), and more and more fanciers will see that you can clock in the Internationals.

There will be people who will try and win Barcelona International into the UK. I consider this possible but unlikely. 800 miles 2nd day is on the cards and will be a new milestone in racing over here. John Halstead with the Untouchable Cock has shown us all the way, and his type of performance will be deemed to be more and more popular and significant in the future.

I see ETS is now firmly in place and its usage will rise and rise in numbers as it becomes accepted. Also there is likely to be a steady decline in the use of antibiotics as they become less and less effective.

That's it for now: I will look in my 'Crystal Ball' again.

TRACKING DEVICES

It is amazing how often you think of something as a fancy and then it becomes a reality. We often think and speculate where our birds are after race liberation. Some are convinced that they know which way they have flown from the racepoint. Only sometimes will your mere guesswork be accurate; most of the time you will be wrong.

What about then a miniature tracking device (GPS maybe) on the leg of your bird? Perhaps you could watch progress on a computer screen all the way from say Pau or Barcelona. Now that would be an entertaining revelation, would it not? This may be advanced and expensive, yet it could be an optional extra. This practice would also yield an insight into the navigated route of a pigeon. Initially one could imagine the work being done as part of a scientific research model. I would imagine it to be expensive, but there are many rich fanciers worldwide. The Japanese are good at miniature technology, so it may be done.

I was always happy not to know the route taken by my birds, yet I often reflected on the measured distance compared with potential actual flying distance.

ONE FOR THE GIRLS

As a new starter you girls will like the 'pretty ones', eg whites and pieds. You will be gentle with the birds, kind and caring. You will possibly talk and sing to them. It is likely that you will be better with the birds than the boys. This is how it is, and a great deal of the top male fanciers owe their success to the work and empathy of the women. Often men take the credit, when the best fancier is in the loft with the birds – the womenfolk. Without doubt a bird responds best to a girl's voice.

I would not be writing to the BHW now without all the hard work that my mother Dorothy did until she was 91. Think about it then men, when you get carried away by your egos, give some more credit to the lady fanciers.

A lot of men are rough and ruthless and see the birds as race objects rather than living beings. I have met some hard pigeon women, but none that would send to Barcelona International at over 800 miles – the ultimate test of pigeon and fancier. Yes, there is room at the top for the fairer sex.

PITFALLS

Sooner or later you will make a mistake and have problems with your birds and racing. One of the biggest causes of unrest can be listening to and absorbing bad advice from well-intentioned or not-so-well-intentioned fanciers. It is wise to question carefully to all you hear, read and see and preferably share counsel with top people who may mentor or help you. Be warned: pick only the genuine ones. Having said that, even the opinions of 'experts' will vary, and really you need to find your own way with your birds by good judgement and trial and error.

Two common pitfalls for novices are: firstly accepting pigeons from here, there and everywhere which may be of dubious quality. Best to buy a family (say five pairs) from a top man. The other one is to train your birds too early in the season, especially in north winds when they can be lost or lose condition. When you listen to the fanciers at the club, ask yourself this question: what have they really done and at what level of competition – club, national or international? My advice is to do it your way, then you will learn the hard way and the experience will wise you up.

CLOCKING/TIMING YOUR BIRD

In order to win or score in a race, a pigeon has to have its exact time registered. From this a velocity in yards per minute can be calculated and the winner of the race has the highest velocity.

For many years I managed very nicely with STB quartz clocks and at the distances I was interested in a few seconds made little or no difference to me. The benefit of least time lost in timing can be gained using a modern electronic timing system. There are many systems which cost money to fit and buy and usually have to be updated. In principle they are effective and accurate, but probably they are yet to be perfected. They are certainly modern and many families enjoy them chiefly because they are competitive and you don't have to catch the pigeon to remove and clock a rubber ring, as with normal clocks like my old STB quartz. Many old clocks like my Skymaster and Benzing wooden case clocks are now collector's items.

It will be exciting for you to time your first bird in your first race and you should remember it. When your birds come home, be calm and cool and control your environment, although I shouted with excitement when I clocked Diamond Queen from Pau 735 miles and had a job to do the paperwork! You will note the atmosphere at the club when times are read out – all part of the game.

LISTENING AND ASKING QUESTIONS

There is no limit to what you can learn about pigeons. The essential and crucial matter is to learn by experience, and any facts absorbed should be hard facts. Learn to separate fact from the fantasy of myth and false belief.

I recommend you try and make a friend and mentor of the top fancier in your club or area. This may not be possible due to the personalities involved. The alternative is to absorb good facts from good books like *Roads to Rome* and Zsolt Talaber: indeed, read all the books. Learn to recognise solid irrefutable fact from fiction and opinion based on belief and fantasy.

A genuine, kind and sporting fancier will help you, but beware that when you start to win races, some of your 'friends' will fall away. However we are in the age of readily-available information, eg on the net – look for the in-depth interviews with the top, record-making fanciers. I am thinking here of people like Chris Gordon and Jim Donaldson, along with other specialists at your chosen distance. Beware of the rogue who will fill your mind with nonsense.

In practical terms, ask about the loft, race preparation, feeding, breeding, training and all up to International level. Think, think and then think some more.

TRAINING YOUR BIRD

A bird should be fit to race and win at any level you compete at. It will help you if your birds fly around at home for two hours plus per day to swell the muscles and improve the breathing. You may keep them flying with a flag or some other device which keeps them up for two one-hour periods per day, or like me you can take the easier route if this suits your home life and give the birds freedom of the skies during the day.

As a new starter, I urge care with your basket training to food and water. When road training, cover the basket of birds with a cloth to quieten them and start them off at say 10 miles with a relative or your father or friend and repeat the distance until the pigeons fly 'straight' home. In warm, nice sunny days get them out to 50 miles before the first race; this applies to young and old birds. Gradually send your birds along the line of flight in the races to increase their fitness. Then good birds may score in the races and think about how far you want to race the birds. I would think 200 miles is plenty for novices – further when you start to gain experience of races.

Remember, birds will respond at home when you call them in to some nice peanuts, perhaps a whistle and some hempseed. Keep to routines of time and make your birds a habit. Hand tame your birds with peanuts, and always be kind and gentle with them.

Many fanciers have a dream with their birds and talk up a big race. The lesson for all to learn is that unless your birds go in the basket to the ultimate distance and at International level, they are not properly tested. This should be the eventual aim of the novice – one for the future. When pigeons are lost it saps the resolve of the fancier, and this is the stage when the tough get going.

Baskets are the traditional method of conveying your birds from A to B on a transporter or in the car, and formerly on the train. They should be nice and light and lined with say, shavings or Easibed. Sheets of cardboard/paper etc in the panniers on transporters is a very bad, unhygienic practice; they spread disease amongst the birds and are covered in soggy faeces. Birds soon get used to baskets and will be calm and rest in them. Keen fanciers get the young ones to eat in the baskets and drink from containers in the baskets. I gave away all my baskets in 2006 when I stopped racing. In 1997 I bought a van which would accommodate just four baskets – neat and tidy in the back. Other containers can be plastic or aluminium. I liked a loose cover over them to start with to calm the birds.

The moral of the story is, if in doubt, basket your birds and send them, to reveal, by evidence of racing, the best birds. You should criticise yourself before the birds and if you have a lot of birds they aren't being properly tested!

BUILDING A NEST

A hen normally sits on two eggs in a nest. The nest may be provided by you as a disposable papier mâché, type eg Dandynest, or some other material like plastic or clay. I used Dandynests since they are warm, light, dry and disposable. Keep it simple – this is the essence of genius.

It is normal behaviour for the birds to bring straw (wheat straw), tobacco stalks, grasses etc to their nest. These can be huge, and let the birds build where they want. I hate to see regimented, over-organised nesting sites. Contented birds may build on the floor, especially in deep litter – a layer of warm shavings or straw on the floor. If your loft is near gardens or fields you can watch the birds come in and out of the loft in their efforts to build nests. When this happens though, watch for cats and sparrowhawks – these are deadly. Allow plenty of space for the second nest by the birds in the breeding cycle. Fit, contented birds may build nests at any time of year and I have seen young street birds in December in York! It is not necessary to use nest felts with the birds; a Dandynest is perfect. If eggs start to darken under the light after eight days they are normally fertile. If not fertile, under careful observation then take them away for the hen to lay again.

RACING METHOD

As a new starter, you will need to develop a system of bird management to condition your birds for racing. There are many, and it will be individual to you as they are all personal and varied.

Widowhood for example can be cocks/hens or both. Basically after rearing you keep hens out of sight and separate from the cocks. This can give outstanding results at all distances and levels. Another method is 'roundabout' – ideally with two identical sections for hens and cocks and exercised to each loft in rotation. This and celibacy all rely on the good form that the bird can attain when parted from its mate.

Note many pair back their birds on Natural mid-season and having been deprived of nest for some weeks can be extra keen to rest, lay and rear – I used this system and also natural open loft. Here the birds were paired in March and allowed free access to come and go as they pleased. I liked a hen on her first small baby of the year for a big race.

Roundabout and widowhood birds often have controlled exercise periods of say 2 x1 hour per day – sometimes with an hour of flagging – forced flying.

For long distances and marathon pigeons usually have combinations of widowhood and natural with as much food as they will eat.

OTHER TYPES OF PIGEONS

I like all types of pigeons and doves. In the UK we have the wild woodpigeon, stock dove, collared dove, rock dove and turtle dove. My favourite is the turtle dove and I have not heard its purring call for years – have you? Boy are they scarce. Note woodpigeons are not stock doves. As a boy I had fancy pigeons and rollers. The fancy came in every colour and type (morphs). Some of my birds were priests, magpies, orientals, frills and balds.

I am especially fond of the sporting types, eg tipplers, rollers and cumulets, and have seen performing high fliers in Turkey and Syria. I have known Dr Graham Dexter and George Mason from the competition roller world. Look up Graham Dexter rollers on YouTube for an insight into the spinning ways of the rollers. Then of course we have feral or street pigeons, which are believed to be descended from rock doves. I doubt if there are any pure rock doves in the UK as they have bred with stray racers, other strags and feral pigeons.

I spent my youth looking at rollers and with the roller men of Derby and kept Barbary and Java Doves. They are all lovely and I have seen green fruit pigeons in Gambia and Senegal.

ACQUIRING WISDOM

As a starter you cannot be expected to be a fountainhead of knowledge, insight and wisdom. This is something you may acquire with experience and time. It is as if a light is turned on in your mind when you will be able to see clearly as near as possible to the actual nature of something. You will see through the scams and tricks of pigeon advertising when someone is out to make a fast buck or two; you will see the real worth and value of something to yourself; you will make judgements of your own; you will be your own person; you will ask questions like what is distance, what is a champion, what is a hype, what is bovine faeces. Eventually, if you persist, whoever you are, you will come to satisfactory conclusions about everything; then you will be a man, my friend (or woman). That was Jim's little visit to the pigeon fancier's oracle.

BEING A GOOD WINNER OR LOSER

If you win often enough they will hate you – this is a mark of your success. It's easy to be popular when you are a loser – 'good sport' and all that. However, it is common courtesy to shake the hand of the winner, even if you do not really mean it. When you start in racing and want to win everything it is very hard to lose, especially if you are really keen. Winning is everything if you are to make progress. If you feel happy with what you have done, then you are a winner in my eyes. We can't all win the Barcelona International into the UK, can we?

At the end of the day it is personal and psychological, as you can be top prizewinner in your club and a right misery, in which case you have lost the psychological game!

I would say, good advice is to go for the first four every week and see where it takes you. Remember though that the ultimate level of winning is at International level.

LEAVING YOUR MARK

Your first success will be memorable. After a while you may be ambitious enough to want to make an impact in the larger world of racing in the UK, and possibly on a global level. Let me tell you that with a little hard work, it is easy. First of all, if you sell a few birds through the weeklies and yearbooks your name will register in the names of the fancy. A good performance or two will lend itself to being written about in the fancy press. You may also initiate an internet article or be invited to contribute to a website. The internet makes the world a small place. It is all very exciting and good fun and with persistent effort you may become a 'great' or a household name. The bottom line of this is your love and passion for your birds and racing as normally you get out of the sport what you put in and perhaps a little more! You may also wish to write articles or books to further signify your presence in the larger sphere.

THE MOULT

The annual main moulting period (ecdysis) of the pigeon is a natural phenomenon. At this period birds (especially your stock) need baths! The food should be rich in oils and proteins – I could feed pellets in hoppers and hand feed in roller bar containers a high protein mix with Hormoform, brewer's yeast and Red Band, including a small amount of linseed and hemp. The birds need all they can eat, especially the latebreds. Replacing all the feathers is a stressful business, so be quiet and calm with your birds and let them out on good days for a fly if they desire and a bath with salts.

I note a lot of very poor lofts for stock birds – they need access to an aviary with the sun and the rain on their backs for good health, a very important fact. There are some very poor practices about – make sure you look after your birds properly. Take a good long hard look at yourself in the Fancier's Mirror – this is where the truth lies. Do you realise that by January even the flights of the distance birds should be renewed? Remember that throughout winter your young birds and yearlings are growing and need lots of good food – no short rations of a poor mix to keep them thin.

Look out for diseases during the moult, eg E. coli and salmonella – beware, especially with latebreds.

WILDLIFE

I like all creatures, although I am not particularly fond of rats. Every day I walk in the country and despite sparrowhawk population levels I see many species of birds, eg whitethroats, yellowhammers, linnets and many others. It's observing them and knowing where to look with a perceptive eye that counts.

Life forms have an equal right to be on earth with man, and believe me the planet does not need man to survive. In my old stock loft I had a fantastic collection of spiders, indicative of the healthy environment for the birds. These looked weird and a little gothic – you should encourage them. However not all creatures are harmless and you should watch out for cats, stoats, mice and rats – you can use traps for these. A Jack Russell terrier is a good friend in this respect.

An intuitive feel for nature will make you more receptive

to your pigeons' needs as sentient beings. As new starters I encourage all interaction with wildlife as nature is a great teacher.

Many people believe in a connection with all life, not just Buddhists, and I see wisdom in this stance.

YOUR VERY OWN STRAIN OF PIGEONS

As young children and new starters, you will love it when you win with your birds. If the winning goes on and on and you manage to do it with related birds bred by yourself, you could be on your way to forming your own family or strain of pigeons. You will breed from close relatives like brothers and sisters and after a time will inbreed and linebreed. Your birds will start to look like peas in a pod – a treat to the eye. Now for the crunch and the test – after say 25 years, you will be entitled to call the birds your strain, eg Jones strain or Smith strain. If publicised, your name may be famous or associated with greatness and may live on for a very long time.

Most fanciers quote Continental names for their pigeons. This is not a unique or individual thing to do, as once they are bred from in your loft the birds are yours in every sense of the word. Big Continental names like Vandenabeele are often used for money and/or reasons of status. The formation of a famous strain of bird is the highest honour and is above just race results. The British strains like Hunt, Gordon, Donaldson and Denney are as good as any in the world. Start now, be different, be unique – start your very own strain of pigeons.

THE OLD STRAINS

You should be aware that Stichelbauts are bred by Stichelbaut, Jan Aardens by Jan Aarden and Vandenabeele by Vandenabeele. Only direct birds bred by the named fancier should take the name of that fancier. If you breed off a family name, it is good practice to name the origin of the birds (if you know it) and state that they are bred by you under your loft and management conditions.

There is a lot of trading on the great names of the past when, at best, some of the 'genes' from way back may exist. How can we guarantee purity all these years later? Pure old strains such as Stichelbaut are a myth, since Alois died in the 1940s. It is probably fine to say that you think your birds are based on, say, Cattrysse or Jan Aarden.

When I talk about my strain of birds I often say that they were Stichelbaut-based. This does not imply that they were 100% of his origin. People claiming to have the pure old strains are making a lot of assumptions on purity. Even if you can prove there were no crosses in your birds, they are still bred from and managed by you. Yes, I am a purist on this matter and you will find that most birds are of mixed origins.

ONE-LOFT RACING

This is one of the modern trends in the pigeon 'sport' and it will grow in popularity. The birds, as paid entries, are raced under a management plan to a single loft location. As an interest and a public spectacle it is exciting and can generate much media coverage. Sometimes many birds arrive together, when it develops into a trapping finish to the race. The distance may increase to, say, in excess of 600 miles at the Barcelona International. Often quite a lot of money is gambled on the birds and I can see the Chinese and others being keen on that.

My abiding criticism (and, as usual, it is just my opinion) is that it is no test of the management skill of the individual fancier, other than the actual breeding of the bird. However, like ETS, we must embrace the new and encourage all reasonable aspects of the modern sport.

I think I am a purist and prefer the small-team, back-garden, long distance 'expert' who dedicates his life to his hobby. Of course, the development of a long-distance/marathon family or strain is the highest goal. I hope you will find my slanted comments interesting.

FUELLING UP PIGEONS

I am thinking of races over 500 miles, yet the basic principles will apply to shorter races and where heavy demands are placed on the birds. You need to maximise the energy reserves of the birds before basketing for the 'big' races. Naturally a balanced diet is required but the modern thinking is to load the birds with fats and carbohydrates before basketing.

Five days before basketing takes place, ad lib Hormoform, peanuts, Red Band and a sprinkle of hemp in the boxes where the birds are. For races in excess of 500 miles the birds will utilise fat reserves in the body, especially glycogen stored in the liver. Thin light birds will go down in marathon races. When my birds went to Barcelona they were large with reserves.

It is important to rest the birds for say two to four weeks prior to marathon races (700 miles plus) – they need to rest and feed up, like swallows on migration to Africa from the

UK. Liquid feeding is very important and to boost the birds I would give Blitzform by Rohnfried in the water.

On a normal week I used Boveil plus Eplus on a Wednesday and Aviform Ultimate on a Thursday and Friday. On a Thursday and Friday, I mixed oils on the corn mix with the brewer's yeast. Light overworked birds will not tackle long to marathon races.

EYESIGN

Each individual pigeon's eye is different and peculiar to that bird. It has been thought that results in racing or breeding could be predicted or discerned by looking at the colours and features and general characteristics of the eye. There are people who passionately believe this, yet I see no positive correlation between eyesign and racing ability that is greater than chance.

In related families of pigeons you may see similar eyes, but these are not necessarily linked to performance genes. It is very nice to see a brightly-coloured eye with lots of patterns in it, but this bird may not win or breed winners – there are many top birds with seemingly unimpressive eyes. When breeding, I would advise you to concentrate around winning birds at your favoured distance rather than breeding eye type, although pretty eyes may win eyesign shows. When looking at an eye it is easy to project your own belief and prejudice into it and as you are the subject it is difficult to be objective. If you examine the eyes of 'top' pigeons you will see how much they vary from any standard eyesign classification.

I based my ideas on experience rather than controlled scientific experimentation and are only my opinions. In practice my senses prefer a nice bright, healthy, lovely looking eye.

BAD PRACTICE IN THE SPORT

My pal Chris Booth of York has highlighted a scurrilous and bad practice. In two years he has had five birds return minus their ETS rings. This means fresh ETS rings are required, at further inconvenience and cost. I can only think that the perpetrators have a point to prove, an axe to grind, or are simply trying to conceal the identity of the birds. In any case and for whatever reason, the principle behind the removal of the ETS rings, which are not your property, is rotten.

ETS is here to stay, and it confers many advantages on its practitioners. We must all adapt to its long-term existence in the sport of pigeon racing. Of course the primary factor is to get your bird home and in the loft. ETS or no ETS, the top fancier will prevail, since the sport is elitist by nature. So that's it.

ARE BRITS THE BEST?

By most standards there are some excellent fanciers in many places of the world eg Holland, Germany, Belgium, USA, Australia and New Zealand. Naturally the winners of the European International races are invariably good fanciers, and I really rate the 800 miles, second day out of Barcelona, into north Holland. However, there is absolutely no need to acquire pigeons from outside the United Kingdom and Ireland. Since we fly the Channel and can get over 1,000 miles with the best of our birds, the quality of the bird and the fancier is as good as you need over here.

Many fanciers, through popular belief coupled with shrewd advertising, will buy foreign birds which may not be as good as those they already have. The external and essential fact and secret is that good husbandry, knowledge and expertise produce good pigeons: if you don't have it, you won't be a top fancier. Take a good look at yourself. Do you pass the mirror test?

We have many fanciers who would stand against any in the world. Names that spring to mind are Neil Bush, Chris Gordon, Jim Donaldson, Geoff Kirkland, the Padfields, John Halstead and York's Brian Denney. Ronnie Williamson of Ireland with 50 plus NIPA wins surely takes the world middle-distance award. All these men are touched by genius.

GOOD SPORTSMANSHIP

If you have a genuine love of pigeon racing and its people, you will show a positive attitude to others who do well. Sometimes this is difficult, due to jealousy or envy. You have to rise above that and give praise to the successful fanciers – that is part of their success and the important recognition of their success. Many of the various problems with pigeon clubs are down to bad sportsmanship. A simple handshake of the winner is all that it takes, plus a 'well done'. I show mine in the writings about various families. I take a high moral stand in this and I know we are only human and therefore imperfect, but it does help if we try. Being a good sport won't necessarily make you popular, yet some will respond in a positive manner. I have initiated the BHW Sports Personality, where you can all judge the top three people in terms of their contribution to pigeon racing as a whole, their popularity and their impact on pigeon racing. Remember, this is personality and not racing results alone – it is much more than good results. As for me, I use my position to promote the sport.

ROOM AT THE TOP

It will be a shock to many that no one has ever won at the top level of racing into the UK. The top level in the world's greatest race is to win the Barcelona International, and then to win it again. Now this could well be impossible for us, yet it is to be aimed at.

Now I do take the above to be a little academic, so that you should aim for the top of your club, Federation, National or perhaps International. Brian Sheppard, Mark Gilbert and Mr Posey are our only International winners, and we should be proud of them.

My advice is not to be overawed by anyone and keep trying to improve with your racing and breeding results. Never, ever think that you play second fiddle to anyone. Carve out your career and aim for the top. The very top is still vacant; there is room for all.

USE OF LAYER PELLETS

I have done much to promote layer pellets for pigeons over the years and most enquiries I receive centre on their use. The facts are that my birds were successful using hoppers of hen layers' pellets at all times. The feeding is of superior quality to just corn, since they are developed by science. Hoppers are supplied at all times for all birds to peck at. The pellets are the basis of the diet of the pigeon at all times, stock, racers and young.

I have explained my use of corn mixes many times before as an addition to the diet. At just over £6 per 25 kilo bag you can't go wrong, and no they do not contain harmful antibiotics. They are easy to digest and excellent for stock and racers. With 100% pellets the droppings may be loose –

this is not a worry. Fanciers are paranoid about loose droppings. Yes, even my Dax, Pau, San Sebastian and Barcelona birds were on layers' pellets. For marathon and extreme distance racing you cannot feed too much. On pellets your birds will not over-eat. Get some now – you will see the benefits.

GOOD PIGEONS ARE GIVEN (MUMS AND DADS)

My sound advice to all is to spend as little money on buying pigeons as possible. It is very difficult to pick a good pigeon on looks alone. We live in a greedy, money-based world and everywhere people are out to make money out of you. Beware, be careful, keep your money in your pocket. Having said this, from 1982 onwards I sold pigeons all over the UK and abroad – I enjoyed it. Let me say I started my work on £3 per week. Money should be put in its place beneath the personality of the individual. By all means charge for some of your birds but make the prices reasonable, as say Geoff Kirkland does – his reasonable prices say a lot about the man!

When you do well with your birds, you will be in a position to be given and exchange good birds with other fliers and friends. Always give of the best in exchange for the best. After a while you may develop a network in the UK.

The prices for many pigeons of dubious quality are astronomical and tend to say everything about greed and little about the real value of the pigeon. If you must buy or sell I would say £60 for a well-bred bird and £100 off a champion – that's if you can't get them for nothing!

RECOGNITION FOR YOUR WORK

In my experience, most if not all fanciers enjoy some recognition for their hard work and dedication with the birds. We race for results and to reach certain targets, or to surpass others. The target or goal may be to be the top prizewinner in your club or to beat the local ace. It is very nice to be popular with, recognised and respected by others in the hobby.

Now there are some singular individuals who do not require publicity and go their own way. This shows an independence of spirit which I admire. It must be stated that recognition implies a security risk for your birds, so keep them locked and alarmed. We live in a world where the lure of fame can be intoxicating.

In my role as a writer, I like to promise people with noteworthy achievements and 'champion' pigeons. Two journalists I can name who have promoted others well are Liam O'Comain and Les Parkinson. There are many others, such as Joe Murphy and Keith Mott. We owe all the magazine people and website holders a debt of gratitude for the way that knowledge has been spread and fanciers highlighted around the world.

PERSONALITY

I so value the individual, the personal subjective qualities of people and all life. In our society, which is based on money and possessions, it is refreshing and heart-warming to see the characters and personalities emerging out of the masses. In the final analysis I think a person is pure spirit in a physical form. If we study our pigeons we can see them and experience them as individuals eg quiet and relaxed or boisterous widowhood cocks. I am pleased to have developed a family, where members are particularly tame and quiet. This is down to my selective breeding and peace amongst the birds. Some of the great personalities that have emerged are Geoff Kirkland, Les Parkinson and Liam Comain, for example.

LOFT SECURITY

Keeping your birds safe and sound is of utmost importance to you. Believe me, it is very soul destroying to have your birds stolen from your premises. It is as simple as this: lock your gates and lofts at all times and think about alarms, CCTV and guard dogs. Another aspect of pigeon safety is not letting out birds that should be in – I refer to your good and/or expensive stock birds, which if prisoners should have access to a wire-tipped aviary. Many, many fanciers will accidentally let valuable stock birds go, ie through leaving doors ajar, never to be seen again.

My advice is to have your prisoner stock in a building within a building, this can be an aviary within a building having an external door. Now when the inevitable happens and a bird or two escape, they will be within the building. When building your family or strain you need to hang on to your key birds for many years; constantly obtaining fresh birds as you lose the originals will result in a loft full of allsorts and crosses. A top fancier develops his own strain.

ALWAYS CLOCK

In any race from the shortest to the longest, there may be circumstances when weather, clashing, peregrines or other orientation difficulties may arise. I recall a race from

Buckingham, 138 miles, when I had sent my International birds for a breather – there were only two birds on the day. It is simple, always clock your National and International birds in race time – they may be in the result or collect money. I did not clock Dax 11 when she would have been 6th Sect K Dax International in 2004. Best to learn the lessons the hard way; then you will never forget!

In clubs which give cards for the first four places for example, always clock the first four. You may miss out on valuable points which count in your club. You may get an arrival in the hours of darkness like some of the 700-milers at Tarbes in '08. If so then clock to show that the birds came on the day or second day of liberation. I recall with fondest memory Dark Enchantment at 10.08pm from Pau, 735 miles. Your good birds deserve their recognition for their efforts and endurance feats. Always try and do the right thing at the time.

Note: thanks to the Cheeky Charmer of York for his exemplary and learned advice on my writing prowess. The Cheeky Charmer is the famous Steve Shipley.

OLD PIGEONS

If pigeons have lived beyond five years in most lofts, they are doing well. Many sprint birds are finished by three and distance birds by five. Normally race birds have finished their career by 10. For breeding birds some cocks will carry on producing at 15 and some hens at 13 – the time varies.

When I was young and ruthless I disposed of unwanted old birds, but in the case of Sister Damien, The Dutchman and Dedication I later regretted it. I believe that exceptional old birds should live out their natural life in retirement. Jim

Donaldson has a special section for his old favourites and I like the kind sentiment attached to this idea.

My racing was so hard that I never had to dispose of a race bird as my distances and the basket were the natural (Darwinian) selectors. I maintain that if you end the season with too many birds then they have not been tested far enough. My belief is that every bird once two years old should fly over 700 miles. Some birds can score from 100 to 700 miles plus, though they are rare. These are the types of birds that can be storm makers, like Dedication.

Do not part with your well-bred stock too early; my The Dutchman bred Sister Damien and Damien as a pensioner. Look after your birds, they are living jewels.

DEDICATED FOLLOWERS OF FASHION

There are many new names in the pigeon world. The birds within the name are invariably of mixed origins, yet we call them by a fixed name, eg Lindelauf. This gives credit to the supplier and often for reasons of commerce, status and deference.

It is so easy to follow fashionable trends and buy and buy; parting with your money to line others pockets. In my mind a really dedicated fancier sticks to his own pigeons, year in year out. He aims to perfect his management to achieve his aims with birds bred by himself. The secret is to find one or two pairs that produce good birds, then line and inbreed to these and the offspring. After a while of long term focus, say 25 years, you may be the fashion trendsetter. People will want your birds, not those of some far-off Belgian. When this happens like it did with say Jim Bliss, you have made your mark as an individual. At this stage if this does not bring happiness then something is wrong.

As a starter I would advise you to make a friend of a top National/International flier and learn and learn. If he is genuine he will supply you with birds from his best. Remember the master was once a novice like yourself. It sounds like an episode of 'Kung Fu', yet the truth is plain to see. Do not follow the herd, go your own way! Be the trendsetter.

SPORTING HEROES

I think most of us have people who we admire, look up to and regard, perhaps, with awe and respect. These can influence and inspire us to go and achieve or be more interested in our sports. People are fascinating in that they often love to compete and to stretch the boundaries of what is possible in the world.

No matter how good you think you are, the world is a huge receptacle of human greatness. Since the 1950s I have watched Formula 1 and I regard this as a peak of sporting endeavour. In my mind the fastest and most charismatic driver was Ayrton Senna. His driving was a metaphor for life and he lived out the extreme. A deeply introspective and mystical man, he left the motor racing world spellbound with his magnificent racing brain.

Of today's sportspeople, I like Usain Bolt, who is a force of nature in running, and in his day Ronnie O'Sullivan was the supreme genius of snooker.

As beginners, you will hold your local ace fliers in high esteem and it is good to do so – it will help you to be positive in your outlook. From my own biased outlook the late Jim Biss and Ronnie Williamson of Ireland are our two greats, and the accolade of great genius goes to Jim Biss! You know I love to praise worthiness and it gets you out of yourself!

WHAT ARE GOOD PIGEONS?

This answer to this is purely one of value judgement, subjective and dependent on the individual. In general terms a good pigeon performs well enough in racing for you as the person to call it a good pigeon. It may win a race say at Club, Federation, amalgamation, Combine, National or International level. You may also consider a bird with a number of positions to be a good pigeon.

In my personal opinion I would consider a bird which flies over 500 miles on the day in a head wind a good pigeon, and all birds that fly 700 miles plus on the second day to be good birds (especially against the wind). Barcelona International birds that fly over 800 miles on the third and fourth day into the UK, I would call good birds. Sometimes, judges decide on the best performance pigeon or trophy in a flying organisation – the recipients can be regarded as good birds.

Breeding of stock birds can be considered good when they are parents or grandparents of 'good' performing birds. The acid test is sending your birds to your chosen distance and proving by results if they are any good or not. A beautiful bird may be useless at racing or breeding. For hard races over 700 miles I prefer small to medium birds which are compact and buoyant.

In the final analysis 'good' is what you agree it to be. Then what is a champion or excellent pigeon? As beginners your winners will be 'good' to you.

I have bred many good pigeons in my time from 71 to 879 miles and from the same family. My own Diabolos won best performance trophy winner in the Yorks Middle Route Federation. His descendants have been successful from 71 to 879 miles and are doing it today. A rare pigeon indeed, a great champion, a strain maker.

My advice is to keep improving with your breeding and racing until you are satisfied that you and your birds are good according to your own judgement. If others agree then all well and good.

I would consider that Barcelona International winners are undoubtedly good birds, wouldn't you?

GENIUS

The definition or interpretation of genius depends on how you feel or think about it. It can mean exceptional intellectual and/or artistic power – a term very much open to analysis and debate.

There are some popular models of genius, eg Einstein and Leonardo da Vinci. It is so relative, yet as humans we like to sing the praises of so-called talented and gifted people. In the world there are some creative and wonderful people – they are in our midst. The human race is a vast receptacle of great achievement. In the pigeon world it is confined to the sublime and unusual insights and results of a few dedicated and singular individuals. These are as eccentric as they are rare, and their contributions have taken pigeon racing onward and forward. With their educative and new methods and stirring achievements they have added to the overall body of pigeon knowledge.

We all have our favourites; for me the greatest pigeon genius who ever walked on earth has to be the late Jim Biss. Geoff Kirkland has set the world on fire as a gentleman one-day racer and Ronnie Williamson is the foremost middle distance man on Planet Earth. An original writer has been Liam O'Comain MA.

For talent and sublime gifts you need look no further than the UK. We are here!

THE PIGEONS

Pigeons have been with people for thousands of years. They are normally fairly tame and easily cared for. Many are beautiful 'fancy' show type birds eg 'Fairy Swallows', 'Priests', 'Lahores' and 'Jacobins'. Some people hate the 'street' pigeon – it depends how you feel – I love all pigeons, full stop!

Once you like pigeons they can get under your skin. There was a man who thought he was one! Young children may find the white or brightly-coloured ones very fascinating to look at and there are some beautiful colours eg 'red ones', 'black ones' and silver ones' – nearly all the colours of the rainbow. Apart from a little peck from a sitting bird, they are totally harmless to humans. I had my first when I was three years of age. You may be like me and become a fanatic.

Hatching from an egg after the female bird has laid the egg and kept it warm for 17-18 days, a bird may live for 30 years in captivity and around 3 to 4 as street birds. Of course pigeons fly with their wings and racers may fly over 1,000 miles – think about that! A good bird has soft rich feathers to keep it warm and protected. If you keep some birds for pets or for racing you will always remember them. Think about getting some now!

THE PIGEON FANCIER

I became a fancier of sorts at the age of 3 at 14 Burgh Road, Skegness. My father, a quiet, gentle and thoughtful influence, started me off with tumblers and fancy birds. Earlier he had kept pigeons and border canaries in his bedroom. I think he was too nice a person to enter the competitive world of pigeon racing

Believe me, the normal pattern is that once you keep pigeons and learn to love them you will be addicted, perhaps for life. As a new starter or novice a good and genuine fancier will give you some good birds for breeding and young birds for yourself – I have given lots away in my time. 'Good pigeons are given' is a good saying to adopt. The love of money drives pigeon sales and I have been guilty of this.

The number of fanciers in the UK and the world is in decline and I am writing these articles to try and inform and encourage all beginners out there, wherever you are. You should seek out the kind and generous man or woman, who will help you; some of these can be found at pigeon clubs, shows, in books, magazines and on the internet. As a beginner, may I suggest you put your questions to the BHW when the 'experts' will answer them.

Fanciers range from simple folk to 'genius' and they all have things in common and all can be beaten with the birds in flying events. We all start at the beginning and there is no end – it is eternal.

THE PIGEON LOFT

A loft, cree, shed, pen etc is the house or shelter for the birds. Mine came from Tadcaster, York in 1976 and at £60 was a bargain. It was old but good enough for me and the birds. A part image of it can be seen on the Prestige Pigeons website by Kimberley Crowley. Pigeons need a dry loft, warmth, air, space, light, shade and security. They are easily caught by cats, rats, birds of prey and dogs, and will feel safe and secure in a building which these creatures cannot enter.

For young fanciers: your father may help to build you a shed or to buy one at a reasonable cost. Pigeons do not need a palace, and elaborate lofts are usually bought to please the fancier. A Petron loft is perhaps the Rolls Royce of lofts. Lofts can be erected in your garden or on an allotment or field site. You should consider some security, locks, alarms, CCTV etc if felt necessary. They can have sliding doors or trays for the birds to enter. I liked my old loft, which had an entrance/exit at the top side for the birds.

The building is usually made from wood or brick; think what the birds' needs are, which should be your needs. If you have neighbours, consider them when erecting buildings and check for planning regulations. A detached house in the country is perfect.

FEATHER AND COLOURS

To me all pigeons are beautiful. In pigeons there are upward of 28 colours (morphs). Racing pigeons are thought to descend from the blue rock (rock dove), originally an Asiatic type thousands of years ago. Many racers are blue bars, blue chequers, so called blacks and reds and with white on them are pieds. Some beautiful show pigeons (fancy) exist and they may be opal, dun, lavender and mottle and grizzle. The iridescent hackle feathers around the neck are often green and purple and look vivid in fit birds.

A good racing pigeon by definition has good feathers; often like satin or silk to the sight and touch. The long distance and marathon birds often have tight, glossy, silky feathers to fly 500 to 1000 miles like my Barcelona International birds. I do not like birds with dry, coarse feather.

Racing fanciers are very conscious of the long primary feathers of their birds used in flight home.

I like white pigeons as partners for my best racers and

decoy (flirt) birds to entice the racers to enter home.

In 1976 I was lucky that Jack Ross introduced me to a pigeon club; I am eternally grateful to him, although frustratingly, I have lost contact with him. At local pigeon clubs and societies, which may be from pubs or working men's clubs, there are some people (eg the Secretary or President) who may help you to join a racing pigeon club or even a 'fancy' pigeon club. This magazine and the Royal Pigeon Racing Association will also help you and will pay special attention to novices and new starters. Some clubs will give free membership for young people to a very rewarding hobby and pastime.

When you join I advise you to think of 20 questions to ask the members as a start. I also think that you should become ambitious with your birds right away and send them to the races. You can always keep breeding more and more.

It will be helpful if you are pleasant and show some respect to the club members and perhaps you can show them a trick or two on computers. Don't be afraid to have a go at the big clubs like NFC and BICC and decide what sort of distances you want to race in, as your interest may last you a lifetime. We are here to help you.

TIMING YOUR BIRD

A pigeon will have a rubber race ring or an ETS ring around its leg. With these devices the time of arrival of your racing pigeon can be recorded using a clock eg an STB Quartz, a Junior or a modern Electronic Timing System (ETS) such as Unikon. The exact time of arrival of your bird is turned into an average velocity in yards per minute in the UK and the highest one wins the race, assuming that you have followed the rules fair and square.

If you are a novice, this magazine will help and advise you, as will many generous pigeon men or women. These may be relatives or people at your local pigeon club.

So get on, race your birds and I will tell you that you will remember your first win (and forget many of the others). Always be honest and never think about cheating. With talent and the right birds you will eventually win. Everyone is there to be beaten.

I do recommend that you learn about the ETS, as this is the way forward, and also rubber ringing of birds at the club.

SPECIALIST YOUNG BIRD TECHNIQUES

Young bird racing can be exciting and lucrative. Good ones will perform with distinction from 50 to 450 miles on the day of liberation. I look forward to the first 500-mile young bird on the day into the UK. In the York area in England, my birds were twice in the first five Open and twice in the first three Open from six races, with other positions. At the time I described my approach as follows:

Feeding: hoppers of layers' pellets at all times. The birds were called in at tea time (around 5pm) to a mixture of Haith's Widowhood Sprint Corn, peanuts, Red Band (condition seed) and brewer's yeast. Water: Wednesday – fruit spoon of Bovril/gallon of water; Sunday – fruit spoon of Bovril/gallon of water; Thursday/Friday – Aviform; Saturday (race day) Chevita Multivit. Before basketing: Mycosan 'T' and Chlortetracycline mixed together on Thursday and Friday. The birds were psyched up to the eyeballs. Exercise: The birds ranged the skies on open loft from 5.30 am onwards (summer). Training: I liked a 90-mile toss on Wednesday. Fielding: My birds sat on wires and fed on barley in the fields around the village of Holtby, York.

My secret was that the night before basketing for racing that day the birds were kept in the house back room with no feed and water in the baskets. They go warm and were really keen to get home. Psychology: I mobilised the birds' instincts to survive and get home as quickly as possible. Result: it was a joy to watch the shiny beauties racing flat out to the loft. Strain of bird: The birds were of the Emerton strain, 71 to 879 miles. You just alter the management systems as the distance gets longer.

RESTORING RACE BIRDS

I have seen some pigeons in a very debilitated state after flights of various distances. This shows just how hard it can be – a life in racing!

We aim to send birds to the big races in peak form though good exercise and nutrition. To restore our charges for further efforts and purely as a love of nature and on compassionate grounds we must act.

In my loft were layers' pellets 24/7, in hopper. These are nutritionally superior to corn mixes and are more easily digested. However, I would first tempt the retiring birds with some quality (bought by the sack) Indian solid peanuts. These have a high energy conversion content of fat and protein – ideal.

The debate about electrolytes is ongoing. Scientific debate thinks that for pigeons they are normally unnecessary, since the electrolytic concentration increases with dehydration. However for many years I administered Chevita Multivit in the water for returning race birds. This detoxifies the bird and restores and regenerates the muscle tissue. Later on in the day feed with the normal corn mix.

Believe me, competing with pigeons is lovely on a simple and well-thought out system.

A good tip – look up Chevita GMBH on Google on your computer – I am pleased to help you

THE YORK RACE SCENE

York is blessed with some excellent racing men and women. These days, in the clubs, every avenue is explored to win and get to the top. We are helped by modern science and technology – you need to be able to get ahead of the game. We have the Acomb, Tang Hall and Haxby clubs amongst others and rivalry is feverishly hot stuff!

Brian Denney as an individual has set the standard at National level as I did at International level. There is a wonderful array of personalities and characters – I am always there for an interview for this excellent journal. It pleases me greatly to be back involved in the breeding and racing game, and I do my best for others.

I would love to see a lot more NFC racing and some BICC racing to York. It can be done, it should be done. In my opinion the Masons are top class up to 500+ miles and have a superb set of birds. Let us all unite and create greatness for the York race scene.

PESTS

There are usually some pests trying to live off your birds. Pigeons are prone to many of these and they need to be kept under control, or the birds kept free of them.

Worms such as hairworms, roundworms, gapeworms and sometimes tapeworms will at some stage infect your pigeons. These reduce condition and absorb food supplies from your birds. Some good vets will examine your birds' droppings to check for their presence. A wormer (vermicide) may be used in water to protect against hairworm and roundworm, eg Moxidectin, and tapeworm will need, say, Praziquental.

Pigeons are also prey to feather mite, red mite, flies and lice. Once again Moxidectin may be used in water, or some fanciers use Van Verminex (a Vanhee product) or dips or sprays based on permethrin.

On summer nights you may see pigeon moths in your loft. I recall a bird of mine returning from Spain complete with pigeon fly. My advice is – keep your birds free of pests; keep them clean and in strong, bouncy good health.

Other pests include rats, mice, stoats, cats and sparrowhawks and you should find out about all of these for the safety and comfort of your birds. It helps if you have some knowledge of the countryside and pest control.

UPDATE ON THE EMERTON STRAIN

In 2009, Joe's Delight, 11th Section K, 155th Open NFC Tarbes, 738 miles, is a beautiful specimen of a pigeon, raced by Jim Weatherley & O'Brien of Yorkshire. Jim was delighted with the bird and we agree that he could be a strainmaker of the future. Steve Wain's hen took 13th Section I from Tarbes, 671 miles, and she was closely followed by another, her sister from the No 1 pair. My friend, Trevor Robinson, won the longest race with a yearling cross and Jim Donaldson won the SNFC North Section with a descendant of Barcelona Dream and Dark Enchantment.

For further reports I can be contacted via the BHW.

TWO

The Jim Emerton Column

From 'The Racing Pigeon'

MARCH 8 2013

THE INTERNAL QUALITIES OF GOOD PIGEONS

There are very many beautiful-looking pigeons with silky feathers, balance and buoyancy in the hand. Some of these judged on external appearance (phenotype), win in the show pen. In reality and to the racing fancier, very few of these will be good racing birds or champion breeders. Do not be conned by sparkling good looks alone. What we need to do is look at the birds as a whole with our minds, with our vision. You see, what really determines a good bird are the 'invisible' factors, the genes and on a more apparent level the heart, lungs and the brain (internal organs). Without the gene carriers for racing ability, a bird will never have the potential to excel in racing. I recall my No 2 stock cock (brother of 'Dark Destiny'), he appeared to be a small, runty cock with a flat head. You see he was a result of a brother to sister mating within an inbred family. Now he was fantastic as a breeder. Why? Because he carried exceptional internal qualities. The message I am trying to convey is to look deeper and further, try and be at one with your birds when breeding. Concentrate around related birds with top results, this way you may hit on the 'good' gene combinations. The acid test is marathon racing over 700 miles, success at distance proves the internal qualities.

THE SPIRIT OF RACING

In my perception, both birds and humans have an inner or spiritual nature. A fancier in a heightened state of consciousness can know the 'oneness' of man and pigeon. This is racing at its very best and most rewarding state; it is a spiritual experience, a journey of the soul. Writers give credence to the mystical and for example, if you clock at Barcelona International, the fact should elevate the ego. When we start at say club level, if we are ambitious we want to win and win, irrespective of the quality of races, I may add. We then set out to be top prize winner at club level, beating the local 'experts'. Now to the initiated and on an esoteric level, racing is a larger playing field than this. We can see the wisdom in testing and building a strain, we can test the outer limits of endurance of our birds. I can say that I did this as a modern pioneer at 687 miles, Dax International into Yorkshire and to verify 3 out of 6 birds at

Barcelona International 879 miles. Now ponder the actual flying distance of those endurance athletes that would dogleg around the Pyrenees. My strain of birds are fit and well after 33 years, rue testament to the 'Spirit of Racing'.

THE PSYCHOLOGY OF A TOP FANCIER

It's all in the mind you see, ladies and gentlemen. At the heart and root of all racing successes and pigeon-racing related activities is the mind of man – the birds being the objective reality of our desires, dreams, plans and breeding and racing systems. The individual personality of the fancier is paramount as the essential source and requirement of success. I know this from my convoluted journey – do you? From my analysis and introspection many character traits comprise the psyche of an expert or champion, i.e. pure focus, dedication, ruthlessness, compassion, empathy, singularity of purpose, patience, longevity, in depth scientific/artistic insights and pragmatism. If these are suffused by possible genius, and in a helpful social context, success is assured. Okay. I am being analytical again and although this is a shallow reflection of a person it helps to explain in some way the complexity of the psyche of a champion.

THE MIND OF THE MARATHON MAN

In my mind's eye, marathon means a distance in excess of 700 miles and can go beyond 1000 miles into the UK. If – and especially if – this is combined with the international element, it is a daunting task for the most hardened, seasoned and mentally tough mind in the UK. To achieve success at these levels takes a peculiar and special mindset, both of the fancier and pigeon. I call to mind the three Ps, perseverance, persistence and patience, for racing a marathon is a task that encourages emotions, unlike the quick, excited buzz that club sprint racing engenders, since it takes you into a mental zone which is akin to a mystical state, like Zen. It is an experience for the initiated.

The mind of the marathon man will have bred birds. The key to inbreeding is to breed around performance genes, inferred from the good performances of the actual racers. It is a fine feeling to look at the same birds today in 2012 and see all my performance birds at National and International level in their origin. This is a very personal and individual thing to do and I say that after more than 25 years of this practice you can your family your strain, ie the Emerton strain. In terms of heterosis or hybrid vigour, I introduced two very inbred hens out of Brian Denney's Dangerman (Stichelbaut-base) which catalysed some of my own birds. To inbreed then you persevere over many years with closely related birds up to brother x sister and always test the progeny in hard racing from 71 to 879 miles. Yes, I can reflect on my breeding over 36 years. Some not closely related birds are introduced from time to time from top birds at 700-plus miles but are absorbed back into the strain. Some inbred birds are too refined and small (may show recessive genes in the phenotype). These can be excellent for outbreeding (crossing). Others may grow into absolute specimens. Therefore, as Geoff Cooper and Deweerdt do, stick to your own and with intuition (stock sense) keep focused. Make the birds your own. Like all lines of birds, I would suggest that less than 1% of mine would fly 879 miles at Barcelona International. Now, other than Rome, this is where your birds should be going. Many of you will continue to buy birds for outcrossing as Vanhee did, yet the pundits like Geoff Cooper and Jim Donaldson keep to their own. To summarise then, you inbreed to performance breeders and racers and send them to International level.

MARCH 22 2013

PHYSICAL TYPE

To me all pigeons are beautiful. Quality racing pigeons come in a myriad of colours, shapes and sizes due to genetic diversity in their origins. My birds were mainly chequers/darks and dark velvets via breeding and race selection. I prefer darks with silky feather classed as yellow and being small or medium balanced birds with nice deep pectoral muscles and smooth and tight in the hand. An exception was Barcelona Dream – a giant of a cock bird. If a bird becomes a champion at any distance it follows *a priori* that its genotype and phenotype are satisfactory in the reality test of racing. There are birds to score from 90 to 735 miles at Pau like my Dedication, which are rare. A good bird usually gives out to the mind's eye an essence of its quality, ie in the eye of the beholder. In practical terms hard racing under optimal management will produce the desired physical type and genotype, since there is no set physical type or eye type at any distance – the latter will manifest family traits and characteristics and it is fascinating to make studies of these. The greatest fancier alive knows little, yet racing will put your knowledge and theory to test in the fire of experience.

CHASING THE RAINBOW

Sometimes in our search for success we may spend money

seeking out much-hyped or seemingly excellent birds or bloodlines. Commercialism in mainstream society benefits by this phenomenon and it fills hungry pockets. Some fanciers near or at a top level via almost perfected racing and breeding systems know in their wisdom that champions often begin at home! In reality all pigeon families can have the potential to produce excellence, as behind the family person's name they can be racing birds of variable innate quality.

A champion results from a fusion of its potential with the racing environment. The limiting and key factor in the equation is the overall personality of the fancier – this variable applies to any human in any sport because of one's belief system. Naturally some believe in God's intervention, or that a study of eyes reveals predictability of racing/breeding performance. I am a pragmatist with a simple rule of thumb which smacks of reality to me: send them and see the results after liberation from the races. We are free spirits, yet may I suggest to some International races. Enjoy it.

FIELDING

Most people frown upon their birds using local fields and in some cases this is wise practice, with notable exceptions. As a freedom lover myself and in the village of Holtby all my birds ranged as they needed to ingest grain, minerals and some vegetable and animal supplements. From 1976 onwards very few were shot, with some predated by sparrowhawks. My birds were pin sharp and almost wild, returning to the loft to nest, feed, drink and roost. Young and old walked the fields, sat on wires and sunned themselves on barns, and they were out all winter even in snow. Dorothy and I would break the ice, feed hoppers of pellets and supply all the birds' nutritional needs. At times it was bliss. Neil Bush and Nic Harvey do something similar, and for marathon races it works, and is beautiful in its simplicity. Ideally this applies to selected rural locations having checked out local conditions. In my system all ages of birds were together on deep litter in the same loft at all times – a free ranging pampered colony of pigeons. We absolutely loved it and recall those days with fond remembrance.

THE NORTH/SOUTH DIVIDE

Humans tend to be prejudiced into believing or asserting that fanciers in the south or north are the best, especially in England. The motivation is often a seeking of superiority allied to the male ego! In UK racing different distances can be involved, say up to 700 plus miles in the south to over 900 in the north of England or 1000 into Scotland. We race for personal reasons from club to international level with success dependent on many factors. Degree of difficulty may be related to time on the wing – distance and environmental conditions being some of the variables. I have lived north, south, east and west and believe me, there are quality fanciers and birds in all those quadrants. For myself, I am biased towards racing in the north of England over 700 miles and in internationals. The latter is difficult and I hope to see more participation in this onerous task. In the final analysis each race is what it is and may you derive pleasure from the activity. In the future many records will be broken and sporting icons will emerge from the heat of competition.

BASKET OR JUDGEMENT?

In racing the key is to get your birds to the chosen race so that race reality will decide the outcome under those particular conditions. You may have been wise enough via a prior decision to nominate your leading bird with accurate decision-making from pure experience of a perceptive, thoughtful and intuitive nature and sound stock sense. Some people develop the art, others rely on say chance. Pooling for money may hone the required skills.

There are too many variables for breeding/racing to be an exact science and much of the success is down to the personality of the fancier in juxtaposition with the intrinsic qualities of the birds. Assuming that we have some control of our pigeon destiny, then with quality judgment I recommend ambitious fanciers to persist with dogged determination until you are happy with the results – plenty of room at the top! The pioneers continue to push the boundaries of possibility, creating champions in the process.

A LEAP OF FAITH

Sending to any race point is a journey into the unknown. The birds primed for the task in hand are at the cruel mercy of the elements. We may feel secure in our guesswork of the outcome, yet the beauty lies in uncertainty. Will we produce the rare champion, a strain maker to propel our name into the future? The race may test our metal, our inner self resolve, in our attempt to triumph over nature or be at one with it. In competition with our peers and rivals we have stirrings of a primal nature – will the ambitions be realised? As man conquered Everest, our highest aspiration may be Barcelona. It is a spiritual odyssey to self-realisation, a giant leap of faith into the future.

MODERN BRITISH STRAINS

In Great Britain are some outstanding, world-class fanciers who dedicate their singular lives to the creation of birds with a distinct hereditary characteristic. Individuals from these groups of related birds may span performances from sprint to marathon distances up to international level, i.e. in excess of 700 miles – my yardstick! Let us just focus on our own stellar fanciers for a little while, detached from others, although I do like the 800-mile Dutch birds, landing on the second day out of Barcelona International – good old Wouter Jorna.

If we look and perceive with a shrewd eye, who appears on our shores? Well there are many leading candidates such as Chris Gordon, Nick Harvey, Brian Denney, Jim Donaldson, Booth and Shipley, Neil Bush, John Tyerman, Padfield family and many others. Wise fanciers exchange bloodlines with each other, and strains result from dedicated good management over time. I hope this article is a celebration of our own good work.

MARCH 20 2013

INSPIRATION

As humans we need to be lifted and motivated to go forward and achieve. Outstanding feats of individuals can drive us towards our goals on a psychological and spiritual level, and history is enriched by leading and classical examples of its impact.

I recall gazing at the blue cock 'King of Rome' in the museum at Derby. As a small boy Mother and I would feed the strags peanuts in the Wardwick Square just adjacent to the museum, and young Emerton would meditate on the charismatic Mr Hudson and his famous bird — a daydream that would change and ignite the fire of my imagination.

On a celebrity level many outstanding personalities have inspired me on a deeply felt level and these include the Bird Man of Alcatraz, Ayrton Senna, William Blake and Nelson Mandela. In the future some of you may become sources of inspiration — just go out and do it.

WHAT'S IN A NAME

Pigeons tend to assume the names of the publicised or famous fancier, humans all! To my knowledge there are no homozygotically 100 per cent genetically pure racing pigeons, ie all with an identical genome. Names become popular due to the media marketing them for ego/sales and a multiplicity of reasons. Janssens and Stichelbaut, who are still famous pigeon people, did not have absolutely pure birds, although it may be perceived that they did. Fashionable strains come and go like quicksilver, yet really top pigeon men are rare, are they not? Now that will be unearthly when the Barcelona International is won into the UK. It is possible but improbable. The real joy is in building a family with a distinct hereditary characteristic that performs at a satisfactory level. Okay, they may take your name, even though they are but a mixture. It is the humanisation element of the sport, and this is only my subjective opinion in the vast complexity of pigeon racing.

CREATING YOUR OWN FAMILY

This can be a very rewarding experience and a long-term target for the dedicated fancier. It helps to specialise with the birds at your chosen race distances from sprint to marathon, or even all distances. Devise an overall management plan and stick to it using related birds from up to brother and sister matings. Logically, severe testing of all race birds in the heat of competition is essential to the goal, and over many years. From time to time a related outcross from top racers/producers may be required, whilst maintaining the overall family/hereditary characteristics of the colony. I like inbred birds, yet each bird is different. As you reap the benefits of your labour of love you may be able to run an exchange network of top breeding to your liking. A little thought and focus will help you on your way to satisfaction.

HOMING & ORIENTATION

As far as we can perceive, the how and why of this process remain elusive to science and the fancy at large. Who can tell what a pigeon experiences within its being or the exact method or impetus that drives a pigeon to home over great distances up to and over 1,000 miles against variable weather conditions? it remains the beautiful mystery! Scientific methodology as it evolves applies experiment and analysis in an attempt to resolve the enigma with examinations of sense of smell, especially magnetic fields, the sun, landmarks and other physical and non-physical phenomena. Having jumped birds over 500 miles into races, it is my belief that a bird may know or otherwise sense a homing impulse sitting in the transporter which may never be properly understood. Food for thought.

SELLING PIGEONS

This is most enjoyable in practice as you expand your network of influence, perhaps in the world! Some good and published results are preferable, yet not essential for success. To be genuine the origin of the birds, I think, should be steeped in generations of related top performance bloodlines, at your preferred competitive distances and levels of competition. In racing and breeding reality very few great birds will be produced — we are yet to produce a Barcelona International winner into the UK. Good selling vehicles via media advertising are the internet/mags/stud books and word of mouth. It all adds interest/spice and money to the pigeon culture — and rewards egos! The most valuable contribution I see as the dissemination and expansion of top strains and bloodlines for the future benefit of the sport. Be aware and shrewd when you buy and sell — illusion and reality!

WINTER EXERCISE

Many fanciers, through continental influences, confine their birds to lofts during the winter months — a practice which can ease management. For marathon and long distance racing at national and international level Nic Harvey and I fly the birds on open loft all winter, being careful in foggy conditions — hens and cocks on alternate days. With hopper feeding the race birds assume good condition, honing instincts and living a free, almost natural life each day. At two years of age, any hardy survivors from a strict racing regime will face 710 miles at Barcelona International, with no exceptions to this practice. In this way a modern strain of endurance birds will evolve from this simple practice. We all do our best within our circumstances, do we not? Having lived with nature for years, it is lovely to be part of it.

APRIL 5 2013

DEGREE OF DIFFICULTY

The severity of a race depends on human perception of it and is a variable concept. We all can conjure imagery of our most difficult race points and races in the whole spectrum of racing. Some 500 mile races are in fact more easily attained than 100, depending on the race conditions. The management and the sheer quality of the bird — the beauty of racing/breeding are the unknowns, and the triumph over difficulty. It is often thought that races over 500 miles are the most difficult and sometimes this is the reality. Pigeon racing beliefs are embodied by prejudice, myth and human personality — I am no exception! In reality testing of your birds, International racing will always sort out your better birds of any named family or strain, a practice which I recommend at least once in a pigeon lifetime. In my experience of looking at the Barcelona International races into the UK, I have yet to see one without a relatively high degree of arduous, mind bending difficulty. Have a go next year and beyond.

INTROVERT OR EXTROVERT?

These are terms created by CG Jung, the Swiss psychiatrist, and are now in common parlance. As a general observation, introversive fanciers tend to be more studious, detached and focused on long term future goals with an enriched psychic inner life. With the right total personality in place they may be excellent long distance fliers where great and enduring patience are prerequisites. I would expect such a character to create a strain and be singular and unique in outward presentation. Extroversive fanciers tend to require fast results and are competitive, being people and mainstream orientated. They may do well in sprint and middle distance events, where quick excitement and rewards are the keynotes. They may seek publicity or financial rewards for their efforts and be fame driven. All very simplistic and floats on the surface of human complexity, yet fascinating yes? Who do you think you are? Look in the mirror – and read the reports. Only takes a life time.

CHARACTERS I HAVE MET

In 1965 I stayed with John Shinn, crack shot and big game hunter, in Kenzie the wild goose man's houseboat moored on the Wash saltings. It was a wild, rugged and remote wilderness of tidal creeks, sea lavender and samphire. At high spring tide the boat lifted on its moorings and you were floating on the edge of the North Sea. At times like this my imagination was fired and intensified – will the moorings break and the boat float out to the eternal sea?

Cooking the potatoes from the local fields was done on a paraffin stove with sea water scooped from the depths. A foggy cloud enveloped the boat and the calls of the common seals intensified in the murky dampness. At dawn the great man arrived, Mackenzie Thorpe himself — artist with Sir Peter Scott, ex-jailbird, middleweight boxing champ, poacher and wildfowler par excellence. His eyes were deep with knowledge, his face craggy with wind and salt exposure — a unique and solitary figure in this lunar landscape.

John and I embraced nature full on as we learned the Wash secrets of the hordes of waders, the ducks and geese, the marsh harriers floating by and the wily marsh pheasants as they tried to evade the gun. We lived the boy's adventure tale and these essential times by the sea, sun and stars framed my life and instincts forever. Old Kenzie passed away in 1976, when the houseboat was torched by Romany tradition.

MODERN MYTHS

It ain't necessarily so! We tend to believe many things, do we not? Pigeon racing is a whirlpool of cherished beliefs. The route that Barcelona International pigeons take is interesting and much debated, yet without an accurate tracking device to monitor the course, just how do we know in individual cases? I never knew for sure my returning birds' directions of flight. In terms of flying systems it is often thought that exponents of separation systems such as widowhood will prevail in racing, yet many good marathon birds —and indeed birds at lesser distances — are being clocked with good effect in simple open loft, free-ranging systems. A lot depends on the man or woman devising the method of action. Many frown on inbreeding, preferring continental-style outbreeding as an avenue to success, yet some of the top men in Britain practise it with a relish, for example Jim Donaldson and Brian Denney, and with good reason, ie to concentrate the best of their own birds and to be used in future outbreeding programmes.

The word 'distance' has quasi-magical connotations, but what does it mean in reality? To me a good bird performing to satisfactory levels between 500-700 miles is a distance pigeon, and it can be from any particular family or strain. With similar analysis we can observe many other aspects of pigeon culture in pursuit of truth.

UNITY IDEAL

Men of imagination and vision aim for the best possible case, to create order out of disharmony and confusion. The old pioneers of long distance/endurance racing sought to stretch the boundaries of possibility with a restless surge, an ardent drive into heady adventure and achievement — a romantic impulse perhaps for hardened men of practical realism. It is this never say die and fiery enthusiasm that creates new levels of accomplishment in any competitive endeavour, and is pertinent with the current movement to International racing in the UK and Ireland.

Now that an infrastructure for race participation is being developed by the BICC, the future is bright for some. I speak with bias and from an optimistic perspective, knowing very well the rigours and hardship of marathon racing, yet success for the few dedicated souls can be sweet. In the final analysis the pleasures and rewards can be great at any level of racing and from the sheer love of our avian companions — I currently feed four species of doves in my garden.

APRIL 12 2013

FUELLING UP FOR ENDURANCE

The BICC and BBC are turning back the popular clock to organise and promote marathon racing into the UK and Ireland. This will result in races of consummate difficulty for fanciers and their birds. We will see record-breaking performances in the future and some new leading lights of European racing. It is critical that the entries are laden with energy reserves in the internal organs of the body. Diets will vary from fancier to fancier with the use eg of pellets, peanuts, Hormoform, hemp, Red Band, yeast, and liquid feeding such as Blitzform, Mycosant CCS etc. The end result is to produce the candidates on peak reserves to fly home over many miles of changing environmental conditions to the secure little haven of the home loft. The Irish fancy will become acutely aware of these phenomena and I wish all participants well.

HUNGER AND DESIRE

What are the feelings inside the heads of champion fliers? They have a yearning, a fire that glows from within to succeed, and it motivates them to achieve great things, to attempt the difficult, the complex, the seemingly impossible. The charismatic greats like Warren and Paley were the epitome of these personality traits, and forged new paths through history. A desire that is cemented in the myth and folklore of pigeons, such men are the archetypes of excellence. In simple practical terms, it means testing all your birds at the top level, good old natural, Darwinian selection in action! I have noticed how many Americans have the juice to excel, yet look at our own sporting stars — the inspiration is there. The results this year will be peppered by those with hunger and desire, and brave young souls who seek to stretch the boundaries of possibility in pigeon racing. Roll on Barcelona International!

COLOUR

Science asserts that blue chequer feral pigeons are the most prolific breeders. I confess my preference in my strain of dark chequer and dark velvet pigeons, since they look businesslike, and stand out to the receptive eye when in prime condition. It is assumed that red or strikingly-coloured birds stand out, reflect more light and readily fall prey to peregrines and other falcons. However many champions have been mealies and red chequers eg 'Motta', 'Woodsider' and 'Early to Rise', all influential performance birds. The reds in some of my later birds are the James Donaldson influence. It is a real test of a fancier to nominate from a loft of all one colour type. Colour will be dictated by personal breeding preference and the genotype. It is conventional belief that the archetypal ancestor was the blue rock dove when pure. Whatever lights your fire folks – race them and see.

THE FANCIER'S DREAM

The future results begin in the here and now and in the minds of visionary men! Fanciers with high ambition and aspiration contemplate their chosen candidates — a highly individual and cerebral matter. Success with the chosen ones can become a self-fulfilling prophecy, the realisation and climax to a dream. Many a bird is dubbed with the word 'dream' after an epic flight, it is part of the nomenclature and glorious romance of pigeon racing. On sending to Barcelona International Dorothy informed that my bird wouldn't clock, it being too far at 879 miles. After his huge peregrination we christened him 'Barcelona Dream'. Men with foresight and a meditative eye look to the future with foresight and plan and hope to make their mark in pigeon racing. Many of my ideas and plans have seen their genesis in sleep and bed. Try and bring a race alive with your mind — what do you see?

TALES FROM THE PIGEON LOFT

Many of us have novel and colourful anecdotes to relate, and these are some of mine. My stock loft was festooned by magnificent and beautiful spiders' webs, which I cultivated and loved to see. My visitors, looking in, thought the film 'Arachnophobia' was made there! Big female house spiders are soft furry creatures in the hand. Glancing along a tree branch, used as a pigeon perch, a large rat scurried towards my alerted eyes. Stepping back I gave it a karate chop and then another as it scrambled up the aviary netting. I gave it a one-two with a garden rake and Dorothy said "good lad Jimmy, put it on the fire back" — she was a game old bird, my mum.

One day I found a lovely little nest in the deep litter, and on examination I found some warm little bodies. To my delight I realised that they were tiny shrews, complete with whiskered snouts, and how lovely they were! That was the day when Freddie the Jack Russell shot up the clematis montana that clad the cottage — lo and behold he got stuck fast, and when I retrieved him he had a big fat rat in his mouth, brilliant.

Dorothy was a charming old girl and used to sing to my pigeons: she must have enchanted a big black old crow as it used to fly into the loft to steal pigeon eggs. Memories are made of this.

SPEED/ENDURANCE

A really good, versatile bird will manifest both attributes with good results from sprint to marathon level, and these are rare. Much depends on the preparation of the birds at the home end. The main systems in operation will produce some rapid birds up to 500-plus on the day and from many origins and brand names of pigeons. A really fast bird, produced well, may score where speed home is the key factor. In my experience all Barcelona International birds that score over 700 miles into the UK will have demonstrated an abundance of total endurance, both mental and physical. Few of this type will win sprint races, and vice versa. You can gauge a bird in the hand, yet the acid test of reality is to send the bird to the race point — this will reveal all to you. A nice endurance type was `Rileys Duchess', 2nd BICC Barcelona at 800-plus. Part of the joy is to test your birds on the edge of capability — suck it and see.

THE PIGEON MENTOR

It is very nice to help other willing individuals in their pigeon racing lives, as it demands concentrated effort and focus on the part of both parties. The immediate aim is improvement and the long-term aspiration is excellence. A union of minds is called for in relation to all aspects that are relevant to success, such as method, applied science and the art and practice of effective husbandry, to produce good stock in prime condition for the chosen races. It is a complex whole that is made simple by analysing and uniting the component parts. The practice will require some lifestyle changes and philosophical adjustments and is a little like coaching, in effect. Each person takes his place within the total system and is as crucial as the birds themselves. Perhaps you may be able to take an enthusiastic neophyte under your wing? We do what we can to secure the noble art of pigeon racing.

FAIR PLAY

Racing is wide open to most folk, irrespective of societal status, which makes for a fascinating and diverse sport. Races with variable distances to lofts, geographical locations in relation to wind directions, localised weather and many other factors will never be entirely fair, not even with narrow radii and corridor flying. They are what they are, racing with the prevailing conditions on the day of action. We talk of overfly, underfly and sideways fly —sounds like the Yardbirds again!

Perhaps best to pursue objectives without fear or favour and with acceptance of the available facts. There are generous souls about who will help you at all levels — these are gems of the fancy and require cultivation. To think that your international winner may be predated en route back home, best to concern yourself with the returnees. Another factor is the design, establishment and interpretation of rules by political administrators, where integrity is paramount! The fairness of the sport then is worthy of contemplation.

MAY 3 2013

THE NATURAL ELEMENTS

I was walking across fields today in half a gale full of snowflakes, and the sheer force of freedom hit my face. How great it is to be out in nature. I must confess I hate to see and sense racing pigeons cooped up in little stuffy lofts, when they can be on instinct in the rain, snow, sun and wind honing their navigation skills and enriching their muscles with red blood cells. The central philosophy of Nic's and my

Barcelona methodology is centred on fitness, familiarity and contentment with the home environment. They will face gruelling conditions on their long migration back home from Spain, and will not acquire race environmental experience in the loft! What a treat they are to behold swirling around in a snow flurry and then the sun as it reflects off dazzling feathers. I have enjoyed deserts, mountains, woods and seas and remain convinced from my biased perspective that pigeons need to have the freedom of the skies as they were born to fly.

THE INDIVIDUAL

With the current accent on general names of fanciers used to indicate certain origins of pigeons, eg Busschaerts, let us focus on the individual pigeon and fancier, which are what create the results and success — each is unique and singular! We use labels such as 'Natural' and 'Widowhood' to describe systems, yet each one is peculiar to the person who practises it. The pigeon culture is awash with generalisations, is it not? Great enjoyment can be derived from focusing on and preparing single birds for chosen events, eg for the single bird clubs, which calls for specialisation. This will be a test of foresight and skill of the fancier in combination with each bird.

We have concluded, then, that all birds and fanciers are different, even specimens of a common name origin. These factors make the sport diverse and interesting, with all the characters available. In the last analysis then, if you obtain a new family of birds they are all individuals — even if cloned.

BAND OF BARCELONA

I have been inspired to write this as a tribute to and celebration of the wonderful feeling of kinship that the advocates and enthusiasts share in their support and dedication to the Barcelona objective. Friendships are being fostered throughout the UK in the spirit of endeavour. Some of these will be life-changing and will endure the passage of time. I think these relationships are fired by the hardship of the task and the sheer endurance required of the Barcelona vigil. The race is gathering momentum, established by early pioneers in the BICC, and we are seeing a renaissance of popular interest in the race where myths and legends are cemented in pigeon folklore. Who will light the torch of recognition in 2013, will it be Goddard, Kay, Gilbert or Harvey, or other aspiring stalwarts of the queen of races? just who is set to make UK and Irish history?

THE LAID-BACK APPROACH

I found that the intense, hard work was in the foundation of a system that would produce birds to perform at a high level. This took me many years of painstaking mind research in books with periods of inspiration. Personal exchanges are fine on a social level, yet I learned most from established experts and academics in the field of pigeon management. After all, the complicated goings on an easy method can induce a nice, controlled procedure which induces calm. I often say that a bright 11-year-old girl can do it! This said, you will be awake during the night during the exciting, big races particularly of an international nature. The complexity then is in the thought processes behind the genesis of a simple system. Watch out that you are not asleep on the arrival of your top birds. I used matchsticks to prop up my eyelids for marathon races. May your individuality go with you.

PIGEON EXCHANGE NETWORK

This is now in operation from Bude to Holy Island to Ireland. We share a joint enthusiasm for each other as personalities, as kindred spirits within a single objective, which is the development of performance long distance and marathon pigeons in UK and Irish racing. In pursuit of perfection we reciprocate with ideas, knowledge, information, quirks and good humour. We pay carriage only for the exchange of quality bred young birds. The central ethos is mutual good sportsmanship in the flame of friendship. It sounds idealistic and naive in character, yet works in practice and is a concept that could be developed.

THE CREATION OF THAT ELUSIVE CHAMPION

Champions are generated out of the fire of competitive racing, and are as elusive as they are infrequent. The essential criterion is entry into the races of significance. Although many are the products of unknown, chance matings or strags, you can endeavour to create one by systematic breeding. In my strain, I inbred very closely to all the best performance birds, particularly liking brother and sister matings for outbreeding in the stock loft. Sometimes when paired to closely inbred birds of high performance origins, birds of outstanding inner and outer qualities are bred, capable of sterling performances. On this premise the foundations of a strain can be laid. Experimentation is the name of the game, followed by severe progeny testing of all race birds in the fireblade of competitions. Stick with your own birds and attempt to improve your husbandry.

PIGEONS AND EDUCATION

Many aspects of the sport can be infused into school curricula, college courses and the wider media for mainstream consumption. We can analyse aspects of it in relation to geography, maths, natural science and psychology, covering diverse topics such as navigation, nutrition, timing and the sport's seating in history, war and tradition. The complete sphere of interest is as wide as the culture is broad — the permutations are endless. I have recently had some of my pigeon articles published in 'Folio', the creative writing special interest group of Mensa for UK and international circulation. If it stimulates minds out there, then the objective is being realised, and I hope to assist a young lady in her masters and PhD researches, giving added impetus to the ancient practice of pigeon racing. Most fanciers do thrive on a little recognition and publicity, perhaps.

PIGEON EGGS

There are some beauties out there in the ultra-competitive world of modern pigeon racing. The dreams, ambitions and desires of man, rewarded by fame, money and esteem, are central to the motivations of fanciers. Why do we do it? Why do we dedicate lives to our feathered friends? The answers are born out of the racing culture itself. What wonderful characters colour the sport with every variation of humanity itself. I do like those who give credit to others —their mentors and early influences, and peers. Yes, sometimes the truth is revealed for us to see, eg when Mark Gilbert gave credit to Geoff Cooper. There are some pivotal egos, yet do we not all share the same melting pot of human emotions and needs.

SINGLE BIRD NOMINATION FLYING

This is a specialist, demanding and very rewarding activity for the discerning fancier. The Single Bird Greater Distance Nomination Flying Club caters for participants in the main races of the leading race organisations, eg NFC, BBC and BICC. For the person the foresight and skill is in the selection of an individual bird in advance, where you can be judged on this particular event. It certainly focuses your mind on one bird in an attempt to perfect the management preparation of one performance athlete. Once you are successful you can apply the lessons learned to all your other birds. I am surprised that this peculiar skill is not practised more widely, as the reports would appeal to continental fliers. It really intensifies the harmony and unity between man and bird and must be good for the collective expertise of the Fancy.

JULY 5 2013

FAIR PLAY

Racing is wide open to most folk irrespective of societal status, which makes for a fascinating and diverse sport. Races with variable distances to lofts, geographical locations in relation to wind directions, localised weather and many other factors will never be entirely fair, not even with narrow radii and corridor flying. They are what they are, racing with the prevailing conditions on the day of action. We talk of overfly, underfly and sideways fly – sounds like the Yardbirds again! Perhaps best to pursue objectives without fear or favour and with acceptance of the available facts. there are generous souls about who will help you at all levels — these are gems of the fancy and require cultivation. Don't think that your international winner may be predated en route back home, best to concern yourself with the returnees. Another factor is the design, establishment and interpretation of rules by political administrators, where integrity is paramount! the fairness of the sport then is worthy of contemplation.

WIDOW VS NATURAL

Each individual fancier will develop a system to try and be successful, eg from club to international level of racing, and maybe skilful with many approaches to flying. Widowhood birds often have controlled exercise periods around the loft, where both sexes are exercised separately, where the desire to mate and nest increases in conjunction with the physiological v. psychological changes precipitated at the hormonal level. So-called 'Natural' birds are often flown free-range and close to nature and the elements, a system that suits my personality. Nic and I use our own system combining elements of freedom with targeted periods of separation to prepare birds from 31 miles to 710 miles, sometimes, eg with the Marmande cock, scoring from sprint to marathon level!

There is a tendency of top fanciers to win with their good birds on various systems. The essence is the expertise and knowledge generated by the focused and dedicated mind of the fancier which may have taken years of research and study to develop – it is a life's work, a grand obsession.

TIME ON THE WING

In preparation for sprint/middle distance races, ie up to 500 miles, many love their charges to be home via the most direct route as soon as possible, where the winning philosophy and methodology prevail. For international races over 600 miles into the UK and Ireland, fresh insights and thought processes are required of the fancier. A nice long first toss, eg 60 miles, first toss from open loft conditions will give the birds sufficient orientation and fly time on the wing when the quintessential factor is endurance and stamina in preparation to negotiate and break out of the international convoy flying into wide areas of Europe.

I like nice increases of time and distance with a 10 to 14 hours fly 3-4 weeks before Barcelona International. I like yearlings up to 500 miles international, yielding ample experience for 700-mile plus racing as a 2yo. In this way you can build a strain to take your name which will have a diverse genome.

PIGEON THEORIES

Believers, academics and thinkers amongst the pigeon fraternity give credence to all manner of ideas about the selection of good birds prior to breeding and racing. Many are based on physical analysis of the bird, its eye, throat, wing structure, feathers, feel, temperature, vents, and pulse etc. All these stimulate minds and foster opinion and belief. Some fanciers do have good stock sense and intuition, particularly within their own family. I place all theory under the test of racing conditions and in fact a champion or bird performing to your satisfaction will have the physical and non-physical qualities of a bird that you require – see if it matches the theoretical judgments you have made. I find that a bird I am happy with has the qualities I desire, after my final decision is made after racing and breeding. In simple terms racing under good management will sort the good ones out – genes, internal organs, brain and body and life.

ZEN AND THE ART OF PIGEON RACING

I was fortunate enough to travel into remote Afghanistan, along the wild and rugged Khyber Pass into Pakistan. and enjoy an area of tribal law. By the time I had reached the snow-clad peaks of the Himalayas, my narrow little Western eyes had been opened by the rich and exotic experiences of the East. Under the spell of Taoism and the Zen Buddhist philosophical tradition, my personal approach to pigeons, writing and all life has evolved. The Zen experience teaches calm contemplation, mindfulness and intuitive awareness of the essence of things, and has been of immense help in my long distance/marathon career, as believe me, relaxation united with patience is essential to cope with prolonged periods of endurance of man and bird in races over 700 miles. The great distance men are often laid back, detached individuals with extended fuses. Zen is the pure and powerful, inner calm, a focus on the meditative moment — I have enjoyed it creating this article.

THE PHILOSOPHY OF WINNING

We win races, but do we feel like winners? I have witnessed

several top prizewinners who at the end of the season are tired and stressed and wonder if it was all worth it. It is in the nature of competition to want to win, but why, and what are the human costs? In my little opinion, if you feel like a winner then you are. I know a lady with no legs who is a cheery soul to talk to – a fine example of humanity. A clever psychological stratagem is to target a key race point and make an intense study of how to fly it. The Barcelona International, the big race in Europe, has yet to be won in the UK. Can it be done and who may do it with what winning bird? The key may be to continue to raise the bar of existential excellence towards the dizzy heights of perfection, an ideal state which is impossible. I find the performances you recall are the ones suffused by euphoria. However in our reflections do we not recall the nectar taste of our first win? The impact of it can be central in our memory in the cool light of nostalgia.

SPECIALIST RACING

The expert fancier will focus and dedicate his racing life to certain racepoints, distances or simply competitors to beat, and will create and evolve a personal system to achieve that objective. He will source and breed birds capable of realising his dreams — a simple formula, and some achieve distinction as a self-fulfilling prophecy from their original conception. He will practise shrewd and sound decision-making from insights gained in the art and science of pigeon racing. The media are flooded with good info, with the onus on the individual to formulate a working, winning method. The birds required are those that will adapt to your singular methods, and they will, given time. What genre of racing then appeals to your life? Nic and I develop the whole year around the Barcelona International as it represents the zenith of racing endeavour — may your race go with you.

SPORTSMANSHIP AND JEALOUSY

Most of us will have experienced these human phenomena, and for better and worse. These personality effects pervade the sport of pigeon racing at all levels from club to international level, and the denigration of a winner seems to be cemented in the English psyche. In the fiery heat of competition, especially in close contact with a peer group, emotions run high, especially green gods of jealousy and resentment! Often these feelings are linked to ego defence mechanisms. The converse is the selfless and beautiful sportsmanship manifested by some generous souls. Oh, yes being a winner with a good bird is the essence of the game, and to some is of paramount importance. Nowadays I target a race point, ie Barcelona International, and the motivation is general improvement of man and bird. A well-structured and disciplined system will enable you to have a go in big races from June to August with a steady and gradual build-up of condition of your charges.

OCTOBER 11 2013

THE IMMUNE SYSTEM

The immune system, which is not yet fully understood, is a complex of biological structures and processes in the bird which protect from and ward off diseases. On this notion a good fancier aims to produce a total home environment conclusive to an optimised immune system. In my experience giving pigeons fresh-air freedom in all weathers is good practice. I never kept any birds hungry and fed Chevita supplements, which were active at the cellular level, pellets and brewer's yeast etc. The art/science fusion is well known to maintain good condition in the flock. The corollary is that some birds will become ill due to genetic or other reasons when effective supplements may be of great help in lifting condition. Try and ape or echo the environment that stock doves and wood pigeons enjoy, ie sun/wind/rain/snow and lively air, plus the benefit of enhanced feeding by the hand of man. This concept is not suitable for all people and lofts, yet for Natural fliers it can work up to Barcelona International level.

THE CONCEPTUALIST IN PIGEONS

We all have unique approaches to performance thinking. Most competitors aspire to and are excited by the prospect of beating other individuals, especially motivated by the big and charismatic names in the area or UK and International levels of fame and significance, eg Ronnie Williamson and Mark Gilbert. History is cemented by men of high impact, and I believe that this is largely due to publicity in the popular culture, as some of the best are little known, the beautiful irony of it all! Personally I aimed for the best with perfectionist tendencies, fuelled by naive and youthful assertiveness. Now in the cool light of day, I take an abstract view in my mind's eye and enjoy the passion fired by a race point, the quintessence of racing aspiration, the unique and intoxicating Barcelona International, the fancier's wildest dream. It is the only race to spawn poetry from my psyche — a powerful obsession.

THE EYE

The most significant eye is the human one looking into the eye of the pigeon! Yes, most of the answers lie in the mirror. Each person makes perceptual judgements on colours, shapes, patterns and forms in the eyes of pigeons, and decisions in the mind on beauty, health and condition. Iridologists have made a theoretical study of eyes with practical disease diagnosis implications. As for the divination selection of winners and breeders, this is not humanly possible in every case, since there are too many external environmental variables to make an enlightened, predictive decision. However, certain fanciers have superior judgement when attempting to select the performance bird from overall interaction with the bird on an intuitive level of awareness. With optimal bird management champions are created, taking their place in starry constellations in the pantheon of pigeon racing. I like a nice pretty eye, like those of a young lady!

RACE CONFIDENCE

The young fancier starts out with hopes, dreams and aspirations, and probably some trepidation and a lack of inner confidence. Racing is a deeply psychological chess game for each person. Sprint and middle distances seem a long way to a raw novice and his feathered charges, and so they are. If the system is right success will be achieved with enthusiasm and hard work, since good birds in all families abound — the key is the fancier! Top men will prevail with birds of different origins — notice how the same names appear on the results time and again.

After this homespun philosophy, confidence may increase as say distances get longer, over years of dedicated time as targets are realised, with the ultimate race in Europe being the Barcelona International up to as far as Poland, Malta and Denmark. A race which calls for obsessive dedication to the point of lunacy and confidence in ultra-marathon pigeons — to be honest 879 miles was enough for me!

In tightly competitive areas, eg amongst the top men at York. it is very hard to combine popularity with dominance and is largely a masculine phenomenon, although there are some outstanding lady competitors. Confidence is determined by mood, is felt and may be ephemeral and transient. I act now as aid and mentor to others in my maturing years and enjoy the people who I count as my friends and they know who they are in the noble sport of pigeon racing.

WEATHER OR NOT

In my long career in racing pigeons, I never held birds at home due to forecasted inclement weather conditions, ie from 71 to 879 miles with my family. In particular I liked north-east winds as a real test of management and bird and mistrusted birds with velocities over 1200ypm. Many sprint/middle fanciers will disagree, liking the birds home sharpish and back under control, purely a matter of subjectivity and personality. To fly 700 plus miles a nice warm up race of 10 to 12 hours was crucial in preparation terms and some birds will go 17 hours on the wing. We do what suits us as individuals and I like birds to experience a holdover in the systematic preparation for International racing where long periods in the transporter are symptomatic of the race. My strain evolved over hardship, such is the nature of the beast.

THE SUPERSTIMULUS

In anthropomorphic terms pigeons home as their being responds to mates and the love of home, food and the fancier. In blissful ignorance we attempt to manipulate these elements to facilitate top race results. With nesting birds, I prefer a hen flown separate and allowed her first chick before the big race, with the added stimulus of sitting five eggs. I believe this can create a physiological/psychological high as subtle internal bio chemical changes occur deep within the bird. `Dax My Girl' flew to her first pure white young bird of the year, and with impact in International racing. The concept is a vast sea of esoteric knowledge waiting to be discovered. In the future men with insight will evolve new methods and stimulus tricks — will it be you? The bond between a hen and cock is little understood, now that we accept that animals display emotionality — fascinating is it not?

BLOODLINES AND GENES

For many years I have raved on about the personality of individual fanciers as crucial and limiting factors in the racing success equation. This is true, ie no fancier, no method, no loft, no birds! By the same token, the origin and performance heritage, ie genome, are crucial too. From humble beginnings in 1976 my intensive strain making is evolving after 37 years and continues under the control of some good men. The birds today are all down from the seven foundation originators, especially 'Dark Destiny' and 'Daughter of Darkness', the No 1 pair. One of the yearlings for Nic Harvey and myself has the No 1 pair on numerous occasions in its ancestry, as were our first four birds from the BBC Niort endurance race of 2013. Good birds thrive on extensive inbreeding with occasional infusions of other genes. You can theorise all you wish, yet performance testing is the master of racing/breeding reality. This may be pedantic, reflecting an academic background, but true. In simple terms treasure your good birds, particularly if related — it fosters success.

NOVEMBER 8 2013

LOFTY ASPIRATIONS

Men with vision and imagination dream of triumph over difficulty in the races of significance to them, the only bird on the day, the record flight, the name carved in the foundation stones of historical time. In this way the collective good of the sport is richly enhanced. Such personal traits are the fabric of folklore. it is very human to seek the elusive perfection in sport. I am delighted that UK success in international racing is the norm, evolving from the original diehards of the great BICC. However we all seek our own levels and credit due to each person who engages in the ancient and noble art of pigeon racing. I feel the future of the sport is secure in a world where companion pigeons are cultivated in conjunction with the competitive impulse of man. Like horse and dog racing, powerful groups will cement its survival. it is an insular world where it means all to some people.

THE MEANING OF COMPETITION

What a competitive set of people pigeon fanciers are! Life at or near the top may bring transient and elusive happiness with the joy of a race win or other assorted emotional states. It can be a *modus vivendi*, a way of life. In reality the world of the writer has allowed vent to my self-expression regarding race birds where I am totally hooked. Levels of success are very personality related in terms of how you react to comment by fellow competitors, which are not always positive. A little pure resolve and single-mindedness should ensure your future participation in the sport at the level you are suited to from club to international levels. The irony is that being regarded as a great competitor is not an automatic formula for success, since life on Earth as a human is more complex than that as it encompasses fleeting moments of total fulfilment and oneness — sounds rather Buddhist in influence.

HOME ENVIRONMENT FOR THE PIGEONS

At Holtby the birds were catered for all their needs with constant open loft to roam and be free as nature intended birds to be, coming and going as they pleased in rain, fog, wind and snow, the seasons through. They mixed with wild pigeons and led a pure, elemental and instinctual life. Dorothy and I were calm and gentle beings with the birds, taking our human place as fellow beings in the colony, supplying all the birds' needs as evolved by applied science and husbandry — the perfect setting for good breeding and racing results. Nic and I echo and improve on this system with the Emerton strain — sounds esoteric, yet it is simple in reality with 5 from 7 so far verified at Barcelona International into the West of England. Central is the concept that we work on the inner being of the birds in juxtaposition with our beings in one harmonious and beautiful ecosystem — the old distance boys call it the love of home. More to pigeons than meets the eye — agree?

TEMPERAMENT

Each individual bird has a unique personality, a factor echoed by the fanciers themselves. It is our job to tune in and cultivate each bird for its racing and breeding tasks. This takes observation and management expertise. Many distance/marathon birds, ie over 700 miles, are quiet, calm and laid back — introverted pigeons in a sense — and they tend to rest well in the transporter especially sweet little hens, that may go almost unnoticed. When coupled with racing potential from the genome they are birds to condition and nominate in Barcelona. I love tame, happy pigeons, a trait that I inbred into my strain via 'The Iron Hen'. I would walk round the garden with her sitting on my head, dam of 'Dark Destiny'. Birds like these inspire affection, loyalty and trust and dedication in us and are strain makers. Marathon racing will test the temperament of us mere humans and can be draining, especially if you do not time in —on to the next race then.

ARE GOOD BIRDS A RECIPE FOR SUCCESS?

Fortunes are spent in pursuit of success by obtaining birds which by outward, often sales techniques, are winners or will breed winners at desired levels of competition. In truth the key factor to excellence is the genetic blueprint or genome of the bird's ancestry wherein the racing performance potential lies. Now the onus is on the management expertise of the fancier to produce the bird in optimal condition for the targeted race. Some can do this and we will see the names at or near the top for years, many with birds of different origins, ie genes, be they obtained for nothing or costing loads of money — shrewd fanciers are careful with their dosh!

There is no one strain or family that is the best, since all are of mixed origins taking the names of the good and great, often for ego/commercial and fame reasons by slick operators in the pigeon culture. In my long career I put breeding at the top and tried to perfect my overall system with the use of extensive inbreeding to brother x sister with inbred outbreeding from time to time, finding more intense control at the loft compared with all the risks engendered by racing. Success is when you derive personal contentment from the progress made, even though one never reaches perfection.

JANUARY 17 2014

HINDSIGHT, INSIGHT, FORESIGHT AND OUT OF SIGHT!

Hindsight reveals wisdom and knowledge of the past, our decisions, successes and failures, and prepares us for the present and future with the luxury of experience. A more valuable mental tool perhaps is insight, when we can discern the reality and potential of a situation in an instant of time and without long-winded and laborious thinking. Pigeon men with stock sense tend to have this trait where snap decisions about people, birds and the weather are required. Living on the edge, travel and exposure to the elements and risk encourage this intuitive skill and it works wonders. People with foresight may have the acumen and vision to predict the likely outcome of decisions or events. Fanciers of good judgement will call upon these personal skills and more on their progress to the top in pigeon racing. I feel the personality and mind are crucial in the ticking clock of pigeon history, along with quality birds which good fanciers will have, breed and race. The above reflects my simple analysis of the deep and profound complexity of a full blown human. Is it not fascinating that each pigeon has an individual personality too?

STRAGS

The one that has just come into your loft may be a champion! It is a fact that many top birds stray, and for a plethora of reasons. Many of my top birds were weeks away, perhaps sitting in a stranger's loft. The mystique deepens in the esoteric world of racing pigeons, a complex microcosm of complexity. I found that returning birds from Ireland to my loft at Holtby, Yorks tended to race well when reconditioned for Saintes and Pau 735 miles, being fixated, navigationally on the loft, a process yet to be fully understood by man. One year a young blue cock transfixed my gaze, and duly transferred it has bred a chequer cock to negotiate the Barcelona International twice at approximately 853 miles into England.

The essence of good management, I feel, is to cultivate each returning bird with an eye on its future: the potential can be great when a bird finds its wings —it may launch you into the stratosphere. A regime, a system may prevail, yet each bird is a unique entity, don't you think? When fuelled up it is amazing what wonders birds may accomplish.

GOOD ALL-ROUND PIGEONS

It is often believed that birds can be differentiated into sprint, middle distance and long distance types, and a whole media and commercial culture is built around this conception. The reality is that this holds water in some cases. The exciting truth is that distance and velocity are very dependent on the efficiency of the system that you devise to create race conditions for the race points in question. To illustrate this concept by practical reality, Nic was 1st & 2nd at 52 miles with two birds that flew Barcelona International at 710 miles, and the next bird had flown Agen International at over 500 miles as a yearling. Although unusual, these are showing tendencies to be good all-rounders, and they are, genetically of mixed origins. With a great deal of focus on externals, ie the names of origins of pigeons and the theory of type and phenotype, I like any bird that performs in existential reality in the fireblade of experience.

ON PUBLICITY

In the modern days of celebrity culture and instant gratification and communication, many people enjoy a little fame and publicity, shallow as it may be. Globally, there are some interesting, original and clever journalists and personalities who parade their ideas and reports in the public domain and for mass media consumption. It is satisfying to receive some wide and external recognition from other humans for the sweat that has dripped from your brow in the noble art/science fusion of pigeon racing. Homo sapiens needs an ego fix, and many will capitalise in hard currency as a by product of the fame machine. Excellent editorial staff churn out magazines and webmasters, eg at Elimar, and PIPA serve the world with features, reports and information. Hard facts are obtained with ease about the most sophisticated aspects of the sport. It is relatively easy now as experts abound, yet who are the innovators who will inject creative ideas and systems into the future? Rest assured that future publicity will launch these icons into the collective consciousness of pigeon racing.

GENIUS IN PIGEON FANCIERS

Genius is a relative, cultural phenomenon seen from a human perspective, and can be defined as exceptional intellectual and/or artistic power. In my biased and loose application to pigeon racing, I use it to celebrate outstanding efforts of racing folk. Others may create another list, since it is all a little fun. In Ireland we have the inimitable Ronnie Williamson, a top class man, in Wales we have the Padfields, in Scotland is marathon master Jim Donaldson, and from Yorkshire we have Neil Bush, Chris Gordon — a peerless all-rounder, and Tarbes specialist Brian Denney. from the south of England Mark Gilbert is still, believe it or not, improving, along with Nic Harvey at Barcelona International. All these men are gifted practitioners in the subtleties of the art and science of breeding and racing and world class in my perception. Their achievements should be showered in praise and glory by the fancy at large, irrespective of their individual personalities.

THE ROLE OF SCIENCE

Certain fanciers like Mark Gilbert in the UK are getting close to an ideal and optimal system of management for their birds and will flourish with birds of many origins, irrespective of cost I may add. The key base element is the brain and personality of the fancier – dedication and psychology are always at the core of success. Top level racing, ie international, is enhanced by the application of modern scientific research. There are many ways to create top racing condition without official doping, and German boffins have formulated a group of active supplements which, eg as liquid feed, will with a good home environment precipitate flying condition. We are narrowing down and improving performance levels with time up to Barcelona International level. from experience I recommend Chevita and Rohnfried products, since these are not bogus and work for the fancier's benefit.

BARCELONA INTO POLAND

It fascinates me that the Polish lads and lasses have mustered over 2,000 entries into the daddy of all races! There must be a strong belief, becoming a tradition in the collective psyche of rugged individualists over there. I bet they have some hard birds, negotiating over 900 miles in race time. let us see interviews with and features on the outstanding fanciers in the media, since wonderful stories abound for our contemplation and admiration. Surely the Polish initiative is the blueprint for UK and Irish racing? I say this in the conscious realisation that entry numbers have increased with due motivation since the pioneering days of BICC diehards. This upward trend will roll with publicity as we are to witness some seminal performances into our islands. Long may this be, and please make sure of your verification procedures and be lucky.

FEBRUARY 7 2014

SUCCESS

Just what are the factors and qualities of a successful breeding and racing loft and person? Firstly a comfortable secure loft in surroundings conducive to the adaptation of racing pigeons is required. I loved my loft at the village of Holtby in the Yorkshire countryside, where open loft, at some risk, could foster the type of condition required for racing. I reflect on it now with sweet nostalgia, where at times man and bird were contented. The personality of the fancier is the key element in the success story, requiring total focus and an enduring dedication in pursuit of excellence! Pigeons are the flying instruments of mind, and a good fancier will source, breed and evolve good athletes. Recognition by people may be the outcome, but surely personal satisfaction is the central objective. However whatever lights up your sky is surely the modus vivendi.

PEDIGREE AND PERFORMANCE

Life is like a box of chocolates, you never know what you are going to get next. This concept often applies to attempts to breed good birds, in that the apples may fall a long way from the tree. By this I mean that winners may be produced many generations down the line of the pedigree from the original performance ancestors. Your mating decisions may be inspired and intuitive, yet the simple and limiting factor is the genome of the ancestors or bloodlines of the bird that you breed. In practice it is wise to pair birds of your liking and test the progeny. This smacks of reality to me. I always bred latebreds for stock out of key birds of the year, and these paired together in the stock loft. There is no absolute science to pigeon racing, I am glad to say, and this is where personal skill and wise decisions fall into the equation. Each fancier works on his own level, since the art and science of the sport makes us all human, don't you think?

LONG-DISTANCE MASTER

This person will dedicate a life to the creation of a strain of distinction from 500 to 700 miles, preferably at international racing into the UK and Ireland and over the English Channel. In popular culture he will gain respect, although some will unload their criticism on to him for the support of inner motivations. Sufficient knowledge and application of science will evolve a personal system, capable of producing performance pigeons at his chosen racepoints. His career will endure, with perhaps the fame of recognition, largely dependent on media publicity. As a personality he may be singular, unique and perhaps eccentric with keen long-term focus on objectives. To master racing at any distance is difficult and the good and great are judged by pigeon society. Interpretation of history produces a hall of fame where the living and the ghosts of the past dwell, men like Jim Donaldson, Nicholas Harvey, Chris Gordon, Neil Bush and Brian Denney, to name a few fanciers of distinction.

WIND AND DRAG

In reality we can but reason and guess regarding a pigeon's return from the race point unless an accurate tracking device is fitted with imagery on a computer screen. Naturally there will be clever and informed opinions which may or may not reflect external reality! Three birds' performances I rate regardless of the wind and drag cliché are 'Flange' by Biss, 778 miles Barcelona International second day, `Padfields Invincible', 2nd BICC Barcelona 750 plus miles second day and `Rileys Duchess', 2nd BICC Barcelona over 850 miles third day. If you look at the first

20 BICC Perpignan birds 2013, all are east or central of England, giving me the thought that the drag can be of consequence to the result, even if the wind appears to favour the west of England and Wales. An interesting concept for good fanciers north, south, east and west to ponder. In my own racing and with Nic Harvey in the west, we aim for the greatest possible difficulty, yet can go to only 710 measured miles at Barcelona International. We make the best of our positional geography, which is the modus operandi.

INTUITION

If asked for the basis of any success I may have enjoyed in racing pigeons, I would have to say intuition. It may be inherited but is developed by living on the edge in the wilderness, in exotic and wild locations and in life or death situations at home and abroad. It is akin to instinct, sixth sense, insight, foresight and acumen etc. It can be described as an overwhelming and immediate perception of reality and truth and is correlated with human mysticism. I can think for England, yet my breakthrough judgments in pigeon racing and breeding are always intuitive, as is my best written/creative work. Try and develop this faculty in life for instant decision making and judgments. Study your system, your birds, what do they tell you in your inner psyche – go by it, sounds like a quote from Star Wars. This is how I operate, it may or may not work for you.

RACING PAST AND PRESENT

How the knowledge in the pigeon culture has changed, from when many saw old hands as the fount of esoteric knowledge. The cultivation of a personal strain was paramount, tic beans in hoppers were fed ad lib and the so called Natural, open-loft system prevailed. We bathed the birds in potassium permanganate water solution and used quack remedies of doubtful efficacy. However records were broken, fanciers became famous and legends evolved in the consciousness of the sport. Today men with ultra-competitive science-based systems are producing entries in almost perfect condition with types of systems developed from classical Widowhood, Roundabout, Celibacy and Natural with innovative suffusions of jealousy and other performance-enhancing techniques so good at physiological/psychological conditioning as to look like doping. The future will see yet more improvements with intuitive leaps by visionary men. The benchmark race will be the Barcelona International with gradual improvements in UK and Irish and wider European performances.

FEBRUARY 22 2014

PIGEONS AND MONEY

I believe the greatest moments of a man's life in pigeons are priceless. Money may buy you some well-bred birds at inflated prices, although good birds are available as friendly exchanges on gentlemen's terms. To me humanity is greater and of more value than currency in a capitalist society. However if you need money, the Chinese will cater for your every need via shrewd and slick advertising of apparently really good pedigree pigeons. There are some men of acumen who trade in fashionable names, when the irony is that each pigeon is an individual under the umbrella of a strain name. Old Jack Ross of Holtby used to say "good pigeons are given Jim", a dictum I have remembered well. However it is wise policy to finance your expenses with a few sales, although I know a man who stands by his kind generosity and gives them away. In the vast infrastructure of modern racing in Western society the fanciers blessed with ability and dedication will prevail with their clever management of good birds, and they will all be different.

SAVAGE BEAUTY

I am inspired by the majesty of this severe test of spirits, of man and bird to give due and bountiful credit to the wonderful birds conditioned by experts that have and will return in this odyssey, this monumental peregrination from the heat-drenched skies of boiling Barcelona to our islands. Years of devoted and dedicated human application have contributed to a truly awesome avian event. Whoever wins my trophy will be one proud individual, savouring sweet memories for conscious life on earth. I think Olympicric to be one of the true greats of a spectacular race and will found a dynasty. It has moved me to be a small part of a great experience for all the ardent and patient souls brave enough to endure the cruel and savage beauty — poetic.

THE WITCHING HOUR

For aeons men hardened by toil and competition, and indeed some women, have sought the heightened and mystical sensory awareness in quiet yet vibrant communication with their long-distance candidates in long and stamina-sapping endurance races. It is the poignant, spiritual anticipation, the visual significance of the final arrival of the favourite cock or hen, which may propel your name into the esteemed collective folklore of pigeon racing. In mindful, Zen-like focus yourself is full of warm euphoria. The rush of adrenaline may offset the anxious fatigue that subsumes the long wait. Time may seem to cease as you unite with the evening crows, the setting sun and the moth-catching bats as the twilight zone absorbs you into darkness of the night, the normal signal for roosting racing pigeons.

ABSOLUTE FACT

There is an absolute fact in pigeon racing, and that is that the Barcelona International is the No 1 race. Fanciers often begin with club races and graduate into races of greater and greater personal meaning in pursuit of more satisfaction, perhaps being bored by other races, or attempting to test the speed and endurance of individual pigeons and a strain. A Barcelona specialist may adopt an obsessive, religious preoccupation with Barcelona as the godhead in pursuit of a mental buzz like a mystical and euphoric state.

Responses to clocking vary. Frank Kay from near Bolton, of profound and shrewd wisdom, likens it to floating on air. Nicholas Harvey refers to it as a rush of reality, like the drug of realisation. Others dream of conquering the mountain, the zenith of a man's career in marathon racing. In a race of ultimate glamour and prestige, like Monaco in Grand Prix racing, fanciers from the UK and Europe engage in the practical preparation of their candidates and if entered will fall prey to pre-race anxiety and hype, followed by the heightened awareness of the long wait. Exponents like Wouter Jorna of Holland may clock second day at over 800 miles — a feat yet to be achieved in the UK with the English Channel to endure. Many continental fanciers are motivated by financial gain out of Barcelona International, here with a different psyche we tend not to be. Apart from inhabiting dreams, Barcelona International preparation is a lengthy fusion of methodical preparation of quality birds by men who are not afraid to be different. In the final analysis I would describe Barcelona people as enigmatic, fascinating, mysterious, folk of imagination and idealism.

MARCH 21 2014

KNOWLEDGE

In pigeon racing knowledge is key at all levels of competition and bird keeping, especially for the successful who apply it in their breeding and racing systems. Much of it can be gained by word of mouth, and via the media such as the net, books and magazines. A good source are the top vets and scientists, eg Zsolt Talaber, and the research bodies Chevita and Rohnfried. You may encounter and learn from good fanciers if they can articulate their wisdom to you. Significant to the collective knowledge of the pigeon culture are insights gained by personal application of fine minds who change the modern face of the sport, eg Geoff Kirkland and Chris Gordon as practising specialists. Knowledge will evolve and change with time as the mantra faster, longer, better takes effect.

Combinations of personal applications of Natural, Widowhood etc are increasing the speed and endurance of racing pigeons in combination with sophisticated feeding and solid and liquid supplementation as more and more discoveries are made in the psychology and physiology of pigeon needs. The emphasis will fall on the total being, ie an holistic approach to individual birds and the fanciers who keep them. A lot can be gleaned from competitive sports science at human Olympic level — so it is onward, upward, forward in pursuit of perfection.

THE INDIVIDUAL

We talk of organisations, clubs, committees, pigeon strains and families — al! are plural and collective groups. OK, the sport requires some intrinsic and basic organisation and infrastructure to survive and flourish. However, in my mind's eye, and from life's rich experience, often spent alone, the sanctity and cultivation of the individual person and pigeon are of paramount importance. There are no groups of related birds by strain or family which are purely sprint/middle distance or distance in race potential — a genetically-based phenomenon. The key is the management methodology of the fanciers which will produce birds capable of certain distances and is under the control of individuals. Racers thus are not as a race for any set distance being heterozygotes, ie of mixed genotype. An example is my strain, where individuals performed from 71 to 879 miles — a question of method to suit the distance as formed by the individual. A distance race bird will do exactly that, ie perform at the distance, eg 5 to 700 miles. I hope this goes some way towards a clarification of the generalisations used in the sport.

THE REALITIES OF PIGEON RACING

With 61 years of accumulated experience with birds and pigeons I have come to realise certain truths to myself in a general outlook on the sport. Weather and environmental conditions will tend to vary with each race and race point liberation, so it is not wise always to blame the officials, the race controller and the convoyer for relatively slow or low percentage returns. I think more insight can be gained by looking at the overall effectiveness and quality of your system, management and birds, when most people are extra-punitive, blaming others and outside influences for poor results. A little mirror searching, ie introspection, can yield dividends as an aid to self-improvement. The degree of difficulty tends to increase with distance/time on the wing and perceived difficult environmental conditions. The need for fame and wealth and to experience success is very powerful and the media is a melting pot of hungry egos looking for gratification, and some find a modicum of contentment and happiness after their hard work. Races are the cauldron of competition, with a biased emphasis on the first place. Some fanciers, partly due to sheer personality, become popular and perhaps icons via results and publicity, yet others who are skilful people shun the limelight, and such is the rich human diversity of fancier folk who keep the humble pigeon in its many forms.

WHAT IS POPULAR IN PIGEON RACING?

I do not necessarily pursue an interest because it is popular or mainstream. I am usually drawn by the degree of difficulty of attainment within it. Let's face reality in that more people partake in sprint to middle distance racing up to 500 miles than any other type. There is a multiplicity of reasons for this, such as desire, publicity, sales, continental influence, tradition, perceived type of pigeon possessed etc. Key factors are the time of completed race in relation to personal lifestyle, patience and personal egos. However, and for some years now, international distance and marathon racing as far as Barcelona International has expanded into the popular psyche as a desirable and serious challenge to be undertaken by more and more folk who believe in the mantra LONGER, GREATER, BETTER.

There is no better organisation than the BICC to cater for all your highest needs in the pigeon sport. Why not take your place in the pantheon of greatness and join this singular club which is evolving into the modern and popular facility for national and specialist racing?

HEROES

Competitive people do not live in a vacuum — we have life influences who inspire us and set the benchmark of excellence. The pigeon sport has a society of fame, publicity and achievement generated by competition and the media. One man's meat is another man's poison in the who's who of pigeon racing. Some of my personal iconic figures were Jo Warren of `Lancashire Rose' fame, and Emiel Denys of Belgium as projected by Louella. The popular give an intensity and richness to history. These days I admire and respect Nicholas Harvey for his sheer character in pursuit of Barcelona International excellence. All can be criticised, yet some set real standards for others to emulate, reach and better, and I am of the belief that this process will continue. In the wider sphere I love summer and winter Olympics, most sports and mythical figures like the complex, charismatic and mystical Ayrton Senna and the sublime boxing talents of Marvin Hagler —each person has an individual story to tell.

APRIL 4 2014

NEGATIVITY IN PIGEON RACING

You know I accentuate the positive and decline the negative in an optimistic mind mode. However, there is a rampant and insidious malaise in our society, epitomised by the attitudes of some fanciers. I think it lies in the propaganda and negative perceptions of the messages in the media, and in response to some of the personalities who govern a quasi-democratic society. At the core of the endemic problem in the sport today is an unhappy synthesis of commercialism, jealousy, criticism and a decline in generous, spiritual and moral values due to the unhealthy rise of materialism as the baseline entity of out-of-control capitalism. People demonstrate their instincts and emotions in a diversity of guises, and the obsessive will to win at all costs philosophy is contributing to a sport that has rejected balance, fun and enjoyment, in favour of exaggerated hype, self-delusion, and illusion. Bring back the long-distance master, poised in vibrant expectation for the arrival of his old favourites in beautiful and kind surroundings.

THE ROMANCE OF RACING

What motivates people to dedicate themselves to years of specialised hard work with their feathered charges? It helps if you have a dream, a vision of what you desire to achieve, or to win, perhaps against the odds. This may be suffused with an obsessive inclination towards perfectionism. A love of wildlife and birds is often key to the whole process. As you mature in your career, you may be intoxicated by one race as reward for years of effort, and a test of ability of your evolving family of birds — I regard this as the purist approach. At the setting of the sun the whole scenario is seated in personal satisfaction, a reward in itself. I still celebrate the traditional philosophy and waking dreams of men who wait in excited anticipation to feel the thrill of arrivals from great races and mind blowing distances, and now in my little world, the lonely pursuit is priceless. I like the spiritual quality, the lofty idealism of it all. Some of these principles maybe inspirational, and are all beyond the material.

THE URGE TO REPRODUCE

Species reproduce via innate urges developed since primordial individuals in the species. A racing flock and a loft colony consists of subtle behaviours within a hierarchy, reminding me of a human committee. Loft territory, eg a box, can be claimed by both sexes, and fiercely contested. Hens will mate with hens and cocks with cocks, with shades of bisexuality. When cocks are fed back into the hens, the predominance will be heterosexuality, as perceived by the human eye. On Natural all my hens and cocks and young lived out their lives as one in the same loft, where the pecking order prevailed. Easy peasy is my dictum — why complicate nature? The aggressive, dominant birds are not necessarily the best racers, especially for distance, since I favour quiet birds that conserve energy. Race potential is based in the genome of each bird. A sure sign of loft harmony is birds nesting on the floor, with you the master in their presence. Loft dynamics should be part of a research dissertation.

SEPTEMBER 26 2014

THE GENEROSITY OF FANCIERS

In the cynical and cold world of the competitive psyche are some lovely people noted for their simple generosity of spirit, like the warm sentiments of old Jackie Ross of Holtby, who said 'good pigeons are given'. I do not take any money now for birds of my origin, although some are sold. I like the kind feeling generated by the exchange of friendship, do you not? Believe me the commercial waters are shark infested, and great whites too. I sold birds to China in the 80s, and now I face the reality that most birds bred from any source will never succeed as racers or breeders —despite the hype associated with fame. Marathon racing hardens and it is nice to share communion with likeable folk. I enjoy the people I mentor, which adds an extra human dimension to my life. My writings over the years have been open as to how I created my overall system, which is in capable hands. Modern racing is dominated by specialists, and I like to see genuine generosity in donation of trophies and charity birds, even though it may be free advertising and self-satisfying. Despite my awareness of many negativities of the sport, my overall feeling and perception embraces optimism, and to fly Barcelona International into the UK, dreams maketh the man and results in good birds.

THE VALUE OF GENES

The racing and breeding potential of a bird are influenced greatly by genes, the molecular units of hereditary. The physical appearance and phenotype depends on them with some subtle effects of the total environment, you the fancier included. When I inbreed for stock from birds saturated with performance genes, I increase my chances of a good bird, especially with outbreeding to an inbred performance saturated bird. The theory is simple, and the practice is difficult. Random cross-breeding, widely practised, I frown upon, as it results in a motley multiplicity of talents and types — seems out of control to me, as I like a systematic and ordered approach to the hobby. A little knowledge of the impact of genes is no guarantee of success, yet is compelling as a long term project. Dogma is vain, as there is no known exact science to the pigeon sport, it remains a challenge, a long journey into the unknown.

THE NEXT GENERATION

In terms of my own racing of pigeons, I have thrown in the towel. After 38 years the strain development is ongoing under the management of many men, including Harvey and Ghent who are using the base bloodlines and genes up to Barcelona International level into the UK to 792 miles. The sustained concept is pure, it is still the difficult marathon racing. The reality is that birds evolve and change as custodians take on their care, and it is delusion to think that pure strains exist — they do not, and mine are not that, although years of close inbreeding has been carried out to the originators. Inbred performance genes are great for outbreeding, a fact known by the cognoscenti. The future of the sport will rest in the hands of the few who will make it and shape it by example, men of intellect, vision and power who support the pigeon culture, its literature, its information, science and esoteric knowledge. The vanguard of racing is unity with Europe in international competition, and men of vision will cement the future of the sport for others to enjoy. The scientists, authors and politicians feed the means for dedicated fanciers to excel.

WHY OPEN LOFT PERSISTS

The sport is flushed by modern regimes of applied Widowhood/ Celibate, Roundabout/Darkness and Lightness systems, yet the irony remains that most 700 to 800 mile UK Barcelona International birds will have been on types of Natural system, perhaps combined with some controlled separation of the sexes. If you can tolerate the activities of birds of prey with occasional kills, relative to your home area, Natural birds may attain optimal race condition. With modern applied nutritional science and working on the total beings of the birds, ie a holistic approach, it is almost perfect preparation for marathon, speed-endurance races. Normally around 10 percent return in race time from Barcelona International, it being the ultimate contemporary test of a pigeon. Study the behaviour of wild doves and pigeons, feel your way around how they survive in the raw elements of nature, on the generations of survival of the species, then apply this lore to your racing management — it works!

RACING WITH HENS

In 76 I started racing both sexes, and we still do it today, on our own system. All the birds are destined for over 500 miles as yearlings, then 710 miles as old birds in the Barcelona International. Some of my favourite birds to serve me well have been hens from 31 to 879 miles. It may be a question of sexual gender, as I prefer the stamina/reliability and endurance of a good hen, eg Oddball, Dark Enchantment, Delta Lady and Mystical Queen, whose genes we cultivate today. My system suits hens and it works. The corollary is that my most famous pigeon, yet not the best, was a cock. At one time I sprinted hens on open loft and combinations of Widowhood as young and old birds in my ardent youth, eg 1st, 3rd, 14th from 6,066 birds. The basic tenet is that good hens will prevail, with the right potential and conditioning, as long as you can fly em!

I note the Northern Lady hen of Denney, quite unreported, was his highest placed bird at Tarbes NFC, ie 3rd Open — a good one, and many of N Bush's exemplary Tarbes and Pau birds have been hens — why? All roads lead to Barcelona International and if the talent of fancier, and innate bird potential are there then you can realise your ambitions and dreams.

THE NO. 1 OR GOLDEN PAIR

Blessed are the fanciers who find a prepotent pair of producers from which a dynasty results. The old boy bred in 78, Dark Destiny, was such a bird. Two of our stock cocks, sons of our Barcelona hen, Musgrove Addiction, feature him over 80 times in the ancestry — a fantastic testament to dedicated inbreeding —when paired to the foundation hen Daughter of Darkness. We are outbreeding the two small cocks to daughters of Padfields Invincible, a pivotal UK Barcelona bird at 756 miles approximately. It is an experiment glowing with potential, and we anticipate some success when progeny testing. I am absorbed by outbreeding, inbred birds for vigour and out and out racing ability. Have a close look, can you spot the golden pairs of Gilbert, Cooper, Denney, Bush & Donaldson? I far prefer the intrigue of breeding, where you have more control of the variables than actual racing.

NOVEMBER 28 2014

THE CRITICAL PERFECTIONIST

A little self-criticism is helpful, as a step to self-improvement. In any competitive sport or pastime, the champions and leaders in their fields raise the bar of their aspirations under the concept of perfectionism, where self-satisfaction remains an elusive goal which fires the cauldron of desire. Isolate goals and targets and focus these in your field of vision. The whole process can be seen in a spiritual/psychic context and may transcend material and money-based values and desires. These folk often manifest and thrive on idealistic and romantic notions of the good and the great and the rare inhabitants of that lofty realm. if they pursue a course of pragmatic and earthy realism, a great career, enhanced by success, may ensue. We all go our individual way, yet is nice to admire heroic figures beyond the ego.

IMPACTING THE SPORT

We are in a fame-driven celebrity culture, with increasing media attention to the humble racing pigeon. The hype is reaching ballistic levels as hungry human egos reach out for gratification. Yes, most people in Western culture are very insecure and in need of wholeness. To make an impact in contemporary consciousness of the sport is easy after the realisation of some excellent results, preferably at international level these days. Publicists and writers will promote themselves and you to the receptive and stimulus-hungry world. I find the greater picture to be most inspirational, and the raising of the profile of the eager and dedicated and perfectionist hobbyist. The largest modern leaps of communication and advancement in the sport are via the internet/films and the creative results of scientists and technologists, in fact the basic infrastructure that is the core foundation of the happy little soul, sat in his deckchair awaiting the arrival of his old favourites. Harness your talents and make a nice impact.

GOOD CORN MIXES

The aim is optimal nutrition. We mix our own probably unique admixture for speed endurance as part of a highly developed system that I have evolved over the years. The basic concept involves Versela Lap Gerry Plus, Superstar Plus, also hemp, peanuts, oils, yeast, Breedrite and sunflower hearts. We have no secrets other than that our birds all go to Barcelona International, since it is the only race that motivates us these days. The future lies with the BICC organisation of internationals, a concept that will endure as long as the UK races pigeons. Think about the top echelon of racing, put it all in perspective in your racing career. I keep researching for any improvements in the system which Nic and Ghenty fly on, and there may be an insight from Dr Colin Walker in his new masterpiece, as I favour the work of academics and scientists for novel insights, as they are the fabric of knowledge. My interests continue to be obsessive and enjoy my contribution to the pigeon culture, as it gives an old boy something to do.

QUALITY IN A PIGEON

Now this is very simple, a quality bird will race and/or breed to your required standards of excellence. A relative concept to nail, yet if we are satisfied then the objective is realised. As with all aspects of the sport, the essence of it all is psychological. Photos for pigeon marketing are often enhanced for sales purposes. Lookers make a visual impact, and may handle like a dream. Many beautiful pigeons are useless for purpose, eg breeding/racing. A good-looking quality bird is the ideal, yet perception tells us that many good birds are plain ugly to perceive with the senses. My No

2 stock cock manifested recessive traits in the phenotype, yet his genes survive in 2014. We may ask why this should be. Simple: the performance potential and interaction with the environment are determined by the genome of the bird, determinants which are invisible to the naked eye. From a scientific perspective I would favour a gene analysis of champion birds, to increase our understanding of the secrets of a quality pigeon.

DONATION OF TROPHIES

It is very nice for some people to receive properly inscribed and engraved cups and trophies for their efforts at presentations. Accurate records of details should be kept in the history of the parent organisations and for publicity purposes. As material objects, even in silver or gold, I value the honour of their receipt, and the remembrance of the donator.

There seems to be a paucity of trophies for the long and extreme distance fliers in the BICC and BBC at Barcelona, for example. With the expansion of the BICC, I hope that generous people will correct this for the lucky recipients to enjoy. I was never bothered by them myself, although Mum enjoyed them, and I gave two nice ones to the BICC. Perhaps they will continue to be presented at BICC Barcelona as the Jim Emerton Trophy and the Barcelona Dream Trophy.

INSIDE MARATHON RACING

There is a modern modification of the traditional values of the long-distance little man in his garden. The accent is now on speed/endurance events at 700 miles plus, and to be purist in international races, which carry the power, the kudos, and the prestige in Europe. The big picture concept initiates a big reaction in the personality of the participants. The UK pigeon culture is poised for a dynamic surge in this direction via the medium of the BICC. The NFC will need at some stage to revaluate its core philosophy on levels of comparative competition. Central to any ambitious plans are the happiness of the fancy and the care and optimal management of the families of birds. I treat the sport in a rather conceptual/romantic and idealistic way with a constant mind's eye on seeking perfection in the overall ethos of the sport. The essence of the fancy is the pulse in the minds of men, and transcends money and material values.

FEBRUARY 6 2015

THE BRITISH OBSESSION WITH
PIGEON FAMILY/STRAIN NAMES

Having practised family breeding for 38 years, I can assert that all birds I have encountered are of mixed ancestry and origins. With the commercial marketing pull from the continent and in the UK, you tend to source into the influence and impact of the ego of a famous fancier, eg Jan Aarden or Stichelbaut, when no direct pure birds exist anywhere. A bird is a bird, every one unique, no matter whose name is applied to them. The old cliché that you buy the bird not the man is very true today. This said, there are fanciers with many good related birds with great results under their management – wise to study the man and go for the best-in theory, bred birds, and let him advise you and become a mentor.

Try to befriend the supplier, bearing in mind that good pigeons are given. It is true that some capable birds can be found under the umbrella of many names, fashionable and not fashionable. In the acid test of race reality very few birds from any source anywhere in the world will hit the ceiling of excellence. Nic and I work on about one from 200 bred, and we have quality genes — look for about 10 percent over 10 days of race time in the BICC UK Barcelona International, which I use as the benchmark. However it is fine and purist to dedicate your life to building a family to take your name — a noble and personal thing to do. I do respect the craving for the new and to spend some brass, and I am experimenting with some outbreeds from Marco Wilson/House of Aarden/Bert Shepherd and Schlepphorst —we shall see as this is just for stimulus and fun, since the strain is established in my friends' lofts.

WHAT MAKES A PIGEON TICK?

Like humans, pigeons have basic survival needs that constitute a life cycle. Attempting to understand one may come from and give insight into ourselves, since we are both lifeforms sharing the same planet. With empathy we can react and respond to the behaviours of a pigeon and perhaps to its mind, which is the essence of being — they are not soulless machines. Lady fanciers are often clever at the more sensitive aspects of communication, and Dorothy sang to each one as it sat on the perch — O Come All Ye Faithful perhaps? Switch on your mind, tune in and focus on each bird in the loft —you may enjoy the relationship. All nice and soft, yet the objective is to entice the birds to race home from greater and greater distances — the good ones will give their all.

This with top overall management is the quintessence of clever fanciership. A bird needs a secure, comfortable home, with quality food, water, breeding facilities and access to nature, so that it can exhibit its instincts and just be in optimal surroundings. My partner knows how to do it, and pigeons will break their necks to return to his methods as seen at Barce. Many good birds just lack condition when race entered, a factor which depends largely on the fancier – the man makes the bird, he is at the top of the pecking order in the food chain, and the intricate web of the sport.

I LEARNED THE LESSONS WELL

The starting point in the sport, for the raw novice, is a maze of myths, contradictions, truths and unknowns. You will be the target for mixed human emotions, eg jealousy or support and encouragement, enmity or friendship. You need to find a clear path through the fog of problems that test your will and perseverance. If you are fortunate enough to find or be pursued by a wise mentor, then stick to them like glue. Some of the best info is out there in books, and articles — the clue is to spot the expert. Word of mouth, enriched by the personality of characters, tends to be entertaining, but not hardcore info that will help you evolve a successful racing and breeding system. If you apply your intellect and full mind, you may resolve the many facets that constitute the diamond of knowledge, and make an original contribution to the sport.

One lesson I learned the hard way, so it sank in, is that every bird is a unique individual from any breeding. Each race has a unique set of conditions that prevail. Pigeon names appear and disappear like melting snow and are ephemeral. Your life cycle in the sport will be relatively short, so make hay whilst the sun shines — grasp the moment. In the vast sea of humanity, it is nice to be recognised for your efforts, a fact which most competitors aspire to.

800-MILE BOYS OF THE MODERN ERA

With great resolve of man and bird, a select group of stalwarts has edged towards the limits with their intrepid birds. They have flown into the twilight zone of distance with their feathered charges. Some have been strain makers, some now figure in sporting folklore. The common denominators have been individuality, imagination, raw ambition and skill — a distillation of traditional marathon values. I admire them all, as people of optimism and belief, and they keep the dream alive. We maintain the hope that these exemplars will light the touch paper of inspiration in the future.

Let's give credit to personalities like Paley and Wales at Palamos, Kay, Robinson, Wilson, Riley, and McGrevy at BICC Barcelona, and NFC Tarbes fliers in the Sportsman Flying Club of the North East. I feel the weight of history upon them, and commentators of the future will celebrate the significance of these brave souls who relished a challenge and pushed the boundaries of possibility. The passage of time attracts new converts, and a new generation dawns, personified by Michael Feeney of Ireland.

FIT TO WIN

The race we take part in has yet to be won in the UK. The birds may win other races in an outright fashion, yet a different psychology is needed for our race. We rate all our birds in race time, and they give us an inner reward. Their genes are introduced into the colony as a reward for their persistence, stamina, determination and crucial navigation skills, and we rate other people who do well in the same event. Our competitors are scattered throughout the UK and Europe, and we follow the race conditions and results with intensity. The preparation to one race assumes a devoted lifestyle with that sole objective of improvement. At the time of entry our birds, being laden with reserves of body and energy, would struggle to win or do well in non-marathon races, yet some of our birds are versatile at different distances. The secret then is to prepare each bird for the demands of distance, the conditions and the racepoint. If you have a bird of potential, the art and skill is to enter it FIT TO WIN. Internal health is vital and a keen fancier eye may spot this in outward behaviour of it and as a sense perception by the human. The corollary is that the fancier has to be fit to win too.

APRIL 24 2015

THE RACER/PRODUCER

In my old family, all the birds were tested over 700 miles as I got into marathon racing. The policy was to breed off all the top birds and thus they became racer producers. We now have some birds bred back to all the key birds, and some of these are poised for an outbreed after 38 years. Some of the lines of the key racer producers we use today in my network of marathon monks are Diabolos, Dot's Delight, Barcelona Dream, Iron Hen and Man, Mystical Queen, Dedication, Oddball and Delta Lady. One bird, Diamond Queen, was a beautiful specimen who did not produce any birds of merit.

The essence and secret is to work with birds of good origins, down to the perspicacity of the fancier to select them in the first place.

Good performance birds in National/International racing over 500 miles inspire confidence, especially if you have the ancestors in the stock loft. The finest thing I ever did in birds was to evolve my family from 71 to 879 miles, and to keep concentrating the performance genes — for further details please refer to The Evolution of the Emerton Strain on Google. Here is a recorded, systematic, and practical approach to a man's attempt to improve and perpetuate performance levels in the humble racing pigeon. It is a life's work, and lofts in England, Scotland and Ireland are experimenting with the same lines up to Barcelona International, which is pleasurable and rewarding. The personal input has seen the formative dream made into a reality by obsessive and persistent dedication. In poetic terms it is a form, a creation of great design beauty.

LOFT LOCATIONS AND NAVIGATION

Let us consider how pigeons may perceive and interpret signals from magnetic fields or other energy forces applicable to certain loft locations, which may assist some of the quality birds of say Jim Donaldson at Peterhead, or Neil Bush at Amcotts, or the Coopers, under their expert management. Will we crack the code, the final enigma of racing pigeon navigation? With the limited mind of man I do not believe it is possible to unravel absolute, total knowledge, although a discipline like science may yield a little human truth on the great question. I believe the great cosmic questions to be beyond humanity, and I rest in sublime ignorance. I take a philosophical stance on all major aspects of life.

The fact that many folk do not repeat the glories of the great fanciers on acquisition of their birds is I feel down to individual systems of management, since I have done well with birds from Denney and Donaldson for example, all being of mixed ancestral origins and not genetically pure or true to type. Each pigeon is an individual. I do suspect that some geographical areas are more conducive to racing or solo navigation of pigeons, and to think that ferals flight to the fields in snow and fog — what are the bearings of instinct and memory on this? Is the basis of navigation in the brain/mind of the bird?

THE ESSENCE OF 800-MILE FLYING

It is not within the win, win, win ego buzz, the obsession with first prizes. My experience was an intoxicating insight, a pioneering step into the beyond, going beyond the conventional norm, to reach a place that many dream of and aspire to, yet few achieve. The degree of difficulty of clocking over 800 miles is the motivation needed. In simple terms a second day UK bird at Barcelona over 800 miles is almost impossible, yet ambition drives men to take a leap of faith into unknown territory. Barcelona fanatics are noted for rugged, singular individuality, optimism and cavalier spirit — we do not do normal. They are, by definition, a minority group, yet not a pariah. With the renaissance, the new dawn of popularity, young men of dreams chase the dragon in the cauldron of marathon racing, where the future will both praise and castigate them from all angles in speech, in print and in the minds of men. Take a walk on the wild side, feel the euphoria when the old cock glides in from faraway lands — yes, the essence is in your head.

THE SPORT — A GREAT ENIGMA

The great writers, fanciers and thinkers have made bold attempts to articulate the secrets, the wisdom, the knowledge, the essence behind the fanciers and their feathered athletes, and will continue to do so in a distinctly human way. With few insights that hint at truth, we delude ourselves with the arrogance of dogma, bias, and belief. The great paradox is that with all the feeble power of human consciousness, the inner nature of the bird remains nebulous and poorly defined, the nature of navigation is opaque, yet we pursue the sport with intense fervour. The wonder of pigeon racing is a true motivational force that drives hardened men to fall in love with their humble racing pigeons. Thus records are broken, fortunes are made and the sting of fame is felt.

PROGENY TESTING

The raison d'etre of a race bird is racing. Many are bred and not tested properly in the various disciplines of racing, down to the people who race them. I like around 500 miles for yearlings and over 700 miles for two-year-olds — stick to that formula, and with clever husbandry some good marathon birds may emerge, to evolve a strain over time. Genius is simplicity – good breeders breed good pigeons, judged by virtue of their racing results, since many theories are academic, based in the thoughts and dreams and prejudices of man. As a practical exercise to prove your birds, race them out to your chosen distances — it gives simple evidence of your prowess as a fancier and the capability of your birds — a clear object lesson for you. I have studied pigeons for 63 years, and these are my insights into progeny testing — the fundamentals.

HAVING A NUMBER 1 STOCK HEN

Nic and I have found one. My old associate Steve Wain gave it to us, and she is a priceless daughter of his top hen bred from the top pair of direct Emertons — all the key 700-mile lines in my pomp. The dam of two Barcelona International birds for us, one of which was 'Musgrove Addiction', her progeny, have won from 31 to 710 miles. Addiction, a great race hen, is a dam of outstanding stock. We refused a big offer from Japan for the hen, as we are purist breeder/race men and I sold birds in my youth. At present our top hen is paired to a grandson of my two Barcelona International birds at 879 miles, and descendants are in Ireland and Scotland. Making hay whilst the sun shines, we line and inbreed to the old top hen to maximise the genetic racing potential of her genome — she is revered like the sacred cow of India. Practical family breeding is easy within a family, as long as you progeny test the offspring to the limit, and no fixed theory prevails. When the modus operandi is concentrated breeding of proven birds to seek a champion.

MAY 29 2015

FACTORS INFLUENCING UK/TARBES/BARCELONA OUTCOMES

The fusion of speed and endurance is a key factor in the successful racing pigeon, in all climates and on a global level. These variables, although innate and fuelled by instinctual   drives, are fostered and augmented by the conditioning regime of the fancier. With collective flock racing, perhaps a group dynamic occurs with leaders and followers in the group over space and time as they orientate and navigate towards home or roost. Many day races up to 500 miles plus, where velocity is key, may be won by birds which have the required speed but perhaps have linked up to navigational leaders en route. Now in extreme and marathon races over 700 miles for example, navigational ability becomes the limiting factor over pure speed, which is very apparent in harsh weather conditions of rain, fog and head winds above 4 on the Beaufort Scale. Most international marathon pigeons into Northern England are proven quality navigators, eg 'Barcelona Dream' and 'Dark Enchantment' at Barcelona International. To home in good time at 700-plus miles most birds will have a total being and brain/body physiology that produces slow release energy and stamina as opposed to explosive speed of many other races. I would like to see a study of the relative physiology of actual speed and endurance proven birds, analysing any similarities or differences. The mechanism and or mind set of navigation remains a mystery, despite the methods of contemporary science.

A BREEDING PAIR FOR THE FUTURE

With an influx of 700-plus mile marathon birds into the UK, we have an idea which is unique, to perpetuate 850-mile Barcelona into genes. We plan to put the grandson of 'Barcelona Dream' and 'Dark Enchantment', both 879 miles, with a daughter of Marco Wilson's champion at 844 miles. It is a pairing of great potential, and may produce some worthy progeny. At the moment we must test the descendants in the racing cauldron to see what develops in practice. It is very nice to aim high, and the experiment is exciting and well thought out, yet true value is in the performance of the progeny in the acid test of race reality. I think the future will see some exemplary performances by the 800-mile-plus fanciers, with the accent on hope, faith, dreams and endurance of this minority and singular group of fanatics.

THE TRUE NATURE OF A MARATHON PIGEON

The marathon pigeon is a singular, wonderful and beautiful creature and quite rare. Its innate potential, under clever conditioning has conspired to enable it to endure and navigate many hundreds of miles to its home loft. Many of these peculiar individuals face adverse terrain, weather and other environmental challenges to split from the flock and fly solo over new ground, drawn by mysterious forces beyond the understanding of humanity to the roost of their birth place. Men of curiosity, vision and dreams and fuelled by wonder devote competitive lives to the cultivation of avian miracles. Physically such birds may project beauty, or common looks, yet the uniting factor of them all is guts and tenacity, to survive against great odds in competitive racing. This fact unites and cements the icons of the sport in true brotherhood — long may this be.

OUTBREEDING INBRED PIGEONS

I produced some good racers using this simple practice — remember, genius is simplicity. A complex mind finds the essence in a sea of confusion. If you inbreed to related, proven performance birds and pair them to similar birds for outbreeding, you may reap the benefits of hybrid vigour or the heterozygotic effect of novel and fresh gene combinations in the offspring. In my long career, 'Diabolos, 'Barcelona Dream', 'Sister Damien' and 'Dedication' were great racer/breeders following such an experiment. It does not happen every time, but it will maximise your chances of a champion. In our lofts we go very close, up to brother and sister, with inbreeding, and I look for outbreeds from fanciers noted for great performances from inbred colonies of pigeons. After 63 years studying birds and other life forms, I know the fundamentals of an effective marathon system, are based on sense, insight, pragmatism and mind as an observer of external reality. The novice must be perplexed and confused by all the conflicting information in the media, yet with a focus on the truth, a practical working knowledge can be acquired.

YOUNG FANCIERS TODAY

I look around in the media and in my contacts, and see very few, a rare minority, of men under 40 years of age who are willing to engage in the rigours required to cultivate and condition a team of marathon pigeons over 700 miles and towards the mother race of the Barcelona International. It's a question of resolve, desire and character that few will or want to achieve. In modern society, instant gratification is endemic, with social media, the speed fix of modern communications and the hype of celebrity, shallow culture and the sting of fame as influences. However rare, singular individuals like Michael Feeney of Ireland are showing us all a fixed purpose to sound objectives. If realised, there is an iconic hero in the making and records and world fame are the consequence of a bold and pioneering quest. A touch of madness is required as well as practical gifts, and time will reveal if this young fancier is touched by the hand of genius.

BONDING

The great fanciers have a spiritual, emotional and empathetic bond with their birds, a great inducement for great racing feats. Men and women of sensitivity and insight adopt a warm, compassionate approach to the flock, particularly to potential champions. It is my belief, akin to animism, that a bird has a mind or spirit that is mutually responsive to your own. This may sound esoteric, yet I take it as fact. Many lady fanciers are the fanciers behind successful men. Observe the bonding in your loft between all sexes and ages; yes, man is not the only sentient life form on Planet Earth. Champions of old knew the wisdom of love matches in the loft and this is how we like to let them pair today, under the ancient wisdom that nature knows best, we are born of it and belong to it.

AUGUST 28 2015

BASIC SUPPLEMENTATION OF THE RACER

I do not favour plain corn mix diets, as the nutritional status of a G10 pellet is superior. We are using science and sound practice to find the optimal feeding sources. The energy requirements of a marathon bird are huge, and serious stoking up of the bird is fundamental to success. My marathon birds are given Hormoform, yeast, peanuts, hemp, tovo, mixed oils, seed and sunflower hearts as solid food. The liquid feeding is Vydex Supersix and Rhonfried Blitzform. These are given as additions to Versele Laga mixes, and a heavier, more proteinaceous mix, all mixed together. The basic concept is the provision of all the needs of the performance racer – it works for us and is easy to do with no breakdown, no weights and measures, feeding to appetite. The flight muscle is developed as the distance progresses along our planned race prog. A good system, yet for results we depend on the intrinsic quality of the racer itself.

BASIC RECOVERY OF THE RACER

Each bird that returns will need to recuperate and rest. The insides of the bird will need some work. Welcome them home with some Supersix, peanuts, small seed and Hormoform. They need to be quiet, so that confidence can be regained in and around the loft and the balance of power in the colony restored. Some birds will fly well for years, whilst others have one big performance in them. I like to put a nice bath down for them with salts diluted in the water. Let the bird do its own thing and avoid overhandling, as you will not see inside it with the naked eye. Many distance birds go feral with time, and your observation may spot one building up to this eventuality. The whole concept of the welfare of the birds is health, fitness and confidence at home – what the old masters said yesterday is acutely applicable to today.

EFFECTS OF INBREEDING IN MY STRAIN

After thirty-nine years of racing and observation, the foundation birds have experienced concentrated breeding around performance individuals. The pick of the best lookers are stocked for further inbreeding and a little out. Some beautiful, small, refined birds are bred, and any inbreeding depression due to homozygous recessive genes is raced out of the progeny. I like nice delicate-looking little birds, far removed from the big bold sprint archetype. I have noted a minority of barren hens, frills and crests, yet some lovely smooth feather and light balance in the dark chequers and velvets, and we do not countenance a bird that will not go 700 miles. Even so, champions are rare enough to keep us motivated. I think strict racing in the early days was most helpful and Brian Denney made us all try very hard to do well. Inbred birds may increase your chances of a good one, especially if you mate them with an unrelated inbred for hybrid vigour. The methodology is best suited to individualists who wish to make a stand and concentrate in an introverted way on birds of their own intensive breeding programme. The corollary is that most continental champions are of mixed origins and a right assorted bunch — have a look at the peds, there being more outbred than inbred champions. The secret has to be in the racing of all the progeny irrespective of breeding system.

WHY SOME BIRDS HOME AND SOME DO NOT

There are many natural hazards en route such as variable weather, predation, shooting, obstacles and other assorted environmental conditions from the race point, and distance tends to enhance all these factors. A contented, well-conditioned bird of sound genome must be able to orientate, navigate, break out of the convoy and fly solo. Then we have the brain/psyche traits of will, desire, drive, tenacity, endurance etc, which can be only guessed at. This constitutes the wonder and mystery of the racing pigeon, and are unknown and quantified by man, his knowledge and science. In race reality, some hack it and some do not — it's always wise to dwell on those that do, since they are the strain and name makers. I know of no one person with total understanding of the humble pigeon, they will always be enigmatic, like the men who fly them.

ORGANISATION

Many are very disorganised in their whole approach to the sport. There are some factors which will help if you have a mind for the job. 1 like a copy, accurate or not, of every new intro to the squad. This will give archive background to your strain if you build one. To me, identifying every bird is important without access to records ie by perception and sight. Can you bring the name of your racepoints to mind and distances? How to sex your birds will test your sensory powers and perception. A breeding/racing plan needs forming and carrying out with efficiency, and do not be deterred in your intentions and objectives. The fanatic lives and dreams his birds, which are afforded priority. Keep your daily tasks simple and easy and let the birds do the work. Records and any writing can be made concise, precise and pointed — this will take a sharp intellect. I find it helps to target a racepoint, after you have been competitive against others. The whole essence of the job is organised mindfulness.

IS THERE ANYTHING IN THE EYE?

The eye is a receptor of external images for brain processing. Humans can see what they like or think they see in it and we all can differ as our brains process the perceptions. From my personal perspective I like to see a shiny, colourful eye that gives me the indication of strength and vitality radiating from the iris colour — a bright, pretty eye. Cocks tend to confer more power in the eye as I perceive it. Champions exhibit a range of individual eye types in terms of pigmentation, patterns and other characteristics, all of which are unique, as is the bird itself. Similarities can be analysed in related birds, and I place no trust in the predictive power of single eye judgement to determine performance levels at different distances. It smacks of the occult or faith and belief to me in the eye and mind of the human judge. A champion needs a keen eye to brain sight and two healthy functional eyes. Like most I do peer into eyes, which may be the mirror of the soul. What does your eye tell you on this complex matter?

DECEMBER 11 2015

DIFFICULTY AND DISTANCE

Any distance can prove to be difficult in racing. I am attracted to those which test fancier and bird, as this shows in the types of birds produced and in the nature of a strain thus generated by persistent events. This is best reflected in the interiority and performance genes of the birds, although I do like the smaller sharp-looking birds. Over 500 miles on the day against the wind is good, and International races over 700 miles test the birds' navigational ability and speed/endurance faculty. In wet weather races, birds with oily, silky feather tend to shine. Good little hens in these races often leave good birds behind, and I inbreed to these birds for stock. Excellent condition produced by the fancier may lessen the difficulty of the race. Too many hard races in a season and you will need a holiday and the birds a good rest.

KEEPING A STRAIN OF PIGEONS ALIVE

After nearly 40 years of focus I cling to the old bloodlines which will be tested in England/Ireland/Scotland and Holy Island amongst enthusiasts. With few surviving introductions, the birds will evolve and change over time, as people reach the ends of their lifecycles. It is nice to hold on to the dream that was created aeons ago. The irony is that the UK has a culture of outbreeding any new introductions on a constant and fluid basis. Certain men, often distance specialists, inbreed as part of long-term planning, as they are masters of racing, with specialist knowledge. These like Donaldson, Denney and Denys, are people I look at for a genuine inbred/outbreeding experiment to augment the basic family tree. People like these keep the quality high by strict racing regimes. Building a strain is a lasting adventure into the unknown and is a self-fulfilling exercise in existentialism.

HOW TO FORGE A CAREER IN PIGEONS

With great enthusiasm, and starting at the bottom in a club, if you are good enough a long career may shine ahead. At first good results are imperative, when others will attempt to knock you off your little perch as part of the competitive, human psyche. Good publicity leads to recognition, deserved or not deserved, and aim to do something unusual or different. Many aspiring people sell birds — a nice way to make contacts. You may reach a stage, after years, where enough is enough, and you wish to contribute back to the sport by mentoring, writing and giving birds of your strain away. With a long career in the bag, there may be changes that define the phases of your lifecycle from young ambitious man to the wise old boy. It will be a journey which tells the story of your life of pain, pleasure and enjoyment.

IS IT HELPFUL TO HANDLE A RACING PIGEON?

It is possible to sense condition, feather type and overall physical type via the hand/mind combination. Other than admiring or criticising the bird in the hand, I judge the breeding of the bird and the pedigree of the fancier in making a decision. The wisdom of my thought is then tested in the reality of racing and breeding, then handle the birds by all means to gain possible insights into the nature of a good one — you will find they vary in phenotype, yet always have good internal qualities, both physiological and psychological. The lesson I learned the hard way is that some great lookers are useless as racers and breeders — beware looks that deceive when you buy. However when we breed latebreds from our key birds we do select on balance, shape, size, feather and character — these are from birds we have knowledge of. I do like nice dark chequers from my own strain, and favour them over a blue or red, which is a bias.

SPOTTING CONDITION

Birds that win or race well will be in good internal condition, when the physiology/psychology is right. From the outside the eyes will shine, along with the nice, tight clean plumage. I like to see trembling, and to feel the vibrancy of the breast muscles. Ironically, birds like this may succumb to viruses when you thought all was well, especially after antibiotic therapy. Birds out in the elements will show rugged, hard condition — I do not like big fat birds covered in bloom. The key is endurance condition by increases in distance and clever feeding, then they will be right. Poorly birds will have fading iris colour and changed droppings and will lose weight. Try and maintain good condition of all your birds at all times, especially when breeding and moulting cycles are on. Study each bird daily with mind and senses. The top men capitalise on condition.

THE LONGER DISTANCES WITH HENS

A really good hen takes some beating at 5 to 700 miles. I have done well with them from 71 to 879 miles. Paired in March and raced with the cocks in build-up stages of distance, they are my favourite for their tenacity and quick recovery, and will do all you ask out to Barcelona. The rub is that they must be brought into sparkling condition by you and sent to great distances in actual racing, say in the NFC and then the BICC. If you can in your area, an easy way is the open loft natural system of your style as this will mirror the types of weather and conditions faced en route. Some hens can score at all distances, and are good breeding birds. The fancier, as always, is responsible for the entry condition of the hens in the races. Good ones emerge from many origins, not just fancy commercial named birds to make money.

BASIC STRAINMAKERS

A minority of modern fanciers, usually men, will have dedicated many years of their lives to the breeding, racing and perpetuation of a group of birds, with distinct common, shared ancestors in the pedigree. These folk, by nature of the task, tend to be settled specialists, with an established winning system to their lofts, and are often long-distance enthusiasts. New introductions into the gene pool are seldom, where some extensive inbreeding will take place. I regard these people as purists and specialists in the old school art of pigeon racing — they are often obsessive perfectionists. Some leading exponents of this esoteric knowledge are Jim Donaldson, Chris Gordon and Brian Denney. It would be ideal for many more of these individualists to emerge in the future. Birds are never pure in a genetic sense, yet these men all concentrate on racing/breeding performances.

JANUARY 29 2016

WHAT WE DO NOT KNOW

Many of us think we know a lot about the sport of pigeon racing. Collective knowledge is yet to crack the code of navigation over great distances. Theoreticians, scientists and other humans do not know. I feel that some birds may have an awareness of the direction home, enclosed in the transporter, before actual liberation. It is easy to think that the brain/mind is at the centre of the mystery in response to the external world – what is the inner being of the bird?

In terms of nutrition I have yet to see the perfect feeding system in print, although my unique one generates optimal condition in our racing regime — we work deep within the psychology/physiology of the race bird. With our good, total system in place we then rely on the quality of the bird under Barcelona International race conditions – always very tough indeed. The greats of the game intrigue me — every man is an island — why do they devote their lives to the humble pigeon? I perceive it to be self-realisation in an existential sense — it is about personal identity, is it not? Fanciers will continue in the pursuit of perfection with their birds, in a profoundly human way, and in many parts of the earth. The great fanciers have the need to prevail.

THE NEW BEGINNING

After 40 years of strain building from 71 to 879 miles, the birds are now in the hands of various enthusiasts who will leave their own mark of destiny on the genes I have cultivated. We hope to realise dreams and create some racing champions. Some of the leading men on the chessboard are Nick Harvey, Michael Feeney, Alan Kelly, Chris Little, Booth & Shipley, Gilbert Chappell, Jim Patterson and John Ghent. All individuals, they will stamp their personality on the birds they evolve. On 25th Jan 2016, I will be 67 chronological years old, with a 64-year interest in pigeons. I have looked for doves and pigeons in 52 countries and islands. Now I see beauty in certain birds that have framed my obsession. They inspire me to both poetry and philosophy, in the realms of higher consciousness, and all because a little boy fell in love with a humble pigeon.

THE RIGHT DECISIONS

An eye and a mind for the right bird are very significant in strain building. Knowledge and focus and a perception of quality and potential are important. In '76 I matched two birds up out of the pens, with value judgements on feather texture, balance and the total impression in my mind, having studied the evolutionary history of the strain origins and a montage advertised by Louella. The image was of the DVH Stichelbaut-based birds from Descamps Van Hasten. I felt that they were the birds for me and would be successful for me. With strict progeny testing, the originals, with two more from inbred, related birds, have left descendants that are raced out to Barcelona International some 40 years later, with inbreeding back to my seven foundation birds — these origins are documented on the internet. The decision to inbreed around real performance birds has been good, with some outbreeding of inbred pigeons in the strain creation. Today top-class UK and Ireland Barcelona marathon performers are rare, especially in excess of 800 miles, ie within three to four days — yet to be a Barcelona International bird into the UK on the second day over 800 miles! Have a go in the race of all races — it is mind bending.

METICULOUS RECORDS

Though they are never perfect in reality, it is important to keep pedantic and accurate records in the recording of the creation of a strain. Over 40 years I have tried to maintain this principle, and the evolution using my seven foundation birds is well documented on Google. Some indication of key, prepotent birds may be seen, yet it is the total ancestry that is of highest significance — the apples may have fallen from the tree 50 years later, for example, when I got the DVH in 76 they were already inbred for generations. It is fastidious and hard work, yet it leaves behind the history of the human who created a group of birds with distinct hereditary characteristics. This type of activity is often undertaken by academic/scientific and intellectual types who may be visionary in conscious perception. Gerhard Schlepphorst personifies these traits — I have bought in 28 of his Stichelbaut-based birds, and the standard phenotype is beautiful —we will progeny test them all. A strain is the outward expression of the psyche of man. Nice to reflect back on birds that shaped the strain. There are often many errors in the recording of pedigrees — we do try.

HARD ENDURANCE PIGEONS

Long-term, continuous, competitive racing from 500 to 879 miles up to Barcelona International level, and in all weathers, will produce some birds of great navigational ability and solid character. In my strain and with inbreeding to performance birds, many small-medium dark chequer birds have contributed to my career. Going very close indeed as a continuous entity, some of the birds are prolific breeders when outbred, and every one must be tested right out. After 40 years my partners and contacts are in this process that will continue. The modern lure is Barcelona into Ireland in race time. All individuals these folk will shape a destiny out of birds and dedication. We are seeking another champion to add to the genome. On perception, the good birds may radiate an aura about themselves, like charisma in people. A bird may mature into a good racer with years of on-the-wing experience, and you will recognise them in race reality. I reflect on the birds I raced and bred with admiration and affection.

BELIEF IN YOUR BIRDS

The breeding and racing of your birds is a test of your total personality – the desire, the acumen and the complete psyche. Racing is an expression of the competitive spirit. As a novice, select with a keen eye on potential and external, physical type. Empathy with a pigeon is based on perception, and how the brain processes images. I have believed in the birds I evolved for 40 years, the type and the origin. The passage of time has made me realise that few champions are born and raced from birds of any name and origin, ie those to excel in the Barcelona International race UK and Ireland. I have a network of fanciers, and we will attempt to produce some good ones in the greatest race on Planet Earth.

THE TRUE VALUE OF A PIGEON

Racing pigeons may raise thousands of pounds and be coveted and valued in material terms. This is mainstream market forces in action, and fuels the international world of pigeon racing. Having sold birds myself, I came to alter my philosophy on pigeons. I believe the real value of a bird lies in its racing and breeding potential and at my chosen distance and racepoint for it. This is a pedantic and purist approach to the intrinsic value of a racing pigeon. In this I place the emphasis on an approach to the actual bird rather than the money generated — unorthodox, yet crucial in my philosophy towards marathon pigeon racing. After a long career, I have bred many good ones, and a few rare champions, yet the satisfaction lies in the creation of a strain of some quality, related individuals. In an aesthetic sense the good ones always look beautiful.

MARCH 11 2016

HONESTY AND INTEGRITY IN THE SPORT

I have a little web of pals who adopt a genuine display of honesty when we exchange quality bred birds from a perception of our best — this is how great genes are obtained. Money can corrupt, rackets are run and the deed is done. I have seen the black market in the Middle and Far East, where every trick in the book under the cloak of honesty is used. Nick and I these days are genuine with our birds, and I did some great exchanges with Jim Donaldson, and got some good ones from Denney in 88 and 90, and one from Ken Hanby from his 'Spitfire' cock, and a son of Trev Robinson's 9th Open Pau. The great Marco Wilson gave us five from his best. The spirit is to improve the performance gene pool over time. Our top stock hen was given by Steve Wain. The purist distance men like to spread the good ones about for no money. However the birds in the big sale of Chris Gordon are straight —in the nebulous sales world there are some real deals.

RELATED MODERN BLOODLINES

Birds of my strain are loaded with DVH Stichelbaut bloodlines. I see many of the old genes of the masters repeated over and over again in the outbred ace Barcelona birds. Nice to see the provenance featuring Van Wanroy, especially the 'Kleine Donkere' line —'Black Giant', Kuyper Bros etc. I am putting some of my highly inbred birds into the best of these lines. I know of no other fancier to have done 40 years of close inbreeding and kept the race performances at a high level. The Continentals tend not to do a lot of inbreeding other than to great performance levels. The innate potential will dictate if a bird can cut the mustard in race reality.

With all this breeding going on, I do like small to medium, pretty, refined, silky, balanced dark chequers that are shiny, radiating health and vitality and that can crack the Pyrenees from Spain. The good racer is always the right type — existentialism in action. Many birds are under the cloak of Aarden — they are all a mixture of diverse, ancient ancestry.

RESULTS COUNT

The essence of the nature of the racing game is hard results — we are never satisfied with ours, which is a motivational source. We need more champions to come from the strain, and there will be some. How do I judge a pigeon man? He has to meet my criteria, as follows: he has to have made a lasting contribution to the collective good of the sport and developed a good strain of birds over 25 years plus at all distances to beyond 700 miles. One way is to mentor novices to get results and donate trophies — a kind of ego-altruism.

Psychologically, if you are happy with a career in birds then it is the result that counts in the end. Personally I would sacrifice all my firsts for one champion out of Barcelona International. Racing is hard grind, and I do prefer my creative writing and mentoring the neophytes and initiates — some of them appreciate it in a genuine sense — I am aware of the Janus Face of humanity.

KNOWLEDGE AND LEARNING

The top men in the game all have advanced, esoteric info in

their heads and at their fingertips. Mine was created from academic study and insights from breeding and racing practices. In 40 years some intuitive leaps have helped me to create a unique breeding and racing system. Others attempt to replicate it, and may become quite close, yet it remains mine. The Zsolt Talaber books are great, as was Schraag, since good applied science is there to help the intelligent fancier. I use a fusion of the wild open loft with quality solid and liquid feeding, which with the man all optimise and maximise the race condition that is crucial for marathon flying from Spain. What works is a fusion of all we think and do with our key genes and inner potential of the birds. The desire has always been to improve the strain — after 40 years some steady progress is made.

RACERS NEED REST

I like my birds to have four weeks or so loft rest at home before a marathon flight of over 700 miles. Before this and in steady increases in race distance a nice fly of up to 500 miles will be under the belt. The birds will have fuelled up on my unique feeding system and will be laden with fuel and fat reserves in the internal organs – glycogen in the liver etc. A short toss of around 100 miles in the week before basketing will add the final tuning element to the condition. Exercise at home then with no stressful basket/road training. The birds are then calmly caught for basketing and marking. Time on the wing to build up preparation is essential, with birds left at home certain weekends from the race programme — BICC/BBC/NFC. The birds are blown up with air/muscle and fat reserves for Barcelona International, where stamina is key. We are not expecting to win this race as no UK person has done it — the essence is the majesty and awesome challenge of the Pyrenees and Spain in the greatest race on Planet Earth.

STOCK SELECTION MADE EASY

I make this process a simple exercise. We choose the best looking and handling latebreds from our Barcelona birds and the proven top stock, going on brain perceptions of shape, balance, feather quality and vitality as seen in the eye expression. A decision on the external appearance of the bird is made, yet the chief criterion is a deep intuitive call on the breeding and innate performance potential of the bird — I like a pedigree packed full of performance genes. With stock sense many birds tell you what to do, with a little empathy. International Barcelona performances prove the quality of the ancestors.

The hardest part is the actual marathon racing of your own strain to your own lofts with the birds you send. This is pure racing and we need to enter every bird into the cauldron of competition. My strain over 40 years is based on the very first matched pair I selected in 76 with continuous back inbreeding to them and five other prepotent foundation birds. I feel the main factor has been my system to a specific, rural loft location and the role of my parents.

THE MYSTERY OF THE MASTERS

Have you wondered why say Vince Padfield, Jim Donaldson and other marathon/distance fliers have become great? It is easy to comprehend – they have developed specialist knowledge in their heads and conditioning race systems for their choice of birds. These men are modern geniuses of the sport, and very dedicated to their own success with the birds. They are rather quiet men to the public eye — deep in thought no doubt. The real nature of these people is enigmatic, and you need to be like them to know them. The finer aspects of the game are subtle, and not understood. Only I know my system, although some get close to it – the subtleties go with the fancier to the grave, it is the way of things, it is immortal. You may copy a system, yet you will not duplicate the man. Why did Stichelbaut become so famous, or Aarden? Think about it.

MAY 20 2016

AGE OF PIGEONS FOR BARCELONA INTERNATIONAL

We continue to enter all two-year-old birds in this epic race. With seven timings in four years, success has been reasonable, and one hen is destined for her fourth go at Barcelona this year. After this year, depending on our result we may up it to three years of age. I reflect on the fact that my cock bird at 879 miles was only two. Our system is good, and we are trying to produce another champion like 'Musgrove Addiction'. For most people the key is in the race preparation of the birds, I like around 450 miles for all the yearlings, then you have some quality to work on. Really good UK birds are rare in this race, and the Irish one will be seminal, and its fame will radiate around the world, with dramatic consequences. Rapid experience in distance races is key to the maturation of Barcelona candidates.

SPEED/ENDURANCE FLYING

Between 500 and 900 miles from the racepoint, it is what you get. A minority of people practise this specialist art, and the degree of difficulty in producing a rare champion in races of this magnitude is what fascinates me. There is no hiding place at this level when race reality kicks in. I find most of the residue of birds tend to leave a breeding line of influence in the strain. The demands on man and bird are large, with waits of patience night and day over many days, and preparation of the birds taking years. A type of monastic mental discipline is required in the execution of these races, with holidays booked and a happy home life. The marathon Barcelona International men are all fanatical, never say die optimists and dreamers, and totally barking. We love the focus required and getting some nice birds in the clock from the big convoy at the Pyrenees. Our chances of the ultimate win are remote, in the UK and that is of no concern, we dream on!

PROMOTION OF THE SPORT

I like to see people of influence raising the profile of people and pigeons, and of themselves in the process. The Elimar website, The Racing Pigeon and other public media do a great job. All the writers have a responsibility to the collective good and knowledge in the sport. It is such a rich seam of communication that all can have their say to intensify our concentration on this absorbing hobby. A site like Elimar takes the written word around the world, and makes grounded, ordinary folk rather famous. I do feel there is work to be done in the area of sportsmanship, and the establishment of the sport is a great hobby, with less attention to the money god. Having said this, I used to sell pigeons to make a few bob. To me the purist aspects of pigeon racing are to be found in International racing, distance, marathon events and strain building, which are a fusion of traditional and modern concepts. I am all for new and creative ideas, especially allied to feeding and practical management systems, yet an effective open loft system will always have its place in the execution of success. Help a novice, donate a trophy, write a book, fly Barcelona International.

SINGLE UP TRAINING

You may think this practice confers an advantage. In reality I have not noticed any ultimate difference using it. At the end of the day, all my birds will have to fly many miles solo from marathon race points; a good pigeon will navigate, it needs to be fit, not just shown the way. Birds in great condition will jump hundreds of miles if any good. In the early preparation races I like time on the wing to muscle up and tune the psychology and physiology of the birds, for big performances later in the season. In early training tosses I like the flock that is racing home in a collective group. Many people work too hard in a physical sense, when it is in the brain where most of the effort should be placed.

We have devised a system where most of the work is done by the birds, which are treated as athletes. A good bird has great stamina and navigational skills, and may spend some time flying in the hours of darkness, a system devised in an attempt to impose some order and fair play logic on the race for the people concerned, since pigeons can fly any time of the day or night. The Barcelona International is on its way. I am looking for a bird into the UK over 800 miles on the second day, as this has never been done in the history of the race, with The Flange of Jim Biss being the furthest in the BICC. In this BICC race, over 800 miles by the fourth day will have sorted the limit out of most of the birds. I love these individual, outstanding marathon birds like the Marco Wilson Cock, nothing else anywhere near it in race time, a singular creature.

AGAINST ALL ODDS

Lads in the far north of England have the vagaries of the weather and extra distances to fly in races of a true National and International nature. I place great value on birds that do well when the chips are down or are on the edge of realistic possibility. I set a yardstick for my strain, and it was that every single bird was sent to a race over 700 miles in distance, irrespective of what others may be coveting. This is the shit or bust philosophy that Nick and I follow today. It sure puts some stamina/endurance origins into the strain we are building. At 735 miles Pau NFC was tough against the wind, and 879 miles Barcelona International was nearly off the scale.

May I applaud the superlative efforts of John Rumney in setting the standards for the far north for others to emulate and follow in the BICC. I have preached this type of participation and success for 20 years, and the Irish should use these men as role models. With clever, practical applications it shows what can be done when sharp brains are applied to the sport-pigeons as flying extensions of human egos.

THE COMPETITIVE SPIRIT

You see it in man, animals and birds. Originating in the brain and being, it is the source and nucleus of inner motivation to create an identity and prevail. The spirit is the essence of all competitions where individuals seek to prevail, and originates in a similar trait to bullying. The trait may be overt or covert, yet is there in human societies and most social species of animals and birds, and may be an important dynamic in groups. A perceptive person can sense and feel it in others, where a pleasant person may be ruthlessly competitive behind the mask. The politics and business in capitalist cultures are based on it. If possible I keep a little aloof to the main thrust of it in the media and propagandist broadcasting, believing only what I prove to myself to be true.

THREE

Ask Jim
a question

Q **Taking your advice, I have been using layers' pellets and peanuts. Would I be enriching the blood too much if I used Hormoform as well?**

A Pigeons for 'hard' racing, ie up to marathon level (over 700 miles) need to be fuelled up like space rockets! I never carried out a full blood analysis but results and practice told me that peanuts, layers' pellets and Hormoform are fine for racing birds. Feel free to go ahead and inform me off your results!

Q I do not understand the concept of inbreeding, what do you pair together and what do you do with the young bird next, race them or put them to what?

A In simple terms inbreeding is the pairing together of closely related birds, eg brother to sister, father to daughter. If you have a 'good' bird say you can pair it to a 'good' brother or sister or father to daughter and so on. My strain is still inbred now after 33 years and some of the seven founder birds were inbred back to the 1940s (assuming pedigrees to be correct!)

With inbreeding we develop our own family, eg the Robert Lee Family, and aim to breed 'good' performance birds like the parents.

So if you have any 'inbred' young bird, either race it like my Dark Velvet or breed from it, and perhaps both. Most men cross their birds, but this is not the way to form a 'strain'. Geoff Cooper is a good inbreeder (top of the National tree). Always races test the result of your breeding, and remember, good racers can come from any pairing of your birds.

Q How far would you send ten celibate cocks that have not been trained as young birds (July hatched '08 latebreds)? Plus how would you implement the celibate system?

A It may pay you to go easy with the cocks and send them in stages to the coast, eg 200 miles. This assumes your objective is sprint to middle distance racing. If I had them they would be aimed at Cholet in the NFC; this may be too harsh for your good self. Give them a nice 50-mile toss and enter them in late April to May, avoiding cold north winds! To operate the celibate system you can exercise in two controlled periods of around one hour each per day or semi-open loft depending on your location. If fed properly (see my 'insights'), they will reach good condition. If possible race the hens (separate of course) as well. The cocks should spend time with the hens on race day.

Q How do you go about pairing your best cocks with up to half a dozen hens to maintain the breed?

A Run the cock with two hens for example and when laid, float the eggs under feeders. Put two fresh hens in with the cock and repeat the process. The birds should be in top condition with Hormoform, peanuts, Gem Matrix and some Mycosant 'T' ccs in the water. Later you can try half-brother to sister mating.

Q Are you for or against rearing the young birds on darkness? As an 82-year-old fancier (starting in 1934) I think nature will find one way or another to pay you back.

A I never used the 'darkness'. However good fanciers report good success with the old ones afterwards. The system is personal and if properly conditioned the birds will be fit. In reality most birds are useless when really tested on any system.

Remember, man is part of nature – we are nature and our egos exert an influence with it. Do what makes you happy. However, we know that darkness, December hatched or lightness young birds will fly 400 miles on the day, if they are any good that is. 'Nature' pays us back when we stand aloof from it – we must work with it. We must be at one (Grasshopper).

Q You experimented with Mycosan 'T' and another product. Please tell me what the other product is and what ratio to each other and how to administer it and what does. Where can I obtain Aviol?

A Thanks Tony. The other product is Chlortetracycline and Raffeisenstra. This is sold by Chevita GMBH 2 – 4 vet Abt, Pfafenhofen, 85276 Germany. You mix sachet (see labels) Friday/Saturday Mycosan 'T', then Monday both together before basketing. Aviol is also available on the continent and like Mycosan 'T' it no longer contains arsanilic acid. The above products are tonics as recommended in Healthy Pigeons by Schragg. NB: Mycosan 'T' from Harkers UK.

Q If you wanted a stock pigeon as an outcross and were offered the choice of two brothers and one had outstanding eyesign and the other had none, but the one without eyesign had been a very good and reliable racer, which one would you pick?

A Normally I would choose a young bird direct from a top pigeon, performance wise, especially from an inbred family of performance-tested birds. I would not choose the bird on eyesign alone since I believe eyesign theory for performance prediction to be fanciful. Proving that the performance bird was bred in the purple, ie from 700-900 mile birds, I would tend to choose it. In my stock loft the breeders were usually from top birds of the year. To conclude, I would reject any notions of choosing a bird on eyesign alone, yet I may choose this bird if it gave me a superior overall perception of quality.

Q I know you have described your feeding methods with which you achieved your outstanding long-distance performances, but during my long reporting career with the BHW I knew one club long-distance champion flier who fed nothing but small seeds. Comments please.

A I would like a definition of long-distance and club long-distance champion. I also question the fact of using small seed only! By long distance I mean 500-700 miles and really in National and International competition. I know nothing of the person to whom you allude and would seek the facts before passing my final judgement. I suspect that the distances would be less than 700 miles and at local club level. Additionally I would have liked to interview the fancier to establish the facts for myself, and in this case I would require empirical evidence of support. I do not suggest that my methods are a categorical imperative and just say it as it is for me.

Q I wonder if you could let me know the address where I could buy your birds (long-distance racing)? During 1970-80s I only raced long-distance races eg SNFC, where I won three North Sections. Then I started sprint racing, but I can't get close to the winners now because I am not going to change to the ETS system. I think it takes the enjoyment out of it, so I am going back to long-distance racing. Also how much do you charge for your birds?

A A book I would recommend is *Roads to Rome* by Cameron Stansfield, as it explains in detail the methods and results of some top long-distance fanciers, eg Neil

Bush to name one. Two more books which are helpful to long-distance fanciers are the big tome by Colin Walker (Australian vet fancier) and the Zsolt Talaber veterinary book. These books are either available now from Boddy & Ridewood, Scarborough or advertised in the fancy press (BHW or RP).

I would like to inform the fancy that my stock of the Emerton strain are in the capable hands of David Barkel. He has the results of 30 years of family breeding including children and grandchildren of Barcelona Dream, Dax My Girl, Dax ll, Dedication, Mystical Queen, Oddball, Sister Damien, Delta Lady etc and the Steve Wain Section winner. These birds were all successful in National or International racing from 579 to 879 miles.

Q I am trying the layers' pellets as you advise and this is going well. I would like to ask what your corn mix in the evening was made up of, as you say in the Parkinson interview that you used to mix brands together.

A It is apparent by the many responses received that my layers' pellets feeding is really taking off! This is not surprising as they are fairly cheap and very nutritious for racing pigeons. I fed them for 30 years, throughout my racing career. For the evening feed I would make up a mixture of Versele-Laga Gerry Plus and Superstar Plus with added brewer's yeast, peanuts, Hormoform, hemp and Red Band. Before basketing for two days add oils to the mixture ie Beyer's mixed oils, garlic oil and Colombine 10:1 oils. Saturday, Sunday, Monday, Tuesday moisten the yeast with pure lemon juice (out of a bottle) and mix into the corn. Five days before basketing for long and marathon races (500-800 miles) give the birds a mixture of peanuts/Hormoform and Red Band in the boxes to appetite. I would also alert fanciers to my use of Bovril in the water – one fruit spoon to one and a half gallons of water on Wednesday.

Q **What method would you use if the open loft was not possible due to hawks?**

A My birds had to run the gauntlet of female sparrowhawks. Over the years they killed many champions, and they will take pigeons at your feet. My maxim was 'if they don't take the good ones then it doesn't matter'. Fortunately by May when she was nesting most of the kills stopped, which coincided with the racing season. However if you definitely can't go open loft, then regular exercise, control periods are necessary eg twice per day for a total of two and a half hours.

Q **Did you ever flag your birds?**

A The answer is no, but I know two ace flyers who do, eg one and a half hours 5.30 to 7am in the morning (when light enough) and one hour 5-6pm teatime. You can create a system to suit yourself, the main criteria being that your birds are fit and contented around home. Racing in the programme will finish the conditioning before the big events.

Q **You can't buy Barcelona pigeons off the shelf at over 800 miles, bearing in mind that these pigeons will have flown well over 1,000 miles by the time they get home even in a good race. How many Barcelona pigeons had he in the loft when he**

finished with the birds and how many Barcelona pigeons has he handled at over 800 miles?

A   In 1995 as the ultimate challenge I sent my most promising six birds to Barcelona International at 879 miles. The winds in England were east and north-east. I was very happy to verify three being the longest flying birds in Europe at that time. To achieve this objective I took a week's holiday from work and sacrificed any Pau NFC claims. Not everyone knows that I lived six miles from the loft and nursed my mother before she died at 92, although she was still helping with the birds at 91. Due to all the difficulties this was my one and only excursion in Barcelona. In my last big race I sent five to the Dax International receiving the two longest flying birds in Europe at 687 miles. A lot of birds will home from Barcelona, but few at over 800 miles in race time. With a concentrated effort in the UK more and more could be clocked; it is up to you!

Q   As I see it, to get a fair number in the loft at over 800 miles all the 2ys would have to go, as you only get one chance per year to send.

A   You are quite right Frank, with Barcelona being the one great test, it is important to send all birds over 2y – fly it or die! The bird that is in the clock is the right one for the job – this is the only theory that matters!

Q   All my yearlings would have to fly Tarbes 726 miles to fly to Barcelona the following year. Is this too severe Jim, or am I on the right lines?

A   I would send your yearlings to say Cholet and/or Saintes with the NFC. In hard conditions you will tend to break yearlings at 726 miles or they won't race, especially at Barcelona. Birds at Barcelona have to be full of 'guts' and reserves and after their race at Barcelona they will probably be finished for ever. I like the idea of experienced old birds sent to Pau International (it's about time the NFC flew this point, it's the real deal). From here you could pop birds over to Barcelona.

Q **A person once said to me that in horse racing, making some horses carry more weight was very unfair, and all should carry the same weight. I tried to explain the handicap system, where in theory handicap races were devised to give mediocre horses a chance of getting some prize money, and that in the top class or group one races, where the better horses compete, they all have to carry the same weight and if we didn't have these handicap races there would be no point in having a high percentage of racehorses, as there will never be any point in keeping them. Jim, do you think that the same principles apply to racing pigeons as so many are lost each year, and some never get in the top prizes? I know that many never achieve success because of management, but millions are bred each year and so many fail to get home from even short distances. I know we have aerial predators, and other manmade obstacles, but we can't keep blaming such for ever.**

A In pigeon racing there is a wonderful opportunity for each fancier, starting from the blocks of a first young bird race, to progress through to the top level, International racing. It is a sport where the small back garden fancier can take on and beat the rich man with his management team and hundreds of birds.

Since there are good opportunities to progress in pigeon racing and with one family of birds as I did, I do not advocate or believe in any handicapping system. The whole essence of racing is that the best bird and fancier win on their day, and I am romantic enough to believe that you never really know the quality of a bird until it is released at the racepoint, be it 50 miles or 1000 miles. It is a fact that most birds especially at the marathon distance are not good enough, hence my 800 mile plus, 2nd day Barcelona Challenge. Handicapping would interfere with the natural selection process of the survival of the fittest and the best.

We all have to start somewhere and I started my racing in 1977 in St Lawrence WMC, winning my first young bird race with a red hen, and I think racing should remain as it is open to all and at every level. The secret is to get your kicks from it at whatever level you decide, with no false results due to artificial and human handicapping. Yes, racing is hard and cruel and many birds are lost due to poor health and basic quality of both the fancier and the bird. The best fanciers have the knack of gathering good birds around themselves. The cream always rises to the top!

Q **Mr Emerton didn't answer the question about how many pigeons he sent across the Channel. That would be very interesting to many fanciers.**

A   In simple terms, I sent all yearlings and older to France (Belgium earlier on) and Spain. I would normally have between 15 and 30 birds to send to the NFC, 466 miles.

Any promising returning birds from this point (sometimes weeks later) I would cultivate for Pau, 735 miles, San Sebastian 737 miles, Dax International 687 miles or Barcelona International 879 miles. A well-prepared 2y bird can cope with any racepoint up to 1,000 miles. Fanciers will realise that I was very ruthless with my birds in an attempt to maximise the individual's performances. From Dax, 687 miles, I had four out of six, and two out of five (Dax My Girl and Dax ll). From Barcelona International I had three out of six at 879 miles (longest flier in Europe). From four races into England with the single bird NFC my birds were 3rd Open Pau, 735 miles, 4th Open Dax International racing, 687 miles and 10th Open San Sebastian 737 miles. I believe my few international results (from only three races) to be the best in Yorkshire in modern times (post 1995). Note: This can easily be beaten. If I had had the facilities to prepare more birds (my race loft was about 20ft x 9ft and over 50 years old) I would have sent more birds eg 100 to 466 miles NFC. In conclusion, as 2ys I may have had between five and ten to send. My losses were relatively large, since I jumped my young birds in (no training) to 95 miles or 138 miles. My philosophy is simple: test the birds as soon as possible to realise their ultimate potential.

Q **You advocate feeding layers' pellets for the distance. I would very much appreciate more info on this method of feeding when you can spare a few moments with me on this subject.**

A   I have experimented with different types of pellets, including turkey and various specialist pigeon pellets eg Harkers Homon, over 30 years with my strain of birds and from 71 miles to 879 miles sprinting, distance and marathon racing. I have found poultry layers' pellets to be excellent! The formulation develops a superior feed source to conventional grain mixes, since it is scientifically developed to supply optional nutritional requirements. The pellets are often soya and barley-based with a proportion of animal protein, and at £6 per bag should be in hoppers before all the birds at all times. The layers' pellets are easily digested and open loft birds will come in to the loft to snack on them as the appetite dictates.

My corn mixtures, fed once per day at teatime in wooden hoppers, have been well illustrated in my Insights and Q & A columns. None of my feeding was weighed, everything was fed to the immediate appetite of the birds at all times. There was no rationing even when winning in specialist young bird races (twice 1st five Open etc) With the responses worldwide I have received, I can conclude that my feeding methods have been influential.

Q Why do many eyesign adherents wait until they know of a pigeon's excellent racing of breeding performances before extolling its virtues? Surely they should visit lofts and forecast such performances beforehand?

A When studying a bird's eyes or any other external object, there is an interaction between the psyche of the individual (the subject) and the eye (the object). However, in a certain level of human perception the eye and the human being are one. The latter normally relates to a 'higher' level of consciousness, or is a mystical manifestation. It would appear that the believers in the reality of 'eyesign' theory, when applied in practice to breeding and racing, regard this process as being definite, predictable and accurate. It is my assertion and belief that believers project their own subjective process into the perceived eye of the pigeon.

I think believers should turn the lens on themselves and analyse the image with great care, when perhaps they will find the source of self-deception and delusion. To my knowledge there are few, if any, top National and International racing men in the UK who use 'eyesign theory' as the sole source of selection in breeding and racing. Most top fanciers at National and International level prefer the basket as the main criterion of selection. Like others, I like to see a richly-coloured eye, perceived to be nice and bright as indicators of health and condition. The development of a strain will produce similarities between the eyes of certain individuals, mine being recessive violets and orange/red irises with yellow around the pupil. I hereby challenge all eyesign theorists in the UK to predict, using their beliefs, the winner of the BICC Barcelona International into the UK.

To conclude, I fail to see any absolute evidence to justify eyesign, other than at the theoretical level of consciousness. Its reality exists only within the collective consciousness of the theorists, who may or may not be genuine in their 'expert' claims.

Q **I expect that millions of pounds are spent in the horse racing world to every few pounds in pigeon racing, so why do wealthy winners of brood**

mares seek the services of the top racing performance stallions? And don't use eyesign.

A   The horse racing world is relatively money oriented, and much more so than pigeon racing. Using top stallions at stud is no guarantee of the success of the racing offspring. There are many factors in the equation, such as future management and the gene combinations of the parents. As with pigeons, good winners could be bred from non-winning parents and grandparents. It is a decision involving the generation of money and the perceived likelihood of producing champions. Sensible racing people will realise the folly of predicting winners by the outward appearance of a stallion's eye. I believe that star gazing into the eye of a pigeon has evolved by hand study of birds over the generations in an erroneous attempt to predict the outcomes of races.

In my opinion a study of the eye in isolation, ie not holding the bird in the hand, will not always predict success in breeding or racing. Naturally eyesign theorists are not always right or wrong. When viewed in totality, sometimes they will be correct. Who knows what is behind the eye of a bird – a spirit, soul or intelligence? Human beings will always be limited by their own humanity and their inability to know anything other than a human absolute understanding of anything.

Q   Do you think free-flying pigeons breed stronger and healthier young than confined birds?

A   Confined birds which have access to an aviary, open to the elements, can breed optimal young birds if managed correctly. It is probably preferable to let birds fly freely in the hope of breeding strong and healthy young. If with progeny testing you are satisfied with your breeding and racing, then the system is fine. A lot depends on your targets and ambition levels. I was happy with mine, especially my strain formulation, although my racing record could have been bettered.

FOUR

Jim's A to Z of Pigeon Racing

A

ACTION

In pigeon racing there are many who talk like champions, and so they are – champion talkers! I have found that is always pays to act on your desires and plans. My old maxim is, 'Think it, do it'. If you act and are good enough, you will win through in the end. Do not let others deter you from your objectives.

ADVANTAGE

You can gain advantage by the application of your knowledge and aims into being better with your birds at whatever level you decide to compete, the 'Formula 1' being International racing. Many fanciers are possessive about maintaining their loft location relative to others within a club, Federation or National. In fact, some fanciers will even move to, say, the 'north-east corner' in south road racing. I always strived to do well against the odds – note Barcelona at 879 miles, Pau 735 miles, etc. Believe me, hardship induces great satisfaction when overcome.

ALOIS STICHELBAUT

Now here is a name worthy of mention in any list. Stichelbaut is one of the historical greats, with the genes of some of his birds surviving today. He was apparently a modest man who did not court a great deal of publicity. However, the former cyclist and butcher Michel Descamps based his stud on four birds from the Alois Stichelbaut sale of the 1940s. Michel formed a partnership with Clara van Hasten, hence the DVH Stichelbauts. In particular the lines of Ware Ijzeren of '57 (a National winner) and his son, Ijzeren Kennedy of '63, enjoyed a great deal of success in champions' lofts and Emiel Denys made Remi of '54 famous. Fanciers may know that my strain was based on four birds of the DVH Stichelbaut strain acquired from Louella Lofts and these are performing with distinction today.

AMBITION

This quality is a wonderful attribute to possess. Provided

every other quality is evident, ambition will take you to the top. The top, in my mind's eye, is success in International racing. Ambition feeds the desire and will do well at any level of your pursuits and they should bottle it! It goes without saying that all 'good' fanciers will have nurtured their ambitions.

AMOXICILLIN (TRIHYDRATE)

This is an antibiotic and a good broad-spectrum antibacterial agent, especially when combined with clavullanic acid. Often bought as Vetremox, it has its uses against E Coli, salmonella and other disease-inducing bacteria. Its usage can be alternated with Baytril and Lincospectin. I have used it, but I recommend antibiotics only when necessary.

ANISEED

Aniseed can be obtained as an oil and I first came across it when mixed with Red Band, which has been copied and copied as a template by many firms. I believe that birds and animals like the smell and I used to drink the fiery, exotic Sambuca and Aniset.

AVIFORM

For many years I used Aviform products and saw no reason to change a good system. I bought the products in winter after mixing Mycoform-T with Ultimate in the water on a Thursday and Avimax before long-distance (500-700 miles) basketing. We stick to what we know by habit, since I did not scientifically research the products.

AUDACITY

An army captain friend of mine (MM) once said, 'It's your audacity that has got you where you are today'. I always thought it was brains, yet on reflection I can see the benefit of good old-fashioned cheek or, as my mother used to say, 'Push your plate forward' and 'Cast your bread upon the waters'. Some people respond and others don't. The art is to keep trying.

AUCTIONS

These are money-making events for the auctioneers and vendors. I am very wary (like Louella) of them. The atmosphere is often intense and frenetic and it is easy to get trotted up into paying the earth for a pigeon. However, bargains can be had and some good birds may be available. Best, in my opinion, to befriend a top fancier with whom you can exchange birds, or a real 'gent' who will give them to you for nothing.

APEX ROOF

It has become fashionable to have pantiled, apex-angled roofs for pigeon lofts. They are believed to confer advantages in good ventilation. This may be the case and they do look nice, don't they? However, my birds were content to look at a flat asbestos roof for many years. It is no good having a loft like a house if you can't manage the pigeons in it.

APPLICATION

All ideas and methods should be applied in practice and

then your ambitions can be realised. I started off at the Grantham racepoint and went through to Barcelona, flying from all points on the way. Try to do what you say. Any more 'A's for analysis?

B

BARCELONA INTERNATIONAL

The greatest race in the world, and the ultimate race for the purist distance and marathon fancier. The Barcelona International race is perhaps the only one that ticks all the boxes and whose prestige and quality is beyond question. It is the race for the purists, magnificent and unique.

BOVRIL

I used this as a conditioner in the water, and brewer's yeast on the food mix.

BOURGES

A famous 500-mile race point for me.

BUSSCHAERT

This man became famous as a sprint man and collector of some quality-bred birds of different origins. They all took his famous name and he cashed in on it. Some of the old genes survive today.

C

CANKER

The different strains of trichomonads (microscopic flagellates) are responsible for the wet and dry cankers in pigeons. The count should be low or zero and most birds in spite of some immunity will need treatment especially when stressed due to racing and other disease organisms. I would recommend alternating Flagyl with dimetridazole and ronidazole (10%) to help prevent disease resistance. Individual birds can be dosed with Spartrix for your convenience.

CANDIDA

Candida or yeast infections in the crop may occur as a result of antibiotic treatment and can be treated with agents such as Nystatin. Swabs will test for the presence of this life form.

CARBOHYDRATE BOOSTERS

Before racing at distance (500-700 miles) I liked to increase the fats and carbohydrates. On a Monday and Tuesday I would dissolve Vydex Super Six or Carbosol in the water. You try everything to lift the birds. These I believe to be effective in combination with creatine and 'L' carnitine, which can be found in Chevita and Aviform supplements. All these substances have been proven by Olympians in the human world.

CATTRYSSE BROTHERS

These great brothers certainly left their mark on the Belgian National scene. Some good fanciers have achieved acclaim in the UK with the famous genes, eg Les Davenport with his Pau NFC winner and Roy Oldfield with Clanfield Expected. I notice that Colin Lloyd and Keith Arnold are doing well in today's racing. Many of the continental champions used them as a cross eg Descamps van Hasten, Vanhee and Pol Bostyn. Today there are no pure direct birds available.

CHEEKY CHARMER

Steve Shipley, who I have known since 1976, is exactly that; he has a quick, optimistic and often witty retort for everything. He has been a real stalwart of the York scene, having been Secretary of the Ebor Fed for many years. We have never had an angry word in 32 years and are both as daft as a brush.

In 1980, whilst looking after my birds at Holtby, he alerted the medics to my mother's plight, she had pneumonia and his actions helped save her! Steve has fond memories of when we stopped for directions on the way to Derek Mitcham's stud, since stopping at a house where I chatted to a young woman in a nightie so much that she finished stood outside and I in the house. We also raced back from Selby, flat to the floor in a bone-shaker of a Minivan.

'Cheeky' has some strong, assertive views and suspects that paramyxo vaccinations were not properly tested and can have negative effects on the immune system. He also thinks that firms should take clocks as part exchange for ETS. A former scribe for the Pigeon Sport as 'Seldom wins', he has enjoyed the Hermans, Imbrechts and Beth's boy van Reets. His ambition is to win the Federation at 500 miles but he enjoys racing up to 220 miles.

CHANNEL RACING

In my first Channel race I sent what I had and was 4th Club Falaise when there had been thunderstorms. She was a settled bird, a black chequer hen (2 x 1st Melun 408 miles) and sat on Jack Ross's loft in a thunderstorm. I frightened her to my loft and clocked her. Many birds will fly the Channel: it is often easy. However, with hard weather the sea can be a graveyard. We are very privileged to have the Channel to fly over, as many Continentals do not.

CHAMPIONS

Both fanciers and birds, these are the leaders. In naming them; whatever turns you on. There is no pure and fixed definition of a champion. Many of them are just good pigeons that we like to boast about. I regard Legend and Lancashire Rose as good examples of real champions.

CHEVITA

This firm makes an excellent range of products that do what they say on the tin. I like all their products, especially Multivitamin and Mycosan 'T' ccs. In the 1980s I sent Swiss francs direct to Petconnect Sarle Chamosson. In the UK Harkers are dealers in Chevita and they also produce excellent information booklets.

CHLAMYDIA/ORNITHOSIS

These are primitive organisms that cause the snorts or respiratory disease symptoms in birds. They are common, especially with mycoplasma and corhyza. At the infected level birds are not fit. A good treatment is Doxy 'T', which is a cocktail of doxycycline and tylosin, sometimes in conjunction with spiramycin.

CLOCKS

These are many and varied and up to the junior level of sophistication, yet many of them will become obsolete due to the invasion of ETS. I remember the old Skymaster that Geoff Farmery helped me to buy from Wilkinson Clocks Racemaster. It was old kit, but I clocked 2 x 1sts Open in it, so it was okay. My accurate two quartz STBs are still in use by Ian Dixon of York. They were given to him, since he was a good lad. I would clock as normal, as the small advantage of ETS would not bother me at 700-900 miles!

CLUB

At every level, from small club to International racing, you will normally need to be in a club. In competition with others you will have a reference point and a yardstick for success and at the top level you can compete against the Continentals. My first club in 1976 was St Lawrence WMC and I topped the Fed at Melun in the last old club race. I remember the characters there with great affection: Freddie Wilks, Steve Shipley, Cyril Frankland, Mick Swallow etc. Now I write about it.

COCCIDIA

These are the causative organisms of coccidiosis disease and their level should be kept low. It is common knowledge that numbers will rise to potentially dangerous levels in the face of stress and other pests and diseases. I recommend treatment of the water with a coccidiostat such as Baycox for 24 hours. Yes, it's a disease that can be fatal, especially amongst young birds when the loft is damp.

CONCENTRATION

In the mood and on my day I am blessed with mesmeric powers of concentration. These were tested when I went to Leeds and took the Mensa test. I would recommend a trance-like focus when looking at your birds.

CONDITION

Birds that win or do well at great distances are normally in condition. This can be indicated by sparkling eyes, smooth, shiny feathers with a bloom and oil effect and general vigour and liveliness. We as fanciers strive for condition!

CORN

Birds should be fed a varied mix to appetite and I always hopper-fed layers' pellets at £6.50 a bag. This is good sense. I like Gerry Plus with Superstar Plus, Hormoform, Red Band, peanuts and yeast. Stock birds for breeding have the layers' pellets and a high protein, mix eg Premier Gold.

CROSS-BREEDING

Fanciers may know that I practised 30 years of inbreeding with my strain. I like crossbreeding inbred birds as some really good ones may follow – it is called hybrid vigour or the Heterozygotic Effect. Barcelona Dream was produced from an outcrossing without a plan with birds from here, there and everywhere.

CULLING

Some fanciers kill to be cruel and think they're tough. My racing was so severe that I never needed to cull an old bird. Naturally you should cull any abnormal or weak young birds. I do not support the policy of killing the old-age pensioners. The basket will sort your racers – try Barcelona for size.

D

'DANCING BOY'

A beautiful white pied cock and a real character and full of the blood of my best distance birds. His vitality was such that he would jump in the air to see me (not for the corn tin as my birds were never kept hungry). I raced him in my last year and he was the most consistent cock.

DANDY NESTS

At about 35p each and disposable, they keep the birds warm and will last for up to say two years and are then thrown away. I would not entertain scrubbing hard, clay nest bowls – very old fashioned. Obtainable from Boddy & Ridewood etc.

'DANGERMAN'

Brian Denney was shrewd enough to acquire this Vanhee-based bird from Louella Lofts. Retired early on, having returned minus one eye, he had been a sprint sensation on widowhood with three Fed wins. More importantly he and his brother produced birds to score up to Pau NFC, 738 miles, and became key birds. Since they were Stichelbaut-based I put two inbred daughters of Dangerman in my strain. Their good impact remains today. I have not hidden the fact of their significance.

DARI

A high energy (carbohydrate) based grain with the white and red (mild) varieties used in mixtures and extensively by some competition roller men.

DEXTER

I first met Graham in the 1960s as a schoolboy near the 'Blue Peter' at Alvaston, Derby. We enjoyed our rollers and Dr Graham (PhD) went on to be a world-acclaimed competition roller expert. A brilliant psychologist and intellectual, he wrote *Winners and Spinners*, still the finest book ever written on pigeons. A very distinguished man in the roller world who formulated many of the modern competition rules and theories behind 'The Roll'.

DETERMINATION

A fixed state of mind that keeps you focused on your goals and objectives. Champions in every field of human endeavour have it in abundance. I recall that I never kept my birds at home because of a bad weather forecast.

DOROTHY

This was my mother's name and she was a phenomenon with the pigeons. Her first job in her dressing gown was to let the birds out at say 5.30am. She kept the perches clean on a daily basis and sometimes talked and sang to the birds in the loft – we had them very contented at home. Yes, she shared in most of my success, and living to 92 was an inspiration to all, having been at the cottage for 26 years alone. We named Dorothy's Courage and Dot's Delight after her. She was a gutsy and true character in the sport.

DIABOLOS

Translated means 'The Devil'. A lovely, dark chequer cock from my famed No1 pair, he was a great Channel flyer against north (head) winds and I stopped him at two years to found a dynasty. He lived for 22 years and his descendants are excelling today. I was lucky to breed him. I have never come across another bird bearing his name. I never stop writing about him.

DOT'S DELIGHT

A lovely dark chequer hen from a brother of Dark Destiny and a daughter of the No1 pair. She was the only pigeon to break 1200ypm from around 2,000 birds in a north-east wind at Melun, 408 miles, in 1984. She topped the Yorks Middle Route Fed at Melun in my last old bird race at St Lawrence WM Club (last done in West Sect in 1956). A rare bird indeed and I paired her with Diabolos to leave a long line of good birds up to 2008. Inbreeding to the No.1 pair and performances paid off.

DOXYCYCLINE

This antibiotic is good against ornithosis (snots) in pigeons, especially when mixed with Tylosin and sometimes Spiramycin. It is the relatively modern drug of choice, largely replacing Chlortetracycline. Colin Walker, the Australian vet, dispenses it from his practice. Do not abuse it as resistance may be built up to its effectiveness.

DORDIN

Dordin was a French 'champion' who produced a beautiful type of bird with some lovely reds and blues of a large stamp. These are not birds I would trust at over 700 miles, yet they were good for Jim Biss and others around the UK. There are no pure direct birds now, only ones carrying the original genes, I recall the champions Spahi and Romulus.

DRUGS

These medicines, eg antibiotics, are widely used by the fancy, but they should only be used when needed, due to bad-bug resistance syndrome. A common example is Baytril. The RPRA has a list of banned types of drugs and substances, yet there is still confusion as to what can be used and what can't. My reason for not opening up the sport to the myriad of drug types is the harmful effects associated with some of their use. The establishment has yet to catch any cheats in the UK, although there have been stings in Europe.

DETAIL

An eye for detail is good to have when studying and observing individual birds. You should know the origin and ancestry of every bird in your loft. For those with a poorer memory, all details should be kept on paper or computer. A hobby-horse of mine is that you should know every bird in the loft. It helps to have the basic of your system written down.

DISTANCE

To me this goes from 500-700 miles, while above this is marathon racing. I always clocked at 466 miles Nantes and St Nazaire and it bugged me that it was only middle distance. I valued a bird when it had scored over 500 miles. I enjoyed short wins in my youth, yet now I am interested only in hard endurance birds up to Barcelona International. Distance birds can be bred out of sprinters and vice versa – it depends on the genes and management of individuals.

DNA

There is a modern emphasis on the genome of the bird and now the DNA (deoxyribonucleic acid) is tested in progeny proofing. For success in distance racing I place great emphasis on the characters through the genes that the birds are carrying. A bird of lovely physical type as seen by the eye might not fly up the garden!

DRINKER

I liked the plastic 5pt (in blue) type from Boddy & Ridewood. They last for years and you do not have to be cleaning them every day. They can be placed on the floor on bricks or whatever and there should be plenty. Very handy for liquid feeds.

DONALDSON

Jim from Peterhead is a genuine and proper marathon man and is the best to ever come out of northern Scotland. He repeats what many find too hard with his birds. My champion Oddball was down from his National winner Doonann and the red birds of my modern breeding are from his origin, especially Circus Boy. A real master of the hard distance and as good as they get in Scotland. I am pleased that her has blended my blood into some of his own as we swapped birds with freedom.

DEEP LITTER

I had feet of old wood shavings in the loft and this was there for many years. It saved scraping and helped to keep the birds clean and modern science says that it builds immunity. In the winter, a warmth generated the air, and the squeakers nestled on it. Easibed is good for modern fanciers. That's it for now.

E

ECCENTRIC

I do not consider myself normal and never want to be. I am on the edge and some of my performances were on the edge. You cannot achieve the exception by being conventional. To me Cutcliffe and others are all eccentrics. I think British culture accepts those with unusual habits or personality traits. Probably a touch of madness and eccentricity are the same; it's purely a matter of judgement.

EGGS

Two of these should be laid after 8 to 14 days – if not, then the birds are not right! I never culled eggs and let them all hatch in season from the stock especially the No 1 pair. I find layers' pellets great for good eggs. There don't seem to be too many egg head pigeon men about apart from Cutcliffe and Clements.

ELECTROLYTES

After racing, salts such as sodium, potassium and magnesium may be depleted in the bird's chemistry. It may be an aid to recovery to dilute them in the drinkers on a race day. These can be mixed with sugar and amino acids and bacterial probiotics and I recommend E-Plus by Aviform and the Vydex products. We use what makes us feel good, don't we?

EMERTON STRAIN (71 TO 879 MILES)

After 30 years of cultivating the same family of birds with my extensive inbreeding I gave them my name. I did this to give recognition to myself and the birds as I became well known in the fancy. Most fanciers are giving credence to continental fanciers when the birds bred by themselves should take their own name. I regard this as being nonsense. There are no Busschaerts, no Stichelbauts. The men are all gone. I believe the great names are used and abused for the halo effect, reflected glory and commercial reasons. Much better to say Busschaert-based etc. I repeat my birds were based on seven foundation pigeons and four of these were DVH Stichelbaut based. I love it when others do well with my birds of my origin, as they are doing today.

EXCELLENCE

We are not all capable of reaching this level, yet it is worth having a go. Excellence is relative to the person making a judgement on it, but it is a nice buzz when we come out on top. In my opinion Ronnie Williamson is an excellent sprinter and Neil Bush (Amcotts) a marathon man. They are both ahead of the others.

EMIEL DENYS

This man is a world famous Belgian fancier, an International winner and twice the Golden Wing winner at Barcelona with the Tee and his son Playboy. He made the Remi of 54 famous and developed his own strain. My Darkness was bred by him being a grandson of The Kennedy. Emiel produces a lovely type of dark chequer bird and I recommend them as a blend into my own. However his birds are not Stichelbauts, they are Denys. Emiel is prone to being reduced to tears when he recalls what the great Tee achieved – regarded as the best Barcelona bird of his time. It was a great day in 1976 when John and Michael Massarella and myself picked out Darkness from many directs at Louella Lofts. Barcelona Dream was bred down from this cock along with all my birds of today. I still have the pedigree which I treasure!

ERYTHROMYCIN

An old antibiotic used against respiratory diseases, once called Dragon's Blood. It also had a tonic effect. I used to get mine from Petconnect in Switzerland in Mycosan 'T' (Chevita) and swear by it especially when mixed with Chlortetracycline+.

ETS

Electronic timing systems are here to stay. There are some clever ones about, eg Unikon, and these will be improved upon with time. Forget all the arguments and get on with the racing. You will find that the top fanciers and birds will win, with or without them. They are convenient, make racing simple and the best bit – you do not have to catch and disturb the bird. If I were racing I would clock just the same and forfeit a few potential seconds – at my distances I would not care! ETS are good aids for the elderly, unfit and handicapped.

ENERGY

Fit birds will be loaded with this and it comes from exercise and feeding. I do believe that the hormonal changes induced by widowhood can have an impact. Many distance birds fail through lack of energy. Sprinters have quick bursts of energy. Energy potential is dictated by the genotype. Peanuts for energy!

EXTREME DISTANCE

In my mind this is 700 miles plus and I first noticed the term in Massarella's advert for the Extreme Distance Family. In latter years I sent all my birds to these distances, a little like Frank Kay today, have it or die. To do this you have to be an endurance fanatic and there are a few about. I think the limit is probably 1,000 miles within 5 days in the UK.

F

FABRY

I think Fabry based his birds on the old Hansennes and he generated enough publicity to be famous. Many of us have heard of the half Fabry as a cross into the Janssen Bros of Arendonk.

FAME

This is easy to achieve but greatness is of a higher magnitude. The route to fame is a few good results followed by advertising, reports and publicity. There are some good fanciers who don't become famous. It's nice to be popular but be sure someone will not like you or be jealous even if you are a saint. Fame can compromise the safety of your birds. Be careful!

FATS

Feeding safflower, rape, peanuts, etc will give an emphasis on fats which have become popular especially for long-distance flying (500-700 miles). They should be fed in conjunction with a balanced ration, but five days before basketing I loaded with fats and carbohydrates. When these are exhausted the bird will break down muscle tissue to keep going. Eddie Newcombe set the trend for peanuts, now they are widespread, being around 50% fat.

FANATIC

It is probably true to say that the top dogs like Jim Biss and Chris Gordon were and are fanatical about pigeons, hence their great fame and success. Fanaticism helps but is no automatic recipe for success. I think it is linked with obsession.

FAILURE

We all fail with our birds, it's how we bounce back that counts. We all know about the good birds and results, and rather less about failure. I will guarantee if you send to the hard races of 700-900 miles you will lose most of your birds. My losses over the years were large and I do not bat an eyelid over it. Some poor souls fail, never to succeed again, it depends how dedicated and resilient you are. Failure is all part of the flying pattern.

FAVOURITE

In my racing all the birds went to the bitter end. If they succeeded they became my favourites, and these I named eg Mystical Queen, Delta Lady, Dark Dynamo, Dot's Courage and Diabolos. My good old ones either eventually went down on the road or lived out their retirement. I think it is inhuman not to have a kind sentiment for your good birds, after all they are living creatures, not machines.

FEATHER

I like silky feathered (yellow not buff) birds associated with the distance and hard weather. By inbreeding to the DVH Stichelbauts I bred some lovely dark velvets like Mystical Queen, and these are my favourites. I do not like dry, coarse-feathered birds, which are usually out of condition. Birds can be good in any colour of feather from black to white.

FIRSTS

The winning of firsts and beating the other fancier is normally associated with Club and Federation type thinking. If you fly south and race in the north of England your wins at National level will normally be zero. Here it is important to have real endurance extreme distance birds that bring you credit. I would give all my firsts for one good Barcelona performance.

FORM

This is a word we use to describe the psychological and physiological high associated with winning pigeons. A losing bird may be 'on form' but not capable of winning. We do our best with the loft environment and overall management to produce superior condition. A bird will sometimes succeed without being on form because it is so good. When I was twice first five Open in young bird races I guess these birds were on form. The good fanciers hit form better than the less successful ones, because they are better at it.

FLOCK

Pigeons will tend to stick together as a flock when they are at home and racing. The exceptions to this tendency are worth looking out for, as they may be exceptional birds. It is usually the case though that the International birds into the north of England will have perhaps hundreds of miles of solo flying to do and these birds I like eg Dax My Girl, Dax ll and my Barcelona birds. I like birds that will race when there are none or very few about in the area. When using water treatments, eg liquid feeds and antibiotics, these can often be given to the flock as flock treatment.

FOLLICLE

This is the base of the feather where the rachis goes into the sheath. It can be malformed due to injury or for genetic reasons. Sometimes you can pull them out, but you risk damage to the follicle.

FRANCE

We are very lucky to race over the Channel from France and we go as far as the Pyrenees, with Pau probably being the most revered point. I like the French people for the action they take over things – good old people power. I do not like their tendency to shoot everything in sight. Some good fanciers have hailed from France, eg Robert Benn, Boizard and Dordin.

FEEDER

I liked the Gaz metal feeders from Boddy & Ridewood for my layers' pellets and wooden roller bar feeders for my corn mixes. I gave all mine away along with all my pigeon things and I kept only one trophy. I hopper fed with layers' pellets at all times.

FEDERATION

Clubs amalgamate into organisations called Federations. In the York area I like the Yorks Middle Route Combine (renamed from the Fed). It is not as good as in the Western Section days but still manages up to 5,000 birds and has a good big radius to the coast and I am a loyal supporter of it. There is credit in winning your Federation.

FLEAS

There are pigeon fleas (not lice) on birds. These can be controlled by a 24-hour water treatment of Moxidectin, Ivermectin (0.8%) or with Pyrethrins. Pigeons will tolerate them, but I like to kill them as they spread many viruses.

FEEDING

The food supplies the muscle and fuel for the energy of the bird. In the early part of the year my birds were slow and fat as all the old ones had big races to fly later on. Then birds nearly always go down at the hard distances. My corn mixtures have been well documented and as a liquid feed I used Vydex and Aviform and Chevita products. Repeat, you will not clock at 700-900 miles with birds fed as 100-mile sprinters. I fed the young birds the same as the old all in the same loft. It was so easy that a 10-year-old could have done it. Genius is simplicity.

G

GABY VANDENABEELE

Birds of this origin were raced by M & D Evans and their excellent winning management and racing systems made them successful in the UK. But they are clever lads and could have done similarly with birds of different origins. I do not believe, as a family, that they are superior to other good families. If I had had them they would have gone to 700+ miles or dropped in the process. They have received some excellent publicity worldwide.

GAZETTE

An offshoot of the BHW, this pictorial magazine was a good periodical and I was happy to be in it in January 1986 with Diabolos on the front page. There is a call to bring it back.

GENTLENESS

I like men to have calm, gentle hands with pigeons and I recall Brian Denney and Jim Wright in this respect. Many men are too aggressive and rough with their birds, which are sensitive creatures and should be spoken to with calm dignity.

GENIUS

Genius is simplicity. It also denotes extreme gifts and/or intelligence or ability. Einstein is the archetypal genius, yet his IQ was just six points higher than mine (160 apparently). I do think that a complex mind can make things, or a system of racing, appear to be very easy and simple; the genius comes as the mental or subjective process, the mind behind it. We all appreciate and favour what we consider to be genius. To me, Ronnie O'Sullivan is a genius.

GIVING

It was Jack Ross of York who in the 1970s told me the wisdom of giving. 'Good pigeons are given, Jim' he said. I realise the essential wisdom of this statement. When I retired from racing I gave away all my birds, clocks, baskets, etc as a gesture to the fancy. An example of giving is the famous '53' of Trevor Robinson of Patrington. I also do my articles free of charge. There is too much greedy exploitation of fanciers.

GENES

The genotype will dictate the potential of each bird right from the egg stage. If it's not there, you are doomed. In my strain I bred around the birds that evidently carried the performance genes. There are thousands of genes that carry

DNA and the factors may be recessive or dominant. I like the vigour associated with crossing to inbred strains. A bird can be outstanding in the hand but with incorrect performance genes it will be useless. Eyesign theories, to bear reality, would have to be linked to performance genes.

GENERATION

We try to interest the next generation of fanciers, yet for manifold reasons the sport is in decline; however, excellence will prevail. A stock pair that generates 'good' birds is a joy to have. I think the young generation will be stimulated by ETS and computer technology.

GOOD BIRDS

There are lots of good birds and as a value of judgement these are purely the ones whose results you are happy with. Good breeders breed good pigeons at the desired distance. Really we are looking for excellence and outstanding breeders like my No.1 pair, Dark Destiny and Daughter of Darkness. Good can also relate to how we treat others and the good we do for the sport; we should all leave the hobby in a better state.

GREATNESS

In the UK there are many excellent fanciers with outstanding results, but are they great? I believe there is more to greatness than results. What is the fancier's legacy? What have they contributed to the sport as a whole?
In my opinion, two of the modern 'greats' are Chris Gordon and Geoff Kirkland. I rate Chris as the best modern fancier

overall from his National young bird races over 350 miles to his marathon exploits at over 700 and 800 miles. He manages the Olympic team and is on the RPRA Committee. His future will be cemented with some International performances. Additionally, like Geoff Kirkland, he has the likeability factor. Now Geoff informs and educates the fancy with his ground-breaking ideas, articles and book. The prices of his young birds are reasonable so that he does not exploit the fancy on price after his fame. The future will look very kindly on these two men.

GROUNDNUTS

Another name for peanuts, and you know I love them for pigeons, especially with their 50% fat, before 500-800 miles. I recall eating them hot and roasted at the side of the road under some trees in Senegal, West Africa. I never had problems with alfatoxins. A poor bird will still fail on them! Some good ones are Indian Bolds.

GRIEVANCE

The sport is full of malcontents. A lot of the negativity is self-inflicted or engendered by jealous rivals. My advice is to do your own thing and avoid the morons – they have hang ups. The RPRA copes well with its grievance procedure.

GLUCOSE

This white powder, or honey, is often used to give a quick fix of metabolisable energy. Sugars are often used in post-race restoratives with electrolytes and vitamins.

GOD

'....and may your God go with you'. I have a concept of the absolute (a bit like god), yet it is not a supernatural being. It refers to absolute knowledge or omniscience and accepts the unity of the whole universe throughout space and time.

GLYCOGEN

When we 'fatten up' pigeons for the marathons we are loading the liver with glycogen, which can be used to release energy for the muscles in flight.

H

HARKERS

They sell a good range of products eg Homon pellets and Hormoform. Although Levamisole wormer is old fashioned I like the Spartrix and I win with Homon, yet these are too expensive compared to layers' pellets. A winner for the firm is that they are agents for Chevita in the UK. Michael Binns is a good man with the firm, and I recall his good Dream Girl.

HEMP

An oil-based, heating seed and I like a sprinkle of it on the corn mix in the racing season. However, when fed to British birds like bullfinches it can be associated with heart attacks in birds. I would avoid the 'skunk' variety, unless you enjoy the trip.

HENS

I love hens for 500-800 mile racing. They did well for me my natural system (sometimes with three weeks on widowhood). I particularly liked a good hen on her first young bird of the season (in July) or on eggs. In my opinion many cocks only waste the hens for racing, and they are so easy to race. Some of my good hens have been Mystical Queen, Oddball, Diamond Queen, Dedication and Sister Damien. Many fanciers overlook their hens. Good hens can be raced to 220 miles, lifted into say 466 miles, rested for two/three weeks and then 700-900 miles. Performance hens are also excellent for breeding with confidence. I do not like hens being kept in little boxes, I think it's cruel.

HEROES

I like individuals who excel and stretch the boundaries in their chosen endeavour. In pigeon racing I have been impressed by Emiel Denys, Neil Bush, Jim Biss and earlier J O Warren. I like what Chris Gordon and Geoff Kirkland do for the sporting profile. A man of great genius and charisma in motor racing was the wonderful Ayrton Senna, and I love to watch Ronnie O'Sullivan playing snooker, he is in a class of his own. From the intellectual world I like Jacob Bronowski, and Karl Gustav Jung and Franz Kafka. It's nice to look up to others in the world.

HERBS

I do not like their use unless there are proven physical benefits in using them. A lot of quackery is associated with herbs, although some are good drugs. Beware!

HEART

Good performance birds have strong hearts and the fanciers who fly a good bird can be 'big-hearted'.

HEAT AND HEATING

I do not like the temperature in the loft to go over 70 degrees F (21 degree C) and never used supplementary heating. Some fliers do to promote early season form. Birds in hot weather 75-100 degree F will tend not to race as well, especially those from Spain into the UK, and need to drink and cool down. Many transporters are not fit for birds, but I like the NFC ones with the controlled environments.

HEALING

Pigeons have brilliant powers of recover from injury compared with humans. You can stitch them up with needle and thread and they don't even blink and are very free from bacterial infections of the wound sites.

HORMOFORM

This is perhaps the most enduring and famous supplement. I first came across it in the 1960s when as a schoolboy I visited a tippler man in Alvaston, Derby. Tipplers (not to be confused with rollers or tumbers) are endurance birds, flown in kits of three. The world record is over 20 hours flying on the wing. Hormoform is good for the birds as an oil and nutrient rich cut cereal, and I fed it as a booster with peanuts and Red Band five days before basketing for long and marathon racing, and on a daily basis. A 20kg bag lasted me the season and it is made by Harkers.

HUMIDITY

Lofts with too much moisture in the air, ie with the relative humidity too high, are not good for pigeons. On the contrary I do not like lofts when the air is arid and too dry. Dry conditions with good air convection should do the trick.

HOMING ABILITY

Not all pigeons have good homing ability from birth. This attribute will vary with the condition of the birds. However, when birds' racing careers are over they will not home from the long ones anyway; they will stay away (very sensible don't you think?) There is a simple truth: If it's long enough and hard enough they will not make it. We do not, with any authority, know how a pigeon homes. Every possible human theory is applied to the concept; and that is what they are, human theories. What does humanity know in an absolute sense? A pigeon that will race 750 miles in two days and 900 miles in three or four days has good homing ability.

HUYSKENS VAN RIEL

A famous old Belgian fancier. I recall Geoff Kirkland had some good ones, eg the Angouleme 1st MNFC Angouleme. Tony Reid sells birds for this (van Riel) apparent origin at reasonable prices. Of course no pure directs are available, only genes.

HYGIENE

I think over-scrupulous use of disinfectants and virucides can lessen the natural build-up of immunity. My lofts were dry but never very clean, with feet of deep litter. I am not in favour of a lot of time spent on hygiene, preferring to spend my time studying form, breeding and individual birds.

HYPERACTIVITY

A bird showing a great deal of extra activity around home may be on form, especially widowhood cocks on a hormonal high. I like young birds to be on and off the loft in fast flurries and flying for hours.

I

IODINE

Iodine is considered to stimulate the pituitary gland responsible for the release of hormones into the metabolism. It can be found as an additive in various supplements such as Impact by Gem and Blitzform by Rohnfried. Both of these have been used with success.

INBREEDING

Some degree of this will be necessary in the formation of a strain. It can be described as the mating together of close relatives, eg brother x sister, father x daughter. My four DVH Stichelbaut based foundation birds were inbred, yet I went brother x sister with the Iron Hen and Iron Man to produce Dark Destiny and his mother. I practised related pairings to the 7 foundation birds for 30 years.

Of paramount importance is that you inbreed to performance birds and their breeders, eg Velvet Destiny. A '99 dark velvet hen bred from Dark Velvet and Mystical Queen. Now in her genes are no less than 14 times the No 1 pair and other relatives as well. She is responsible for 1st Section NFC Nantes for S Wain & Son; my second bird at Dax International (687 miles) and two birds in '08 at Bourges 570 miles for the Barkels in the Up North Combine. Crossing inbred birds can produce champions.

To inbreed you need to focus on your own birds and test them and test them. Most fanciers are constantly acquiring fresh continental-based birds – dedicated followers of fashion. In the early years I had a vision of breeding around my birds and this propelled me into the future; I believe in pursuing my intuitions!

INTELLECT

There are some bright sparks in the pigeon world such as Zsolt Talaber and Liam O'Comain from Ireland. The intellectual types sometimes make good pigeon journalists. However in many cases the top fanciers have good practical intelligence with their management and systems of racing the birds. The top fanciers have usually thought about it and planned their success.

IMAGINATION

This quality gives you the vision and foresight which are particularly needed when used around good individual birds for future long distance races. You should be able to hold an image of a bird in your mind for the 2-3 years before it is ready to score in the big planned events.

IMAGE

An idea of the fancier is created by the publicity that he or she generates. Sometimes the person is like the image, sometimes not, since there is a lot of confidence trickery, often for reasons of profit. The people who do not worry about image and just get on with their racing I admire. With enough publicity people believe allsorts, wholesale people will believe what they want of me; but what you see is what there is!

IRON HEN AND IRON MAN

These were two dark chequers, brother and sister. When paired together they produced my No 1 stock Dark Destiny. The hen was 1st Section Clermont and the cock 4th. Both were nice small, medium, silky feathered, balanced birds of the DVH origin. They were tame and the hen used to sit on my hand in the garden. With hindsight I would have bred many more off these two birds as they were inbred performance birds of 1979.

IMMUNITY

We do not normally have any accurate scientific measure of our birds' resistance to pests and diseases. It is part of modern thinking and practice to build up as much immunity as we can. This can involve the minimal use of antibiotics, the use of garlic and probiotics in the birds' nutrition. There are some people who do not treat against anything in the hope of immunity. The use of deep litter is also thought to enhance it, with the build-up of good ingested bacteria.

IVERMECTIN 0.8%

I first came across this Ivermectin when chatting to Dr Graham Dexter of the roller world. When weaning young birds I placed one drop on the back of the neck. It controls worms and external parasites. It now has a licence in England and is freely available. For the water, best to use Moxidectin rather than Eqvalan (horse wormer).

INTERNATIONAL

You know I keep plugging this level of racing and for one reason – it is the best. Our No 1 organisation the BICC offers races at Pau, Barcelona, Tarbes, Marseille and Perpignan. This is the way forward in the UK, and Barcelona is best. Once you have raced internationally you will know what I mean and I hope you have the inclination to achieve!

IDEAL PIGEON

We search for the ideal; it is the best that can be realised. My ideal type was probably the dark chequer cock Diabolos. It fell short of my ideals but enjoyed it trying to achieve them. They are a product of inspiration.

INFORMATION

By and large I think my information has been fairly accurate. There are a lot of old wives' tales in the sport and sometimes you are hard pressed to glean good hard facts. However there are some excellent books, eg by Colin Walker and Zsolt Talaber, also the old Shraag, and I recommend you to read these and sift through the gossip very carefully. We live in the information age and we can become 'experts' with relative ease. Beware of inaccuracies, especially on the internet. From this we gain our knowledge.

J

JANSSEN OF ARENDONK

These world famous brothers developed their own strain through intensive inbreeding. Although highly acclaimed as sprinters the genetic variation is such that birds of this origin have won at all distances. Vanhee used them as a cross, and was very good at Barcelona International into Belgium. There is a trace in my strain through Jean Pierre-based introduction from Brian Denney. However, to be true Janssens they have to be bred by the brothers.

JAPANESE PIGEONERS

The Japanese tend to be demanding and fastidious with regard to pigeons. I am flattered to have received several enquiries from dealers and fanciers for the progeny of Barcelona Dream. I never did sell, instead I gave them away. I did have fun sending birds to China, that was a laugh, receiving calls at 2.30am.

JEAN

I met Jean, the salvation of my life, in 1978. Jack Ross said 'You are living like a monk' and took me to a club. Jean has listened to my obsessive chatter about birds for 30 years. We have travelled the world together and have had many happy times at Holtby waiting for the pigeons to arrive. She is a kind and jolly soul and lights up the room wherever she goes. In her modesty she does not crave publicity, yet she loves singing and dancing.

JOHN MASSARELLA

John is a wise and shrewd pigeon business man. At Louella Pigeon World he has helped no end of fanciers achieve fame and glory with their birds. In 1956 I spent a good hour with John and Michael as we debated the merits of the direct Vanhees and Denys. I chose Darkness, a grandson of Emiel Denys' The Kennedy. At the time John thought he looked like a Vanhee. Later I rang John and he picked out the dark chequer hen from DVH Stichelbaut-based birds. She was John's pick, 'a roomy hen', he said. A key bird for me with winners down from her today, Delilah. Not all birds from Massarella are champions but they do their best and the most I ever paid was £55 for the Denys cock. Birds do not have to be direct from the champions to be good; it all depends on how the genes combined at the fertilisation of the egg.

JOURNAL

I read the RP, the BHW and sometimes the Pictorial of England. I have had reports done in foreign parts, eg America and Australia. The BHW is the best and most comprehensive of the weekly papers. I enjoy writing for the BHW as it gives me the opportunity to have published what I have to say, most of which I believe to be good for the sport. In particular I like reading Liam O'Comain, who I consider a leading pigeon journalist.

JOB

I don't get carried away by practical tasks. My job with the birds was to observe, think and plan my strain of birds. It was largely a mental and spiritual journey for me. Good pigeon management and its tasks should be made simple. My maxim is genius is simplicity. Dorothy was a great help with the practical jobs around the loft.

JEALOUSY

This is a destructive and negative emotion displayed by human beings. I bear the scars of having been on the receiving end of it since my youth. If you are talented, the green-eyed monster will rear its ugly head. I am glad to say I am jealous of no one, yet there are many I admire. Jealousy is rife in pigeon clubs and has been for many years. I set no clock, just sending the birds as trainers. I see that many of the National and International boys do this.

JUICE

I used both garlic and lemon juice on my corn, garlic on Thursday and Friday, lemon juice Saturday, Sunday, Monday and Tuesday. I believe the citric acid in the lemons is good for the gut flora of the birds. It was an old practice which I picked up from 101 Methods.

JUMP

I believe in big lifts for all birds to find out their potential and orientation ability. In the later years my young birds were sent from the loft to 95 or 138 miles. On open loft if they have it they will come. Old birds were jumped from 220 to 466 miles, then 735, 737, 687 or 879 miles. The distance and weather combination will sort your birds whether or not you have trained them. A good 2y should be ready for any distance into the UK. My Barcelona Dream (879 miles) was on his third trip over the water. Remember, most pigeons will never make it – save costs, save fuel, jump them.

JUDGEMENT

Judges at shows are known for picking fine-handling and fine-looking specimens. With racers and breeders, it is the genes that dictate all. When you have learnt this lesson it will help with your breeding. Good racers and breeders have good genes. It was a moment of inspired good judgement when I paired Mystical Queen to Dark Velvet to breed the little hen Velvet Destiny. I chose the right name, it was prophetic, her grandchildren are excelling today. In her breeding were 14 x No 1 pair.

JOY AND JUBILATION

This is what we feel when we get it right. There will have been much of this after the NFC Tarbes race with the birds flying around 750 miles in the day.

K

KEEL

I like pigeons with good strong, thick sternums. I note that a lot of good distance birds have a bit of depth in the keel to carry enlarged breast muscles. Good ones come in many guises. A bird can recover from and race well with a deformed or broken keel. I do not like thin and/or wavery keels.

KINDNESS

I believe this to be a great quality in a man. Pigeons respond to quiet, gentle, kind treatment. As a youngster I did a lot of shooting and wildfowling on the Wash Saltings, actions which could be described as cruel. These inclinations have now gone with the mellow fruitfulness of age. In the ruthlessness of competition we struggle to show kindness to our rivals. I we can do so, however, I think it elevates the spirit.

KING

'Champion' pigeons are often given the word 'King' eg Whitehaven King, Solway King. The naming gives a feeling of elevated status, royal-like to the bird, and has become popular. I like the sound of 'King'.

KILLING

In hard distance racing you should never need to cull a bird. In this type of racing it is essential to keep the plodders; they could well be the marathon birds of the future. I never saw my Dark Enchantment home in under 466 miles, yet she flew Barcelona International of 879 miles. Some men like killing birds as a macho gesture. I admit as a youngster I shot a lot of woodpigeon; now I feed them in my garden.

KIRKLAND, GEOFF

Who has not heard of Geoff Kirkland? He is one of the most consistently brilliant fanciers that the UK has ever produced. A leader by example with his wins in the BICC, NFC, and MNFC, he has contributed greatly to the general knowledge of the fancy through his writings and ideas. By the same token, you can approach him for squeakers at a proper price, and this factor shows the spirit of good intention of the man.

KIRKPATRICK, JOHN

A Scottish National winner whose strain of birds has taken a central spot in collective folklore. The genes still exist today through birds like Solway King, Stan The Man, Grizelda etc. You should note that proper directs are now available. Kirkpatrick has evolved into a cultural icon.

KNOWLEDGE

I know I am a bighead! However, my knowledge is hard-earned through application and study. I take pleasure in helping the fancy whenever I can, yet I am still ignorant. I hope the imparting of what I know has interested some people out there. I believe the good and top fanciers are all full of knowledge. This can be learned from excellent articles and books and sometimes the web – all freely available.

I respect the practical pigeon wisdom of some fanciers, which is very difficult to acquire. However, it still annoys me when fanciers do not recognise and know each individual bird without reference to a ring number – this I believe to be a matter of perceptional judgement. I used to say that I would have liked to have been an apprentice to a top Continental fancier, but now I know that some of the best are in the UK.

K (SECTION)

Section K is a National Flying Club Section for some of the Northern fanciers; Chris Gordon won Tarbes at 725 miles in this section. A special note should be made of Ken Hanby with 13 x 1st Section K. although a controversial man, Ken's wins are unmatched by any other leading fancier. Some of the greatest fanciers in Section K are also in the North-East 700-mile Club, flyers such as Neil Bush, Brian Denney, Mick McGrevy & Co and other top dogs. It is just a matter of time before the NFC is won again by the dedicated men in Section K.

KUDOS

This word relates to renown or fame. Not every fancier seeks or requires it. I enjoy my 15 minutes in the sun and, yes, I have encouraged it. I do enjoy highlighting other people's successes as a little enthusiasm goes a long way. We are all part of the whole and impact on each other. I like the lift that Parkinson gives to others – all those tiresome hens on the computer! I think his 105-question format to profile the fancier is unsurpassed. There is enough limelight for everyone!

L

LAMBOURNES

Lambournes produce plastic leg information rings for pigeons and are brilliant. I like the telephone, no rings. Slipped onto young birds at weaning, they save stamping the flights of birds. I like the flights for race markings. I think they are made by Nelson Engineering and are advertised in the mags.

LITTLE HENS

I love quiet, hard little hens for the distance. My Delta Lady was a little cutie at 466 miles, four times on the day, Saintes 569 miles twice and Pau 735 miles. The dam of Oddball, she was killed by a sparrowhawk. On the contrary I am very suspicious of big, fronty pigeons, associating them with sprinting.

LEMON JUICE

The citric acid in lemon juice is apparently good for gut flora. I applied PLJ on my brewer's yeast Saturday-Tuesday on the corn. We believe in all sorts don't we, with or without research.

LEGEND

A qualitative term denoting high praise indeed. Our first International Dax winner for Brian Sheppard is called The Legend. We all rate it very highly. You would think the UK would be International crazy after this – it isn't! Legend, icon and genius are all loft terms for the exalted ones.

LAY

Not all hens lay. I once sold a daughter of Barcelona Dream that was barren. A good hen should lay between 8-14 day, if not, look out. I like the laid-back approach to life and racing. A good hen may lay for up to 14 years, but when the follicles are totally shed she will lay no more. Layers' pellets are fabulous for good eggs. We all like to be good eggs, don't we?

LANDING BOARD

My old loft had a good old landing board for racing, and above this was the entrance and exit to the loft, and for the open loft system. The birds would sit and sun themselves on the landing board.

LIGHT

If birds go light look out for a number of diseases, eg salmonella, E. coli, viruses, coccidiosis, worms, etc. Good pigeons, when inflated, should feel big, light and buoyant, yet should not be thin. For Barcelona I like some fat reserves – it's not a sprint, it's a marathon. Nature does not have hours of darkness – it just is. Pigeons will race after lighting up time as it is never black dark in England. We have invented pigeon hours of darkness in an attempt to bring fairness into racing.

LIGHTS

I had fluorescent tubes in the race loft. In my youth, and living six miles from the loft. I would pick out the pool birds on a Thursday evening under artificial light. At this time you can usually pluck them off the perch and will notice any pigeon moths.

LINE BREEDING

This is a traditional and popular concept in pigeon breeding. The children, grandchildren and down the line are bred from a 'champion' cock, or sometimes a hen. Often unrelated mates are used and then the progeny paired together. The idea is to try as closely as possible to replicate the champion ancestor. There was a certain amount of line breeding in my colony, yet most of the time I was a confirmed inbreeder. The line can also be interpreted as concentrating on winning lines of birds, where you are looking at replicating performance.

LINEAGE

In a successful family you will be able to trace key pigeons (breeders and racers) in a line. We refer to them as good lines. In my strain all but Diamond Queen have left lines in the performance birds of today. All my birds can be traced back to Dark Destiny and Daughter of Darkness. With further research you can attempt to trace these back to Ware Izeren, Yzeren Kennedy, Creonne Witooger etc. In your breeding you should concentrate as many performance lines as possible to maximise the impact in racing.

LIQUIDS

The basis for life is water, and this should be given daily. It doesn't have to be as fresh as you think. Water is the matrix for liquid feeding with vitamins, boosters and many other supplements. Many racers are doomed because of dehydration on archaic transporters, and this needs serious examination. On many races birds will drop down for a drink, sometimes floating on water.

LONG DISTANCE

To my mind's eye long-distance racing is 500-700 miles. My Nantes and St Nazaire clockings at 466 miles were middle-distance only. I started off with club spring racing and was a young bird specialist, yet graduated to long-distance racing as soon as possible. I do appreciate the skill behind a team of sprint stars, yet I am always looking to test the stamina and endurance of individual birds. As you know I promote long and marathon racing as the Holy Grail, especially the Barcelona International into the UK. At over 700 miles this is marathon racing which to my biased view is the ultimate in sport. However we have to accept the reality that most people enjoy 0-500 mile racing (sprint to middle).

LICE

Pigeon lice cause irritation to the birds and may vector viruses. I have seen my jumper covered in bloom and lice. Control: 24-hour treatment with Moxidectin in the water or one drop of 0.8% Ivermectin on the back of the neck. Now that Duramitex is unavailable we use Permethrin sprays. I understand that Vanverminex by Vanhee is efficacious. Controlling lice show you care about your birds.

LOUELLA PIGEON WORLD

I have a great deal of time for the Massarellas of Louella Pigeon World. Although a commercial outfit, they try to obtain the very best and sell them at reasonable prices. Many fanciers in the UK can trace the origin of their birds or strains to Louella. All but one of my magnificent seven came from there. If you want strain names bred in their purity you should shop at Louella. These can be ideal for cross-breeding, and this is what usually happens.

LONG-LIVED

We aim for a family with longevity, as it is associated with vigour. My Diabolos made it to 22, Donaldson's Circus Boy was 26. I can't imagine pigeons living to beyond 30 years. Most breeding hens are finished by 12 and some cocks by 5.

LUMPS

As pigeons age they are susceptible to benign and cancerous lumps. Sometimes these are operable, although when a hen has an enlarged oviduct she is usually finished. Often birds have blood warts due to high rich feeding. The latter often drop off on their own. Many lumps are best left well alone. Recall that Champion Woodsider had a lump over one eye.

MANAGEMENT

The No 1 priority in pigeon racing is management. The fancier is all, everything is down to him or her. I mean everything: the lofts, the birds, the planning are all stemming from the mind of the person. Mind over matter mind is the absolute. A good pigeon will never win without good management. It is often the case that women are the hands on fanciers behind the success.

MARSEILLE OF 2008

I am so pleased for my friend Trevor Robinson of Patrington, who has won the British International Championship National Race at Marseille with his good cock. The distance was 748 miles and the birds were liberated with the International convoy of nearly 14,000 birds. I have known Trevor for around eight years and find him to be a modest dedicated man with his feet grounded in common sense. Although I tend to be a bit of a bighead, we have never had a cross word. The bird was very consistent, being 4th in the NFC Averages up to 722 miles in 2007.

During the build-up to the race Trevor said he would like to see his name on the Marseille Trophy alongside the great Jim Biss, a target he will have realised at the first attempt. The bird was motivated being with his favourite hen, a large youngster and looking to nest again. I hope this win inspires more people (come on, you Tarbes lads!) to enter the International races. I am thinking of people like Brian Denney, Dave Fussey and Gordon Ridgeway and others like Dave Impett – in fact all of you. We can do it!

MASSARELLA

One of the greatest names in pigeon racing. Many of the family, like John and Michael, are dedicated to supplying bloodlines of the best of the breeds at very often reasonable prices. Openly or secretly they have supplied birds to be the basis of many a good strain in the UK. It is well known that nearly all my originals came from Louella Lofts. However, not all the birds are good as the Champions do not always produce good birds. Massarellas do make people famous if fame is what you want.

MAIZE

This is what the International convoy is fed on, and it is a high carbohydrate food. There are many types, eg popcorn, cribbs, plate and red flame, but they tend to have similar nutritional value. A good mixture may contain several varieties for balance. Feeding it to youngsters was traditionally associated with spreading canker. I never fed extra maize, although some do. I would reduce its content for rearing and young birds and replace with peas, beans and peanuts to increase the protein proportion.

MARATHON

In my mind's eye races over 700 miles are marathon events. They are my favourite as they test the stamina and endurance of both bird and fancier. The top test in the UK is to send your birds in the Internationals, especially Barcelona (here I go again). For an excellent performance in 2008 see Marseille. I think the limit is 1,000 miles within five days racing.

MICE

I like little mice, they are comical. Watch them though, and kill them. They may spread disease like salmonella. They can be caught with traps or killed with Neosorex bait etc.

MITES

Mites are tiny, often predatory, arachnids and can plague pigeons. A good fancier keeps mites under control. There are the red mite, northern mite, air sac mite and feather mite. They are all pests and should be eradicated. I often see feather quill mite on people's birds. Now that Duramitex has gone you can dip and spray with Permethrins. Try one drop of 0.8% Ivermectin on the back of the neck and a 24-hour treatment of Moxidectin in the water.

MUTATIONS

I used to think that Barcelona Dream was a sport or genetic mutation, since he was extraordinary in every way. If people believe that racers are originally descended from the rock dove, then there have been many mutations on the way. Consider all the different fancy breeds. Viruses have been known to induce mutations. I bred just one true mosaic. They may be induced by radiation.

MUSCLES

Some good birds do not have very well-developed pectoral muscles. Syndale Express has very large ones. Muscles are used in the power proportion of the bird. Any bird which performs with distinction has good muscles – this is the acid test.

MOULD

I do not like to see mould on corn and pellets. Sometimes there is a top layer of green fungi on a bag of layers' pellets. Just take off the top layer, then everything will be fine. You should store your foods in dry bins. Do not feed mouldy corn, and especially peanuts, as you might infect the birds with aflatoxins.

MOTHS

On summer nights you may see moths around the lights in your loft. The pigeon moth may eat away at flight feathers – spray your loft out. I love moths in general and find them magical, especially the Elephant Hawk moth.

MONEY

I started as a £3 a week garden boy apprentice in 1965. In the 1980s with little money I sold birds, including some exported to Malta and China. Now I am not motivated by money and monetary prizes. What I do, I do for pleasure and self-satisfaction. The love of money brings with it trickery, avarice and corruption. I prefer a society whose values are based on humanity and spirituality. I believe the development of the individual self within society is everything. I am an idealist and an egotist. Why does everybody call me a bighead if they don't mean what they say? (An old song).

MIND

Cogito ergo sum – I think, therefore I am. Our minds and

the joint mind between man and bird are paramount. There are some great intellectual minds in the sport like Cutcliffe, Liam O'Comain, John Clements and Zsolt Talaber, and there are some great practical fancier minds like Chris Gordon, Brian Denney and Geoff Kirkland. The great writers and fanciers focus and dedicate their minds to the task in hand. People now amaze me with their talents. Humans at their best are a wonderful group.

MOTTA

A lovely old mealy Vanhee Champion and made famous at Louella lofts. His descendants are performing with distinction today through his daughter Madam Motta etc. Note the origin of the lofts of Brian Denney, Ian Dixon and Gordon Cooper. I handled this bird and he was a beauty, an iconic pigeon.

MOTIVATION

Trevor Robinson asked me to mention this. In both the mind of the fancier and the intelligence of the bird it means a lot. Many motivational methods lead to Barcelona (used to be Rome), such as widowhood, roundabout and natural. In its essence you should keep plugging away at your targets until you have success and then plug again for some more. Keep raising the standards until you are satisfied.

'MYSTICAL QUEEN'

An inbred hen, being a granddaughter of Diabolos and a daughter of Sister Damien from a brother of Diabolos (the Dutchman). She was the apple of my eye, being dark velvet and a good bird out of San Sebastian, 737 miles. Being inbred to the No.1 pair her descendants are winning today through her sons and daughters, especially Velvet Destiny and Eric (after Gibson). With age I get more and more sentimental!

N

NATIONAL FLYING CLUB

This is a nice big, genuine National club and the two longest points of Saintes and Tarbes are good preparation for International racing. I believe we will have a hard Tarbes race in the future to really sort the birds out. My biased opinion says that the Secretary, Sid Barkel, is a dedicated, conscientious official facing a lot of bureaucratic and procedural difficulties. May I suggest that the International liberation site at Pau could be used for the National since this is potentially more difficult than Tarbes. Then again the National could link up with the International convoy at Tarbes. These are progressive ideas, however with some hard weather the NFC programme is testing. Once again come on you Tarbes lads, get some birds to Barcelona International.

NATIONAL CLUBS

The radius of a true National club must encompass the whole nation, otherwise the club is a National in name only, this is simple logic. The three true National clubs in England are the BICC, the NFC and the BBC. The British International Championship club is the best since it races at the top level. The British Barcelona Club should race from Barcelona to be true to its name. I noted the performance of Chris Gordon at around 845 miles second day – a proper marathon result.

NAIVETY

It's amazing how naive many grown pigeon men are and often part with their money on top of some scurrilous advertising for pigeons, a bit like selling snow to Eskimos. What a rude awakening it was for me to go and live in London for over three years. I met many types of people from different cultures and although I hated a lot of it, it was a great education for a naive country boy. I graduated from the Royal Botanic Gardens Kew and such was the training that I still talk in Latin. I believed horticulture to be my great passion, but now realise it to be pigeons.

NAME

Many fanciers make a good name for themselves; this takes dedication but is not impossible. Big names are generated by publicity and the shrewd fancier realises the essential truth. Most of the top studs name their birds. In my case I only gave names which were personal to me and to my better birds.

NARCOTICS

This is a loose term for drugs, and there is plenty of abuse of them in the world. In many cases I think performance-enhancing pharmacy to be ahead of the testing procedures. I see the future to be performance-enhancing genetic engineering. On one level of consciousness I can see a case for the 'anything goes' philosophy in practice. I object to this on the grounds of cruelty to the birds. Believe me, rules and regulations will never stop the abuse of dope and other methods. On a personal level I have fond memories of smoking a water pipe and looking out over the Himalayas – very mind expanding!

NATRIX

A lovely dark chequer cock raced by the genius of Jim Biss and his management crew. The bird won BICC Marseille three times and it was nice to see Trevor Robinson wining the same trophy in 2008, a performance which will filter into the consciousness of the fancy.

NATURAL

Natural birds, once said to be a thing of the past, are still doing the damage in the hard endurance races. Many fliers change mid-season from widowhood and roundabout systems back to natural with great effect. This is due to the form generated by hormones and motivation. Natural racing will never be lost. Ideally I raced separate for three weeks early in the season and switched to natural. Jim Biss was a very clever man with widowhood cocks, as is Chris Gordon. It depends on what you find suits you. I like the freedom and kindness of open loft home flying.

NAVIGATION

Good birds have good navigation to say 1,000 miles in five days or less. Human beings, with our blunt tools of science and perception and built-in limitations, will never know in an absolute sense how birds navigate. There are some clever theories and that's all they are.

NERVOUSNESS

I do not like excitable, nervous pigeons, which are often born this way. Nevertheless 'Oddball' was of this ilk and raced well in the hard Pau of 2002 at 735 miles, being 3rd Open Single Bid, NFC. I was a nervous and sensitive, introverted boy on my long immaturity (not any more). I often think nervous people feel more, don't you?

NEW

There are many new and modern advances in supplements and medication. Many bacteria are keeping ahead of antibiotics as new strains of immune bugs breed in their natural resistance. New is not necessarily best, but it can be. Many fanciers, instead of creating their own families of birds, buy in new all the time. New 'strains' are often promoted as the best for reasons for commerce and fame; this is how markets are created. You should make a name for yourself, not basking in the reflected glory of another name.

NOMINATION

I have lived in the north, south, east and west of England, but you know my writings are biased towards the north of England. The latter is for one reason only: up here we get the real distance, 700-900 miles in the big races. These distances are the acid test for both fancier and pigeon. In

A happy five-year-old Jim Emerton with Charlie Fantail and a young pied

Jim at primary school in Skegness (front desk, on the right)

With my class at the Royal Botanic Gardens, second row, second right.
Alan Titchmarsh is just in front of me, front row, second right.

My mother Dorothy, aged 17

With 'Dorothy's Courage', 1989

In Yugoslavia, 1989

With a copy of the Gazette

In the loft

Mum helping in the loft

Pigeon man!

Jean in the garden

Pigeon man at rest

Jean and Mum (Dorothy) at Sycamore Cottage, Holtby

The late Eric Gibson, NFC clock man

Mum

With the '53' bred for T Robinson –
2nd average NFC, 4 races up to
Tarbes 722 miles

Dark Destiny

Daughter of Darkness

Dark One Two

K. Emerton
1994

"DELILAH"

PETER BENNETT

G880V84359

Delilah

Diabolos

Dot's Delight

my mind's eye the southern fanciers should stretch their birds out to Barcelona. I have friends in Yorkshire and some of them are very blunt.

NOSTRIL

The bird's nose should be nice and healthy and dry, free from obvious respiratory disease. Keep your eyes open for a mucoidal discharge. Treat when necessary with Doxy 'T'.

NEWTON PAIR

A famous duo of Busschaert origin pigeons (a little like the Larkins pair) made famous by Dennis Newton and propagated by Dr J J Horn of Up North Combine fame. I would imagine that the genes of this distinguished pair are alive and well today.

NORTH-EAST 700-MILE CLUB AND NORTHERN CLASSIC

The former duplicates from the NFC and is a band of dedicated souls with some of the top NFC lads in the country. I learned some of my trade in this club from 1992 onwards, yet disagreed when they did not incorporate Dax International into the programme. I thought that was a retrograde step. I did not cause a fuss though and did my own thing. The Northern Classic tests the birds and has a nice fly out of Saintes. Tony Savill is a very clever fancier indeed and on his day can beat all the big names in Yorkshire, etc. He enjoys his racing and is a genuine non-greedy fancier.

NON-CONFORMIST

Since I am a bit of a nutter (some would say a lot) I stand on the edge and tell it as it is. I do believe that genius and greatness await the talents who try a different approach in life. Some of my best friends and contacts have broken the mould. I think advances and changes are made by these very people. In my younger life as convenor of the Joint Unions of York, I learned in the corridors of power and saw officials as they were. I am proud of the work I did for people, yet I was a thorn in the side of the establishment. Now I think some people enjoy my articles because they have a ring of truth. I do believe in opening Clubs up to all (except mass murderers etc). May the best bird win!

OATS

I eat these for breakfast, so they must be good. They are often to be found in corn mixtures or fed as pinhead oatmeal, where they are thought to be good for pigeons. I never fed extra oats, although some do.

OBITUARIES

Every fancier deserves a nice, well-written obituary in the weeklies. These often say a lot about the perceived character of the deceased and their accomplishments. There were some excellent ones for the late Brian Long.

OBJECTIVES

Dedicated and serious minded fanciers will set themselves targets or goals that they want to achieve in the external world. Often this amounts to wanting to beat successful fanciers. I did this at one time, later becoming a conceptualist by visualising certain racepoints, eg Barcelona International. Whatever motivates you is fine and achieving your objectives should bring you satisfaction. As for me, I keep plugging away with the articles, the rewards from which I harvest internally.

O'COMAIN, LIAM

Liam has emerged as a leading light in world pigeon journalism. He is not just a dry, abstract intellectual with a large ego, he expresses himself in a fluid, lyrical and somewhat spiritual style. An Irishman, he is a great enthusiast of long-distance and marathon racing, and if you are lucky you could be on the receiving end of his generous and lofty style, based on a good grasp of hard facts. Yes Liam, your work will live on when we are both but dust. We are all waiting for your book to appear, as like Zsolt Talaber's it will be a volume seller. By the way, put the cheque in the post!

ORNITHOSIS

The causal organisms are chlamydia and may be in association with mycoplasma and coryza. All are respiratory affecting organisms producing loss of form, eye and nasal discharges and impaired breathing function. Good ventilation in the loft is a priority. Doxy 'T' has proved efficacious as a control of ornithosis. Administer as prescribed and remove calcium-bearing grit and pellets. Like most antibiotics, the wrong dose will lend to resistant bug build up.

OPERATIONS

You can perform minor stitch repair operations on pigeons with needle and thread. For anything major you should consult a vet. Ask the question: is it worth the trouble and expense? Many of the small swellings are benign and the blood-based ones drop off. A persistent swelling between the vent of a hen often means that as a layer she is finished. Swellings of the wing joint can spell salmonella and you should be vigilant.

OPIATES

These drugs are derived from the opium poppy. I have stood in the poppy fields of Darra, an area of tribal law, in Pakistan. Most of the derivatives, eg heroin, produce a feeling of drowsy euphoria. I do not recommend these banned substances for pigeons, as they will not win races.

OBSERVATION

What is the real nature of your birds? What do you see? How do you interpret what you see? Good fanciers will observe small changes in appearance and behaviour of their birds. They will note illness, injury and changes in behaviour which may indicate fitness issues. You can notice the decline with age of a bird, or the extra feather quality and intelligence of a future breeder. For all fanciers out there, do you look in the mirror, what do you see? Think about it.

OFFICIALS

Many humans are noted for their power of office within a hierarchical organisation. However in officialdom there can be the abuse of power and bully-boy tactics. Good officials are idealists with the objective of being the best interest of others rather than using trickery for gain. I am very wary of officials, yet someone has to maintain rule and order. I have no desire to be the president of anything, preferring to operate on the edge. Democracies are often dominated by self-seeking, charismatic individuals. Many clubs have secretaries, committees, presidents, chairmen etc. There is often much infighting and gamesmanship, yet sometimes these hierarchies do work.

OILS

The modern trend is to load the food with added fats for slow-burning metabolisable energy, especially for long-distance and marathon racing. For my racing I fed peanuts, Hormoform and Red Band in the boxes five days before basketing and in the mix at all times. On Thursday and Friday and/or the last two days before basketing, I poured the oils onto the corn and yeastmix: Beyers garlic oil, Beyers mixed oils and Columbine 10:1 oils. Traditionally linseed was the oil seed of choice for the moult etc. Now I prefer a sprinkle of hemp on the corn mix. Many of the oils in pellets will come from soya. The overall diet should be loaded towards fats and carbohydrates with higher protein for breeders and squeakers.

OYSTER SHELL

Grit for the digesting gizzards of birds is essential. Good old-fashioned Kilpatricks' Universal contains oyster shell as do many pigeon and poultry grits. I did not need to give my racers grit since they went fielding on exercise. I recommend it for marathon pigeons on 2-3 day flights. Sometimes I gave them some red stone mixed grit in the roller feeders as a treat.

OXYGEN

Fit birds have maximum uptake of O2 into the muscles for the liberation of energy. We aim to keep the air sacs and airways of birds in good condition. The loft air should be fresh and rich in oxygen, with little dust. I have noticed that young birds fly well in fresh, cool air between 5 and 7am on a summer's morning. Diseases which affect the oxygen intake of birds should be treated.

P

PARASITES

Many birds harbour internal and external parasites. Feather parasites can be flies, fleas, lice and mites and all these should be controlled with Moxidectin and/or Pyrethrins. Worms may be tape, hair, gape and roundworm and may be controlled with Panacur out of the moult season or the avermectins eg Moxidectin and Ivermectin. Avoid the indiscriminate dosing of antibiotics against bacterial infections. Pigeons should carry low levels only of the many parasites, and natural immunity should be encouraged by good management.

PARENTAGE

The way to practise actual parentage is individual pairs in isolated breeding areas and/or by DNA testing procedures. Within a strain and if you know your birds you can normally assess the parents of a young bird for origin. My birds were all relatives so that I did not care, because you do not always know where the quality is going to come from. In birds there are many tricksters who sell phoney birds which are not as advertised – beware.

PAIN

I think we suffer more mental pain in the pursuit of excellence than the pigeons do from physical injuries and ailments. Pigeons have a high pain threshold and race and recover from serious injuries. You can stitch them up with ease and they will win having broken a keel. Yet how do we perceive in our mind's eye what a pigeon experiences?

PASSION

A complex mental set that probably arises from applied love and devotion. They say a passion for pigeons brings intensity and strength. How much if at all do pigeons feel it, say when they fight or defend their young? Aren't we really ignorant about everything?

PATIENCE

Quiet, calm patience is an absolute must for the long-distance and marathon champion. I notice that a lot of sprint men are impulsive, aggressive and have a short attention span. You should be able to see through a target to the end with a 2-3 year build up with relentless focus.

PECKING

In most living things there is a pecking order or hierarchy in which a balance of subordinate and dominant beings in maintained. I do not like to see scalping and eye injuries in birds but simple pecking will always take place.

PERFECTION

This is a human hypothetical construct and in its absolute form is unobtainable, because we can always raise the bar of difficulty and apply our critical faculties. Make no mistake, the top fanciers seek perfection in what they do. A mealy cock named Barcelona Miracle with 2 x International wins for Demaret came close don't you think? In the final analysis, whatever turns you on!

PERSISTENCE

This is a great human quality and the ability to tough it out and keep going with dogged perseverance will take you a long way. Marathon races are all about persistence for both man and birds.

PILLS

In terms of medications and supplements I normally give flock water treatments. I find it very fussy to give pills to birds apart from the occasional Spartrix against canker. Make sure you know the active ingredient of your pills and research them.

PLUMAGE

The feathers of a pigeon should be deep, silky and rich, evenly distributed throughout the body. I like to see a shine on the bird and good bold, clear colour. The acid test for quality is that a good racer must have a good feather because of its racing success and stick because of their breeding success. My preference is for yellow rather than buff feather type for the slip factor through the air. A useless racer may have lovely feather. The essence is the genotype of the birds.

PHOTOGRAPHY

Since I did not advertise birds after 1997, and preferring the written word, I have been fairly shy of photographs of my birds. However in 1985 Peter Bennett visited my loft at Holtby and produced a lovely montage and individual photos of my birds which I keep today. The excellent photo you see of Barcelona Dream was taken by Brian Siggers. I think pretty colour photos often lure the fancier into buying birds based on external beauty – this can be folly. Birds should have beautiful performance genes. To me what is in my head is of greater value than physical looks and that is how I judge all – the inner rather than the outer. It is easy to be misled by good looks.

PEDIGREE

It is so easy to create a 'good' pedigree by hand or on computer. These can be accurate or they can be nothing but bovine faeces. The pedigree is the playground of the con man. In my latter years I stated the parents or grandparents only. Nevertheless pedigrees are nice to study if you keep the salt pot handy.

PRIDE

They say 'pride goes before a fall'. Why not enjoy this emotion if you have success? Be proud of yourself and others – it is only human. You are a sad case if you can't feel it.

POL BOSTYN

This Belgian ace was a larger than life character with a great deal of skill in the long-distance National and International races. It is reported that he could barely read and write, yet he became world famous for his knowledge and command of methods close to nature and for his International wins. He had some early Stichelbaut-based birds and Descamps van Hasten used the Sister of Passport in their breeding. Some of his noted birds were Chico, Denoni and Passport.

Q

QUALIFICATION

Chris Gordon will tell you of the criteria that your bird must reach to qualify for the Olympiad. Since I studied so long ago I gained many qualifications, the hardest being the Mensa test, which really is tough. For expert advice go to those with formal qualifications and/or with proven practical experience.

QUARREL

I am not an aggressive type and refuse to quarrel, yet I will debate and argue for fun. A few have upset themselves with me, yet I fall out with none. Clubs are often full of quarrels and I do not believe in them – a waste of time. No, I don't have quarrels!

QUALITY

Top winners and performance birds prove that they have the qualities you desire either in breeding or racing. Show judges choose winners on a perceived subjective quality and this is what showing is about. In racing some of the best-looking physical specimens that may do well in shows are useless in racing and breeding. Beauty is as beauty does. Birds that do well in the distance and marathon Internationals in the UK have quality, and the genes are right for the job.

QUANTITY

The more you breed, the more you are likely to come across a champion, assuming your management is correct. I bred say 60-80 young birds and would be happy with five good ones from these. Most birds from any family are useless at the top end of racing. Better to race hard and have a few good ones than have a loft full of uninterested maybes. In my last big race at Dax International I sent the only five birds I had to it. For marathon racing you should aim to lose your birds; then the best will come through. For stock I kept around 25 pairs to secure the strain of nearly all related birds. The single bird NFC is a good test of quality, as you nominate a single bird into England.

QUEEN

A nice regal term, traditionally applied to favoured good birds. I recall Storm Queen of Ritchie & White of Fraserburgh and my Mystical Queen. It gives a pigeon a degree of permanency and status.

QUESTIONS

An enquiring mind asks questions. I continue to ask many questions and sometimes I get the correct answers. Try to look beyond the obvious – is this really the case, or is there another answer? About life on earth I have asked the major questions and come up with the answers that satisfy me. The right people to ask questions to are those who you think know more than you do in their chosen fields. One of my columns has been questions and answers. I enjoy this format.

QUESTIONNAIRES

A good format for detailing and analysing the thoughts of the fancier. When you have done well, you may be lucky enough to answer the 105 questions of Parkinson. These are normally published in the BHW and may go on to the Elimar website. All good informative stuff.

QUIET

I like quiet birds, especially hens in a quiet loft in quiet countryside. I love to hear bird song, not the hum of the city. I feel that quiet birds, well within themselves basket and travel best for the distance. I know that birds may become more boisterous with form. I often find that quiet, laid-back men are best at the distance (500-700 miles).

QUEST

The fancier goes on a journey, a quest for perfection and success. All very good as it helps to keep you motivated. The secret is to be happy with your success at the end of the quest.

R

RACING

I set and enjoyed my targets in racing, yet on reflection I preferred the breeding aspect of the sport. Race at whatever distance suits you and your set-up. I would say that breeding is gold and racing is silver. Racing tends to be labour intensive and many fanciers have loft management, often in the form of women. I will plug it again – the top level of racing onto the UK is that which is international – all you need are a few quality birds and then it is on!

RALES

An abnormal respiratory and often associated with ornithosis, mycoplasmosis and coryza or combinations of these. Doxy 'T' can be efficacious. Other problems may be air sac mites or injury.

REDS

Birds can win in any colour from white to mosaic to black, although many fanciers prefer blues and chequers. My first win and first into York from Grantham was a red hen given by Jack Ross of York. My second win was with a mealy hen stray from Wimbledon that I had caught at Flamborough Head on a piece of apple core. Reds can be beautiful to look at, yet my strain was developed around chequers and dark chequers. It is said that reds are more susceptible to peregrine attack (note these are falconidae and not hawks). Two of the best mealies ever to fly into the UK are Woodsiders and the Marseille cock of Trevor Robinson. The sprinter Marcelis became famous for his reds.

RED MITE

These and northern mite are serious pests. In my stock loft I had to spray in May every year with Duramitex to combat them. I would also administer Moxidectin in the water. The red mites can seriously weaken or kill the young with their nocturnal predators. They are also the scourge of the canary keeper. I recommend using a garden plastic sprayer from the garden centre.

RED BAND

I used this or similar for years. Although expensive and from Haiths I like it, being a multi-small seed mix with a high energy content. I mixed mine with Hormoform and peanuts. I believe the cheaper copies are just as good.

RED BLOOD CELLS

These are the oxygen carriers in the blood to the muscles for racing. The fancier aims to increase these by legal means. Non legal means would be using GPO. In the 1980s I used Mucosan T which contained arsanilic acid, also found in Aviol.

READING

I recommend you read all the expert matter on pigeon racing, especially Colin Walker and Zsolt Talaber – they are serious authorities of thought. You will normally have more success from reading than listening to gossip and old wives' tales. Some of the old BHW stud books and Squills are nice historical reading. Whatever your interest in life, there is normally a good book on it. Beware of a lot of waffle that you can find on the net. A good pigeon website though is elimar.com.

REARING

A nice team of 50-80 young birds should do the trick for you.

Your stock birds should manage five rounds a season. Feed should be a high protein mix with peanuts, yeast and Hormoform. In hoppers should be layers' pellets and I recommend Matrix by Gem. I have also fed Tovo.

RED CELL

This nutrient-based additive, along with Propel, derived from the equine world of racing. I tried it and didn't notice any difference. My notion here is that if the birds are satisfied in all their needs then extras are a waste of time and money.

RESISTANCE

It is topical and important to develop as much natural resistance in your birds as possible with minimal use of antibiotics and the use of probiotics, garlic etc. Deep litter is beneficial in this respect with the exposure to faecal bacteria.

REGURGITATION

Do not panic if your young birds sick-up food, as this can be stress induced. Your birds do not necessarily have any of the young bird sickness syndromes which have taken on mythical proportions.

ROLLERS

A good competition roller will spin with speed, depth and frequency. They are stunning looking birds in many colours. Two of the top men are George Mason from Derbyshire and

Graham Dexter. Traditionally they were called Birmingham Rollers. I had a nice kit at Alvaston, Derby for years and would visit the roller men, eg Harold Adams, Billy Burdett and Frank Bryant. My head was always in the sky observing my rollers. They are often fed for judged competitions on depurative and flown in groups of 20 – a very skilled test of fanciership up to International level.

RUPTURES

Birds may sustain these, many of which will heal naturally.

S

SATISFACTION

Some fanciers are never happy. Small fish are sweet and you should take your pleasure when it arrives. After many years I was finally satisfied with some International performances. To be honest I liked breeding the best and now writing. I can do an article in 30 minutes from the top of my head and this gives me a buzz – it is liberating and cathartic.

SECRETARY

Now this is a tedious and laborious job. At one time my father was Divisional Secretary for a big firm, yet I would hate it – BICC. You can't be perfect, and believe me both are overworked and need more support and help. Ladies often make good Secretaries. They are the backbone of the sport and we all rely on them.

SEX

Birds are either male/female or hermaphrodite. The modern systems of racing, ie widowhood and roundabout, depend on the condition attained by the release of sex hormones. There is no doubt that it is easier to gain top condition in birds through separated birds deprived of sex until after the race. Some birds though never do mate and remain celibate. Combinations of sexual deprivation and gratification can be used by combining celibacy with the natural free nesting system.

SHINN, JOHN

John Shinn and I met in 1960 at Spondon Park Grammar School, Derby. We were well known for our rude noises, particularly in English and Geography. This must have impressed Bill Cunningham, because he gave me a lowly grade G for English and my report read 'Insolent and a thorough nuisance in class, especially in English Literature'. Now John was good at English Grammar and I gained inspiration from sitting next to him. John is a big, strong, rugged fellow and his dad supplied me with a twelve bore gun and a .22 rifle. We grew up together playing for the school rugby team and rough shooting, which I loved.

Through John's influence – he was the mature one – we stayed in the houseboat with Kenzie Thorpe, the 'Wild Goose Man', on the Wash saltings. We were two adventurous outdoor sorts together. Sometimes John would watch my Rollers, yet he was more interested in pigeon shooting. Nowadays John is a first-class all round shot and engineer, and his affinity with working labradors and spaniels has to be seen to be believed. He is a regular character on the shooting scene with the rich and famous, including Michael Massarella, and recently loaded for Liz Hurley. He can perhaps be best described as a hard case with a soft centre and is a definite one-off. A book of his would be a best seller!

SECRETS

We used to fly under the cloak of secrecy. Nowadays many fanciers are revealing all and there is enough collective knowledge for emergent genius and expertise. All mine have been revealed and my conscience is clear, because at the end of the day you can't take the mind of the man, his individuality.

SIMPLICITY

The complex mind of the genius makes a rational simple system from its inner constituents – the pattern is seen as a simple whole from the kaleidoscope of consciousness.

SELF

The human self in all its complexity and when found and realised is a wonderful and beautiful entity, an intricate and united whole. We spend a lifetime finding and realising it. The process in Jungian terms is 'individuation'. We can find ourselves through immersion in the sport of pigeon racing.

SKENDLEBY

A lovely village in the Lincolnshire Wolds, not far from Skegness and Spilsby. From ages 5-11 I roamed the countryside there and I loved it. Nearly all my inner sentiments and desires were cultivated in the big outdoors of the village. We had the post office with three acres of paddock, orchard and gardens. I can best liken it to the Darling Buds of May by H E Bates. Years later I returned and the old loft by the house was still in that lovely unspoilt village, 'the village that time forgot'.

SPRINTING/SPEED

Most fanciers in the UK are 50-250 mile fliers, where first prizes and beating their fellow men are oft the essence. Likewise most pigeons are managed to give their best over the short haul. The sport is noted for a short term fix, a bit like a drug. I recently saw the first six arrive for Brian Shipley (brother of Cheeky Charmer) and I enjoyed it and could see the birds that Brian was getting. In my mind's eye I still retain images of some of my early sprinters, which were flat out before breaking for the loft. Sprinting is more associated with out and out wins than extreme distance racing, yet only tests up to 250 miles. To produce a team of sprint stars demands a great deal of skill on the part of the fancier. Many birds will do it and family names like Vandenabeele will always have their day.

SPORT

I regard pigeon racing as a sport like lots of others abroad, yet there is no official recognition in this country. This should change since we have our own Olympiad. It is purely a question of politics and semantics. Many fanciers certainly regard it as their sport.

SPECIALISATION

Racing today is a serious thing and you should specialise by focusing with great intensity on our chosen distances. Hit and miss attitudes won't work. Create an overall plan and stick to it with gradual modifications if necessary. The top continental heroes we read about are nearly all specialists with a professional approach. You can be a small back garden loft fancier and still be a specialist.

SPERM

A fertile cock bird produces millions of these, a small percentage of which will fertilise the egg of the hen bird. The sperm is a powerful instrument transmitting the DNA along the generations. An old cock may be 16 years of age and still fertile and capable of producing winners. We like to keep the old boys going as long as possible with good management, vent chipping and hormones eg gonadotrophin. Eventually senility arrives and the male will cease to be fertile and die – it is eternal, it is immortal. Fathered sperm can be used for artificial insemination and may be stored in good condition for years.

SOONTJENS

A family name which became famously linked with sprinting. Believe me there are plenty of crossbred birds about. Now Frank Sheader has a good name with Soontjens-based birds, especially in the Up North Combine, as did John Kirk I believe.

STRAINS

I am noted for creating my own strains, and apart from my words I see this as my finest work. The racing was purely to test the results of strain making. Strain can be described as a family of birds with a distinct hereditary character. I have told you all I know about inbreeding, which is the quintessence of strain making.

T

TARBES

Tarbes is a lovely location near the Pyrenees which affords marathon racing into the north of England. As a racepoint it tends so far to be easier than Pau in the NFC Grand National. Sooner or later we will have a hard Tarbes when the birds will be really tested like the Pau of Old. As a greater challenge and for a 'harder' race, try some of the Tarbes International and watch for a totally different result in England.

TERRIERS

Terriers tend to be wonderful little characters and great rat and cat dogs. Dorothy and I had little Freddie the Jack Russell for 13 years, and we loved him. He curled up in my mother's bed at night at Holtby and he was a canny, knowing animal, with far more acute senses than a human. I walked him every day, until, like so many Jack Russells, he was run over. I used to tell him stories in his ear and he loved it all about his fellow animals and birds; a bit like

Beatrix Potter. My mother said the animal kingdom was far superior to man!

TESTING

All our stock and racers need to be tested to see where the quality really lies. Send all your racers to your chosen distances and test them in true National and/or International competition. With severe progeny testing you can gradually develop your own strain or family – this is the real test of a good fancier. To get to the top is the ultimate test of a fancier and to do this you are in for a very testing time.

TITCHMARSH, ALAN

On 6th October 1969 Alan and I posed for the course photo at the Royal Botanic Gardens, Kew. My first digs was a room with him at No. 83 Mortlake Road, Kew. This was described in the book Trowel and Error. We had a dingy attic room with a bare flex hanging from the ceiling with a light bulb on it. With the cost of paraffin and the smell we had no heating and you could shake the dew off the bedclothes in the morning. After a couple of months Alan moved and I helped him with my Minivan. We studied for three years at the gardens and both graduated with credit. He was a confident and bright fellow with a theatrical twist. We were both very fond of the written word. The boy done good!

TIME

We pigeon fanciers are all obsessed with chronology. Even now I am always asking about the time of events, along with my many other questions. When we are sprint racing, fractions of a second count and we always refer time to overfly – which one are we in? In the marathon races you may look at days rather than minutes.

THIMBLE

I used plastic thimbles in my STB Quartz clock and was happy with this. You will find that as an aid to keeping up with ETS the use of thimbles will not be allowed at the NEHU. Anything that saves time is a good idea.

TOULET CLOCKS

These are good old clocks that are still in use but not really sophisticated enough for modern racing. They were often puncture clocks and still serve many people well yet our absolute technology has taken over.

TOXIN

Beware of poisonous plants in your garden and aflatoxins in infected peanuts. My birds walked the fields for 30 years and my local farmers were kind to me with no obvious shootings or poisonings in the fields. The days of DDT and other organochlorine toxins have gone. For mild poisoning use Chevita Multivit in the water. If you overdose drugs like Emtryl this has a neurological toxic effect.

TRAUMA

Birds will recover from physical and mental trauma at a wonderful rate after breaking bones, muscular damage or shooting. Mostly they will heal themselves.

TRUMPET

Some say I blow my own. Let me be straight on this – I don't
– I play a full brass band. If you have talent, why not assert
it – plenty do.

THONE

Jos Thone, the Belgian ace, cemented an international
reputation. His most famous bird, the Sumo, is responsible
for the Legend via the Emperor of Brian Sheppard of Dax
International fame. His birds command high prices yet will
only excel in the right hands. You can choose the stars all you
like, but you will be a champion only if you are good enough.

TIPPLERS

These are endurance birds and will virtually fly around the
clock. They are lovely hard little birds and I remember them
flown in kits of 3 by the old stalwarts of Derby. They are
different birds to tumblers or rollers which are flown for
their acrobatic manoeuvres in the air.

TUMBLERS

Performance tumblers are beautiful coloured birds flown in
kits where the acrobatics in the air are looser, rather than
the fast spin of the true Birmingham or Competition roller.
I got used to tumblers and rollers from the age of three and
I love to watch them – my neck is still elongated from
staring at them. They make excellent drop birds for racers
and the hens are good affectionate companions for
widowhood cocks.

TIMING SYSTEMS

To register time, we have a clock or system. I recommend ETS to everyone yet, I would be happy at 800 miles with a clock.

TRICHOMONIASIS

This is the disease caused by canker-inducing Trichomonads. There are many canker strains and we should control them with Anti-Protozal agents. In the racing season I would recommend a treatment every six weeks. The modern thinking is to try and stimulate some immunity to the strains.

TRAVEL

The world is a very large place, and I have been to over 50 countries and islands. Adventurous travel will change you forever – it develops character and rounds out the personality. I have been to so many places I've forgotten them all, yet I recall the deserts, the mountains, the forests and the beautiful fish in the oceans of the world. In the words of dirty Dancing, I've had the time of my life. Many men like to visit fanciers abroad, and I loved it in Malta at those roof-top lofts. One of my most exciting countries was Afghanistan. I went from the Khyber Pass into the remote Bamiyan Valley and into the poppy fields of Darra, Pakistan – an area of tribal law. All in all I am very lucky to be alive to tell the tale. Some of my memories still frighten me.

U

UNIVERSE

In my student days we pondered the Universe. It is good practice, since it develops thought. All we think and do changes the Universe, as it consists of physical and non-physical elements. This paper is part of it. I do not necessarily believe the Big Bang Theory, and prefer to think that a form of the Universe was always there and probably always will be. No start and no end. Think about it.

ULTIMATE

Swainsons made a very nice mix called Ultimate which I fed for a while; it contained a good mix with mung beans and peanuts. We all have the most that we can achieve and we should all go for it. In terms of birds, the Barcelona Miracle by Demaret came close to it with two Barcelona International wins. The ultimate level of racing into the UK is International, you cannot improve on that.

UNCOMPROMISING

My advice, with the wisdom of hindsight, is do not dilute your intentions for others, go for it, aim as high as you want to achieve, you owe nothing to anyone. Then you will ring with the sound of truth.

UNCOMPLICATED

When planning a system of racing for your birds, make

things as simple and repeatable as possible. The complex mind makes things look easy and with pigeons they are; send them as far as possible with as little rest as possible. The requirements of a pigeon are its basic needs, comforts and security.

UGLY

There are some birds which to the senses just look plain ugly. The brother of Dark Destiny looked like a double recessive, yet was a great breeder. Watch how beautiful these ugly birds become when they win. Like everything else in life, it is subjective. My preference is dark and dark velvets; the feather tends to be better.

UTENSILS

I like wooden roller feeders for my corn and metal Gaz feeders for layers' pellets. I used five-pint plastic conqueror water fountains. My mother kept these clean with wire wool in all seasons. I was never bothered by a speck of dirt.

UNIQUE COCK, THE

This lovely old dark iron cock, owned by Jim Donaldson, is the last son of Barcelona Dream and Dark Enchantment and is breeding a good line for Jim up at Peterhead.

UNITED KINGDOM

I receive calls and letters from both the UK and abroad. A lot of people talk and ask about layers' pellets. They should be fed all year round in hoppers on a help-yourself basis. The feeding quality is much better than corn and they are cheaper than pigeon pellets, the cost of which hurts your pocket.

UNUSUAL SIGNS

The sharp eye will notice any change or difference in the birds, loft or environment. You may see changes in behaviour for form birds or signs of predators. Try and tune into the instincts of your birds. The world is big enough to accommodate all sorts of people, including the unusual.

UNBALANCED BIRDS

I am very aware of misshapen, unbalanced birds, yet Dark Enchantment, a deep little hen, surprised me. It is the inner qualities that carry most weight. Balanced birds feel nicer in the hand, that's all.

ULCERS

These I have yet to see on a bird apart from in the eye. Cloramphenicol in the eye may be beneficial.

V

VANHEE

The father-and-son partnership of Gerard & Michael Vanhee was very successful in Belgium, winning many Nationals. The name is alive today through the Vanhee products and, of course, the birds. The men liked to crossbreed (outbreed) from top sources and like the

Stichelbaut-bred birds and Janssens. A famous pairing was the Oudeizeren Stichelbaut hen '813' and the Creonne 12eren. DVH introduced progeny from this pairing and the line is in my birds today. Massarella introduced many fine specimens in the 1970s, taking the names Jean Pierre, Splendide, Napoleon etc and the famous Motta. Some of these lines are in good families today, especially Brian Denny's and my own. Louella still markets the old lines today.

VACCINATION

It is a requirement to do this against PMV. For many fanciers this is a pain and various fiddles are taking place. In practice the vaccine has varying degrees of success. Other vaccinations can be used against pox (diphtheria) and paratyphoid. I am not a great fan; yet if your loft gets PMV then it is a nightmare.

VALE OF YORK FEDERATION

This is a small Fed that flies the south route. I far preferred the Yorkshire middle route with a much larger radius and bigger birdage. I always think biggest is best with Federations.

VAN

A very handy vehicle for training and carrying the birds about, and I bought one in 1997 for this purpose as four baskets fitted into it. A nice diesel van is very handy to have. I traded mine in for a Toyota Corolla. I love it.

VAN REET, STAF

This man has been a good sprinter in Belgium, mainly from Quievrain. Through publicity the name has taken off with fanciers like Mark Caudwell and the Mardons. Some of them can win if the management is correct and at different distances. Once again I hammer the point home by saying that van Reets are those birds direct from van Reet – all the others are based-ons only.

VAN DER WEGEN

I first noticed these birds of Adrianus & Anton on the video 'The Greatest Story Ever Told' and thought I must have some of these lovely dark chequers. They had performed impressively in the marathon races. Louella Lofts are keeping the strain pure. Birds of this origin have been significant as a cross.

VANDALISM

I hate this, especially when directed against pigeon lofts and heir birds. It's a practice often associated with allotment lofts, which may result in arson. Security is No 1 for the top fancier and everyone, dogs, CCTV, alarms etc are all useful.

VELOCITY

We are obsessed with velocity in yards per minute and have an immediate understanding of a race by the velocity. I like races between 700-1200ypm. Races above this I thought were easy and often too much so.

VERIFICATION

In most Classic/National style clubs you must register your bird with the authorities. This is a necessary chore and must be done – you can relax afterwards. You should do it by habit.

VERMIN

Pigeon lofts are prey to vermin such as rats, mice, crows, magpies, foxes, stoats, weasels, polecats, ferrets and cats. Aim to keep them all out and set traps where required. On the other hand, crows may dissuade sparrowhawks from your area. The birds must feel comfortable and safe at home. Boddy & Ridewood sell some good traps.

VIOLA

The viola tricolour, or heartsease, once popularised by Old Hand, was used as a heart conditioner for the birds, and is a very pretty little flower.

VIRGO

A white bird from some Kirkpatrick origin is the longest-flying YB National winner for Fountainhead. I believe it flew over 400 miles from Rennes, and well done for that.

VISION

Pigeons have varying degrees of good vision and are excellent at predator spotting, and may use a degree of it for navigation (a process which is not understood). The good fancier has mental acuity or vision; he projects himself into the future on a mental level. The marathon man will have targets that he sets years in advance, and with a self-fulfilling prophecy these are realised.

VITAMINS

The current consensus of thought is for adding vitamins eg A and B complex to the water and food. Mine were supplied by layers' pellets (scientifically formulated), Bovril, yeast and Aviform. I used Chevita Multivits in the water on a race day. It is thought that corn mixes are lacking.

VIRUSES

There are more viruses and strains of viruses than we have discovered. Well-known ones include herpes, circo, adeno etc. We cannot cure these. They run their course with the help of immune-stimulants. It is thought that the archetypal young bird sickness syndrome is a complex involving one or two of these viruses or their stereotypes.

VECTORS

Vectors, or spreaders of virus, may be birds, man, clothes, dust particles, or pests and diseases.

VERSELE-LAGA

This is a giant company which makes some good corn mixes and products. For distance racing try Gerryplus with Superstarplus seven days before basketing. The young bird mix with added peas will see you up to 400 miles. They are dear but noted for quality.

VITALITY

Good birds and fanciers have super energy. Sometimes you can see it and feel it. Inbreeding sometimes tends to decrease it, but watch for it later when you outbreed these.

VERHEYE

Maurice Verheye was a famous sprinter and was made popular by Louella in the UK. Two of his famous birds were Rainstorm and Miss Polly. The good old lines are still cultivated today, although somewhat out of fashion now.

VERMICIDE

This is a posh word for a wormer. Worms degrade performance and should be eradicated if possible by using eg Moxidectin, Panacur, Levamisole etc. Try and keep a worm-free loft with dry conditions and wire aviary floors and grids.

DARK VELVET/VELVET DESTINY

In my inbreeding to my DVH foundation birds and my no 1 pair I produced some lovely dark velvets. I like the smooth silky feather. The above two are in the pedigrees of some very good distance birds today and are keynote pigeons.

W

WEAKLINGS

Most birds will not perform at the marathon level. The way

to select out the weaklings, whatever the cause, is the basket – send them, and send them to 700+ miles. As a result there were no weaklings in my loft. Any obvious genetic variants or substandard babies should not leave the nest. Most birds in most lofts are pretty but not worth their salt – send them on!

WORK

To arrive at the place where I am now has taken dedication and then some more. Most of the work, however, I have done in my head. To develop a top strain takes years of thought, but it is something I recommend to everyone out there. Any rich fool can keep buying in expensive pigeons. The true test of purpose is to create your own. In terms of a racing system, put your mind behind creating a system that you can manage with ease from year to year. My 91-year-old mother could do mine as could a child; genius is simplicity. You may have to delegate some of the tasks to others; this can be fine as long as you have control.

WEATHER

All races are dependent on climate changes. I never liked fast races above 1300ypm, preferring races in north-east winds, the harder the better. I am never comfortable when there are lots of other birds about on a similar velocity. I looked for exceptional birds in my strain, not group birds. However there are many who are obsessed with speed and fair dinkum! Beware of the north winds in April, if you send your yearlings. I have never kept my birds at home because of a bad forecast. The Pau NFC of '02 at 735 miles was tough in a north wind.

WEBS

In my stock loft I had a 30-year-old collection of spiders, festooned in great webs. It was gothic and used in the film 'Arachnophobia' (joke). It was pleasantly weird. I call them 'Boris'.

WELL-BEING

The management system will do everything to develop the control, contentment and well-being of the birds. You should do this not just on merit grounds but out of love for the birds. By putting birds first, if you have things right then success will follow for the fancier. Keep stress to a minimum and be as relaxed as possible.

WHEAT

I never fed extra cereal wheat grains, yet sometimes the young birds found these in the fields. Manitoba wheat is good and grains can be found in many mixes. Wheat lacks sufficient protein percentage for young bird rearing on its own. In terms of humans it is the most important grain in the world.

WINNING

To win is psychological and you need to feel it for it to be a reality. You can be miserable with 30 club wins per year. Believe me, if you time a good one into the UK from the Barcelona International you are a winner. It is all relative, so do whatever turns you on.

WOMEN

Few women sell birds and boast of their achievements with them. Suffice to say that many women are the chief architects of the men's success with the birds. Women often have the gentle touch and dedication required. Eddie Newcombe wrote that my mother was the best lady fancier in the world, but yes or no, she was good. Women are not always drawn by their egos to political excellence, but we have room for them in high, high places.

WRITING

With words we take ourselves through print and reach out to others with relative permanence, especially in books. My words keep me occupied and others enjoy them when I tell about racing from 71 to 879 miles into the UK. At the moment I can see the intrinsic quality of the mind of Liam O'Comain and Zsolt Talaber.

VAN WILDEMEERSCH (FRANS)

Birds of this origin are popular. Remember if they are not direct they are not Wildies, only Wildemeersch-based at best. Walters & Broadhurst were famous for their dark chequers and Leadbeater has some good ones. My friends the Barkels have some. Some of them are good, but as always not all!

WEBSITE

A useful information tool, but beware of bovine faeces on the net. I can be seen twice on www.elimarpigeons.com (loft reports and articles). I prefer letters and the phone rather than being a technology addict.

Y

YEARLING

I liked to test my yearlings at 466 miles in the NFC, the survivors being promising material for 2ys. Many yearlings will go down in the early races of April, due to their immaturity and cold north winds. I would breed out of all my yearlings, as I never knew where the next good one was coming from.

YEAST

I always mixed brewer's yeast onto my corn mix in a tin. I first came across it in the book '101 Methods' and Dorothy brought the tip back from Malta. Yeast is noted for its proteins, B vitamins and minerals and my racers always had it. In fact my mix did not look like corn at all.

YARDS PER MINUTE

We are all familiar with YPM as an expression of a pigeon's velocity home. Of course, the highest velocity denotes the winner. For my purposes I liked velocities between 700 and 1200ypm. Anything over this I tended to think was too easy. I like races that test the stamina and endurance of the birds.

YOUNGSTERS

A young bird should be strong and vigorous, and this comes from good racing management of the stock. At the marathon distance for old birds very few of your lovely-looking young birds will make the grade – they will nearly all be lost before Barcelona.

YORK

We are lucky in York in that we can fly marathon distances (over 700 miles) from France and Spain. We have some very good sprint men and the celebrated Brian Denney of Strensall. In 1977 in my first young bird race my birds were 1st, 2nd, 4th into York – I was hooked and I can see them in my mind's eye now!

YORKSHIRE MIDDLE ROUTE FEDERATION

Now a combine, this is a nice big organisation sending more than some so-called Nationals. In my youth I loved racing in it, with its large birdage and radius and won it three times in the Western Section. My birds were then winning from 71 miles upwards; the same strain is now doing well in marathons. The creation of a strain is the finest thing you can do with pigeons!

YOUTH

An old fancier, Cyril Frankland, once said 'You can't beat youth'. To a degree he was correct as many birds are finished by the age of 4. Men between the ages of 20 and 40 shall be going at it big time.

YOLK

This is the yellow, nutritious food supply for the young pigeon. Sometimes eggs have two and sometimes none. It is a modern idea to give pigeons canary food, eg EMP, and I bet this is good mixed with the yeast.

YELLOW

A colour associated with the Kirkpatricks and nice to look at. My birds were mainly yellow-feathered, ie of a tight, silky type texture and structure and finish.

YOGURT

A 'natural' probiotic yogurt I would say would be good for the intestinal flora of the birds.

Z

ZEAL

Frank Kay of Bolton shows a great deal of enthusiasm and zest for beating Barcelona at 870 miles with his team of birds. In due course he will do this if he keeps at it and can become famous because of it. His fanaticism can take him far!

ZEN

The Zen experience is best described as a trance-like meditative state often accompanied by insights and intuitions. It does not always suit the Western psyche with its object orientation, but it suits me and I often experience it for the better.

ZENITH

I feel as though I am approaching the highest point in my pigeon career, my zenith (not my nadir).

ZEOLITE

A mineral-laden substance marketed by Osmonds for pigeons.

ZSOLT TALABER

This Hungarian vet is an intellectual scientific genius of pigeon books. He is compulsive reading for the intelligent fancier. Read his books now!

ZYGOTE

The cells in the fertilised egg multiply and form a primordial pigeon in the form of a Zygote.

ZOO

For a short while in 1974 I was a bird zoo keeper at Drayton Manor Park. I shared a caravan with the chimpanzee man, who became mentally ill and was sectioned. I got the sack, chiefly because I told the manager off in front of his deputy and his wife. The 'ape' man did some way-out paintings inspired by David Bowie. I recall scoffing bird food (nuts and raisins) for my breakfast – I eat these to this day!

FIVE

The monthly cycle

JANUARY

Your early young birds will need ringing at say seven days of age. Record the details in your BHW Stud Book pair pages. This will be a very handy record of your families. Check after ten days to see if the eggs are fertile – with experience this can be done by the look and weight of the egg. Hold the egg up to the light and you will see the developing embryo. If clear, take the eggs away from the stock hen to let her lay again.

Food for the stock birds at this time is hoppers of layers' pellets, and a high protein mix with Hormoform, Red Band and some peanuts. I recommend Gem Matrix for the birds to peck at. Allow the stock birds into the aviary every day, where they can soak up the rain and any winter sunshine. Aviaries with a closed top are not good enough. All should be peace and harmony in the stock loft. Bed the stock down on some Easibed and shavings, for warmth and comfort.

The birds in the race loft should be nearly through the moult now. If separated, let the birds out on alternate days. If racing marathon and long races, let them field and sit on wires for total contentment in the area around the loft. The birds become very much on their instincts. This is what Neil Bush (see his 700-mile results since 1982) and I have done. Remember 'distance' starts at 500 miles. Look out now for hen sparrowhawks and feral cats. When weaning young birds at say 28 days, place in clean Easibed and shavings with plenty of food and water (same feed as the racers). No daft young bird mixes are necessary, give all the racers and young the same feed. I had my racers and young birds in the same loft on open loft at all times. My open young bird race results in York still stand.

FEBRUARY

As I write this it is the 25th January and I am 61 today. As it happens I am listening to Lady Gaga. This month lads and lasses, please keep the ice off the drinkers. Allow your weaned young birds to come and go out of the loft. Beware of sparrowhawks (females) and cats. Many will have paired their racers: this is the trend. For natural racing or partial widowhood I prefer love mates; it is so simple to let the birds run together. Some of the sprint boys will have heating in the lofts. Not for me this early form, and I do not pair racers until March. My latest was 16th April, when I had the first two birds into York from the Saintes National. Treat against worms with Moxidectin, Baycox for coccidiosis and use either Flagyl, Ronidasole or Dimetriadazole whilst on eggs against canker. When weaning young birds, ring with a telephone number ring; it saves wing stamping. Place one drop of 0.8% Ivermectin in the back of the neck. This comes from Vetrapharm. Allow your race birds to range the skies at will – sharpens them up with the hawks! Feeding of the race birds is high protein mix when you call them in, eg Bamfords' Premier Gold and hoppers of layers' pellets at all times. Allow the natural young birds out with the old – this will wise them up. No training this month. Study your stock intensely and plan your future.

MARCH

Feeding for the racers is the same as February, ie hoppers of layers' pellets, and birds called in and fed on the floor with roller-bar hoppers of high protein mix.

During the first week of this month and for distance racing, using natural and some separation widowhood (about three weeks); you can open the hen's door and let them en masse into the cocks. Let them choose their own mates, the cocks having selected their own bowls (Dandy nests) and boxes throughout the winter. On each day open up the loft so that the birds can fly the sky and go about their business in a natural way. Love mates produce as many champions as if you plan and confine birds in pairs to the nest boxes.

Long-distance/marathon racing is all about ease and contentment. Keep your work to the minimum and that way you will have enough stamina and motivation to be racing at the top in June to August (the big races). Many fanciers tire themselves out early on – they take a knock and then back off for the rest of the season. This is no good.

Hen sparrowhawks will still want to fatten up on your birds.

As for breeding off your racers, if they are well-bred, then breed off them. Your best birds may come from these rather than your stock.

The stock birds are in full breeding mode now, with layers' pellets and your own mix including Red Band, Hormoform and plenty of peanuts. Give Matrix by Gem and mixed grit and minerals. Mix oils and brewer's yeast powder on your corn. Feed all they can eat at all times.

Young birds should be coming out of the race loft to fly now. These are fed the same as the racers – make everything simple. In this way you should enjoy your racing. Genius is simplicity!

APRIL

This month you can toss your birds, in good, warm weather only. Don't take the sting out of
your birds in cold north-east winds because you sprint lads are too keen! On open loft, one good 50-mile toss is enough to start them off slowly. With birds on controlled exercise-around-the-loft periods, give, say, four 25-mile tosses. Daft five or ten-mile tosses are too short! Naturally, the above depends on the condition of your birds.

Start the race feed one week before racing, using hoppers of layers' pellets at all times. Call in with a mix of Gerry Plus, yeast, Hormoform, Red Band, hemp and peanuts; Saturday and Tuesday with lemon juice on the mix; Thursday and Friday (or two days before basketing) mix garlic oil, Beyer's oil and Colombine 10:1 on the corn to moisten. The last feed before basketing should be as many peanuts as they can eat. Five days before basketing for big National or International races give ad lib Hormoform, peanuts, hemp and Red Band in the boxes for the birds and give Superstar Plus.

In a normal week add the following to the water: Wednesday – Bovril (a fruitspoonful) to 1 and a half gallons and E-Plus by Aviform; Thursday and Friday – Aviform Ultimate; Saturday – Chevita multivitamins in water. Before National or International Channel racing add the following to the water: Friday and Saturday – Mycosan-t CCS; Sunday – Vydex Super six; Monday – Mycosan-t CCS and Chlortetracycline Plus; Tuesday and Wednesday – try Rohnfried Blitzform.

Every three to four weeks treat against the canker strains on Sunday and Monday in the water. I recommend 10% Ronidazole to be sure. Have droppings and swab samples analysed.

RACING

On open loft, jump your hens into the first race, say 95 miles; second race – cocks at, say, 138 miles; for the third race send both hens and cocks. After this send all birds every week to about 220 miles once or twice. You can separate them for about three weeks if you desire to keep the wing in good condition and improve the condition of your birds. After 220 miles you can easily lift them into the 460-mile range. After this give three to four weeks' complete rest before the big one, say 700 to 900-miles, depending on your selected programme. For your further interest, just go to

Pigeons on Google, where I will help you!

I like my birds paired for marathon races, but they will perform well on roundabout or widowhood systems. The ultimate test, of course, is the Barcelona International. This is the last bastion of excellence.

MAY

The old bird season is in full swing, and the breeding cycle is well advanced. The full race mix is used at this time and early YBs will need training. Start to race and rest the old birds ready for the big tests in July.

JUNE

Now is the serious build-up time for the big races. Young birds for racing this year should not be bred after this month or they will be latebreds.

On the open-loft, natural system birds can be out at 5am and in at, say, 4pm (some are out 24/7). An alternative is to flag them at 5.30am for one and half hours and let them stay out at, say, 5pm for an hour.

Don't forget, five days before basketing for long Nationals and Internationals, ad lib peanuts, Hormoform, Red Band and a sprinkling of hemp with layers' pellets in the hoppers. Many people are reporting success when incorporating my methods into their own.

Open-loft young birds will fly and fly, disappearing in kits, like dots. If you have wire injuries, stitch them up with black cotton – it's easy. Many sparrowhawks will be no bother now, but watch for hunting peregrine falcons. Look out for feral cats and other vermin. Boddy and Ridewood do some nice traps.

Continue to plan the success and development of your name and family or strain. Enjoy your birds and your friends and look to exchange stock. At all costs, avoid buying in expensive stock (tightwad). Be ambitious and try the BICC, BBC and NFC races. I must mention some of the Welsh clubs at Barcelona and Tarbes (International) with the NFC.

Treat your birds against worms with Moxidectin and give your stock birds a tonic of Mycosan-Tccs. Study your stock, learn each individual, focus them in your mind. At this juncture, formulate a long-term plan for your birds – where are you going? What are your aims? In long races, learn the art of quiet patience, perhaps over days.

Finally, take pleasure in the lovely summer days, when you can be at one with the nature that surrounds us and absorbs us all into itself. On a philosophical note, so long.

JULY

Now you will be heavily into young bird racing and training. If you can get your young birds to the first race point before the first race to test your birds before the list of racing, this is good practice. Look out for moths and other insects in the loft and if present spray with Cypermethrin-based insecticides. Before your 500-900 mile racing give two to three weeks' rest – no daft training to burn up your birds' reserves. Rest, rest, reserves and reserves are required. Consider selling a round of latebreds off your birds for funds and friendship. Look out for young bird illnesses or stressed-out young birds. These need rest, a light diet and probiotics/vitamins. I recommend you test young birds to at least 200 miles once or twice. Consider a few for the 300 miles plus naturals if you can – these are often young widowhood cocks paired to old hens. I managed to clock Little Darkie at 262 miles NFC Sartilly, she being a May-hatched dark hen jumped from 150 miles. You may need young bird Club points to be the top prizewinner. Fuel them up with Mycosan T, CCS and Blitzform. Tame them with plenty of peanuts. You can separate your stock – I kept mine together. Selling latebreds with a nice, sharp honest advert at say £300 for 6 is plenty. I sold out and enjoyed putting on the sales act. Life for many is one big act!

AUGUST

If well, I would aim to send your YBs every week. Consider a few selected candidates for your National races. It is preferable to fly lightness or darkness birds for the long races in September. After due consideration I recommend you send YBs to at least 200 miles, when you will have confidence in them later. Be wary of young bird sickness involving adenovirus, circovirus, herpes, E. coli and salmonella. As a last resort use Baytril, giving probiotics, eg E Plus and a tonic of Mycosan T CCS.

To combat respiratory problems and when required, give Doxy T – a mixture of doxycycline and Tylosin. I like consistent young birds and of course those that score – if they make three mistakes then I would cull them. Although my No 1 and 2 stock cocks were bred in September, I would stop breeding this month. Have you taken latebreds from your top racers for stock? This will keep your family alive. For in-depth articles please refer to Pigeons on Google.

SEPTEMBER

The old hens and long YB races are upon us. These are normally won by specialists, and often using their own darkness system. Reflect and study hard – Where did I go right? Where did I go wrong? Now that the moult is upon us, feed a high protein mix, layers' pellets in the hoppers and plenty of Hormoform, some hemp and peanuts. I recommend Matrix by Gem. Train your latebreds up to 50 miles on good days.

By this time all old birds should have been tested, and if so you will not need to dispose of any, unless you are a sprinter. Check the health of your stock, which may be run down due to breeding and moulting. Treat for worms with Moxidectin, give Mycosan T CCS and Blitzform as tonics.

I like Chevita Chlortetracycline+ since it still contains arsanilic acid. Remove the old Dandy Nests from the stock loft. Monitor the health and progress of your latebreds from your top racers and stock for your family. Some separate the nice birds – I kept mine together as a Community until January!

Do not get carried away and buy expensive birds in, yet look out for bargains and good exchanges. You know my hobby horse – cultivate your own family!

OCTOBER

Make a moulting mix which is of high protein, eg Bamford's Premier Gold, with Red Band, peanuts, east and Hormoform. Supply Matrix (Gem) or equivalent and hoppers of layers' pellets. Use a tonic of Mycosan T CCS.

If you have separated the cocks and the hens, let them fly out on alternate days – pigeons are born to fly, not to be cooped up n sheds. Occasionally let the cocks into the hens' side and the hens into the cocks' side, whilst keeping the birds separate. Keep on with the Aviform Ultimate on a Thursday and Friday and Bovril and E Plus on a Wednesday. Order and buy all your new sundries and loft requirements. Keep adding shavings/Easibed to your loft floor as warm, dry, deep litter. Mine was about a foot deep. Allow your birds to have natural exercise in the elements and fresh air. Remember, the moult continues until January.

Watch the health of your latebreds and plan to get them into breeding condition for December – March breeding if stock. Watch your pocket – breed your own pigeons, as most birds are just not worth a perch. Start building your plans and ambitions for the future. If it has been a good year, have you recorded your total management system, to reproduce it next year?

NOVEMBER

Let your cocks and hens out on alternate days. Watch out for fog, as in the autumn latebreds and hens easily hit the wires or are lost.

Many will be conditioning their stock for a 5th December pairing. Check the health of your birds with throat swabs and dropping tests. Enjoy studying and planning around your race birds and stock. Have a vision of the future with your racers and family. Which birds do you think will be successful? Of course we are still on with the moulting feed. Enjoy your friends and fellow fanciers. Watch for rats coming off the fields and control with bait.

The fieldfares and redwings may be here, and this month I had little trouble with sparrowhawks. Watch out for hungry feral cats if you live in the country. Is the loft stoatproof and foxproof? I used to sit our all autumn and winter in hard weather on a chair, watching nature and the pigeons.

Once again, do not spend big money on pigeons; better to improve your pigeon management and skill as a fancier. This is the secret to success.

DECEMBER

Carry out all the pest/disease treatments prior to mating stick and early racers. Apply extra lighting for stock birds if you need to, and unfreeze the drinkers. We continue with the open loft for the racers and enjoy our birds. In the cold weather feed plenty, as the birds are still growing.

SIX

Myths & beliefs in pigeon racing

THE MYTH OF GENIUS AND MADNESS

We are all here for society to make vital judgements on us with the language and thought of the day. I believe that if you sit in a creek all night in January waiting for ducks and geese with fingers frozen to the gun barrels, then you qualify to be called a little mad (or a lot). I did many such things in my 'hard' wildfowling days. I always believed in mind over matter. Today the snow is on the ground as I reflect on genius and madness. Similarly and in terms of our pigeon experiences waiting in a north-east wind for birds from Barcelona into Yorkshire is assisted by a little madness. If you stretch your mind to the limit, it will definitely make you what could be described as psychotic.

In my life I have been labelled both, but at the end of

the day we are what we are. Genius and madness then are just words to try and describe the undesirable. As a fancier, using the word genius, I rate the late Jim Biss as the nearest to its definition. Some of the great people now and in history, as we see it, are both mad and geniuses depending on what they achieve. In our society the verbal fluency of Stephen Fry is fabulous, the snooker skill of Ronnie O'Sullivan is sublime. What about the artistic genius of musical savants? The pigeon world is led by outstanding individuals, either great fanciers or intellectuals like Zsolt Talaber and Liam O'Comain. These people stimulate and change the consciousness of fanciers who are able to read.

What a wonderful group of fascinating individuals is the flux of society.

THE LOOKING GLASS AND THE ART OF ZEN

Introverted and introspective people have the quality of self-criticism and analysis. The great Jim Donaldson and I were commenting favourably on the need for a pigeon man to 'look in the mirror'. If you do this and sense an image of your own psyche, then there lies the source of much needed knowledge.

The biggest reason why we fail with birds at any distance is ourselves. There are many bad birds but the good or brilliant fancier acquires, trains and breeds good birds to suit his racing distances.

Auctions rely on the compulsions of men who don't look hard enough in the mirror to buy more birds and so the cycle goes on. To be successful you need only a few good birds and the Single Bird National Flying Club promotes this type of racing in the top events and up to international level. The above may be hard to understand with the extroverted Western psyche which blames the abject. I suggest you practise meditation and see the dawning of reality. As for me, in my innermost self I am an introvert, as many good writers are.

Just imagine the mind of J K Rowling or Blake – both geniuses. Sorry to lecture you, but I write the truth.

AND NOW FOR A DOSE OF REALITY – LAYERS' PELLETS AND PEANUTS, WHAT TO BELIEVE?

Layers' pellets and peanuts are two excellent foods for pigeons which have been fed for many, many years. If I were limited to two foods only, it would be these. I have known about them both for over 50 years. In terms of personalities and mythology, the chief architect of the mindset for peanuts was the great Eddie Newcombe, a living legend in Malta. Peanut popularity has grown in pigeon racing culture and they are absolutely brilliant for supplementing distance and marathon pigeons and also for sprinters. I bought two large sacks for a season and fed them to racers, young and stock. With peanuts the belief in them is realised in reality and the birds prefer them to any other food.

As for layers' pellets, most of my phone calls that filter through refer to them. These have come from the UK and Europe and I have been involved in them since 1963. The facts are that they are superior to corn in nutrition, cheaper and more easily digested. My method was to have layers' pellets in hoppers (metal gaz from Boddy & Ridewood) for all birds at all times. My main racing strain was built on them and peanuts. Yes, I have become famous for layers' pellets and the irony is that Eddie Newcombe was a good friend to Dorothy, my marvellous mother.

COLOUR PREJUDICE

When we produce a 'champion' or 'good' bird we experience it in terms of its colour, unless we are blind! Now it is a fact that pigeons will perform with distinction in all colours from black to white.

We know that any colour prejudice preference is for dark chequers and dark velvets, which are just beautiful to my eye when they have silky ie 'yellow' feathers. Some fanciers are convinced that certain coloured birds, say, types of red, are superior to others. From experience, this may be the case with the gene linkage in certain individuals from certain families. The stereotype is back breeding to an ancestor of a particular colour eg blue bar (perhaps an old favourite champion).

The genome of a pigeon is so complex that it is not frequent that a descendant of the champion of the 'same' colour becomes another champion. My practical experience told me to test all birds as two-year-olds upwards at over 700 miles and, if possible, at International level, no matter what colour they are.

I think that most of us will have our favourite colours of birds and some fanciers breed for particular colour traits. One thing is certain, and that is that a good bird is a good colour. Thanks for your interest.

YOUNG BIRD LOSSES

First of all, young birds will fail if you send them far enough. Having said that I can conceive of a 500-mile young bird on the day into the UK. Now what a sensational result that would be. Young birds are regularly doing around 400 miles. These are often darkies or lighteners, young birds on widowhood. Spend what you like, but most birds are not and never will be good enough at any distance. However, with optimal management we can get the best out of them. The key really to not dropping young birds is good health through correct feeding, supplementation and training and breeding.

There are many, many hazards such as wires, natural predation and shooting, but most should come through up to the 200-mile mark with the specialists 200-450 miles on the day. Perhaps the biggest reason for losses is the fancier him/herself. Yes, the young birds were not properly fit. I broke my first young bird records in York in 1983 and they still stand today. You have to be ahead of the game and standards are rising all the time. I liked an open, country loft for youngsters and in my last season, and as a first toss I sent them to Leicester, 95 miles, with the first nine home, vel. 800+. Now that's condition. Some of these birds are now at stock with 19 of my direct stock.

In my youth I was hell-bent on winning with youngsters. Today I like to see them to the coast, approx 220 miles, with rich feeding and large full bodies. A good young bird which can come from any pairing will take racing in its stride. Remember to keep them nice and calm and quiet at home. Usually the best people to do this are women, with their compassion, feel and understanding of living creatures. Sometimes I would be on the loft floor and happily let the young birds walk all over me. I also like the idea of a mannequin in the loft to kid the birds. My advice is to focus your mind on your objectives. and if you are given enough the rest will follow.

Yes, young bird racing can be very exciting, but don't burn them out on drugs and training. Handy though are Blitzform and Mycosan 'T' CCS. Keep off the EPO, Clenbuterol and designer enhancers, they are unethical and banned. Sooner or later someone will be caught out. Therefore breed plenty, get them fit and send 'em.

THE WONDERS OF PEDIGREE

It is so easy to write or compose a pedigree for a pigeon on a computer. The information featuring all the champions with a glossy photo can make a pigeon look special. Yet what are we really looking at? Is the pedigree a statement of fact? A DNA test might help here.

In reality many pedigrees are possibly the work of imagination on the part of the creator. However, in my family I could really tell by eye the results of haphazard pairings. I once received a pedigree where the parents were both hens! I ask you, what is real?

To reduce risk, you should buy from a man of integrity and repute, even then you cannot necessarily guarantee all the origins of the birds. In my strain I only assumed that the pedigrees of my birds were correct. What is a fact is that my seven foundation birds were all proven to be good pigeons that projected their genes into the present day. At the end of the day we have to work off our own good judgement and like all in life it is psychological and down to discernment and sense. Pedigree or no pedigree, we all like nice handling lookers, don't we? It is what you prefer, isn't it? Look in that mirror again.

ANTIBIOTICS

Once there was a craze to use Daytril ad lib for all manner of diseases. Yes, there was a strong belief in antibiotics for pigeons. Of course they should be used, but only as and when necessary. As we know, many bacteria have mutated to give some resistance against many antibiotics. A causal effect is the under and over dosage of the drugs.

My philosophy today is to encourage and tester a degree of natural resistance in the birds and this often means letting disease conditions run their course with the resultant increase in vigour of your birds. I still love to see birds in pen loft and well fed, these birds will see you proud at the greater distances. Speaking of greater distances, thanks to Dave Bycroft for his comments and I wish you well with your Brian Denney-based birds on your retirement. Note to all fanciers – it's time we put Barcelona Dream to bed – enough said.

Good antibiotics are Doxy 'f', Lincospectin and Amoxicillin with clavulanic acid.

ETS – ELECTRONIC TIMING SYSTEMS

We believe or do not believe in it, don't we? Personally I think the Unikon is a good system. There are some great advantages with ETS that inspire confidence – mastery of the system fosters ease. The future tells me that more and more people will enjoy its benefits. My judgement tells me that normally the good flyers will in the main win ETS or no ETS, although seconds can be vital.

Out of the huge furore and controversy the positives will benefit the 'sport' now and tomorrow. ETS or no ETS in clubs is fed by personal politics. I believe in harmony in the fancy and have yet to fall out with a fellow fancier. We are all part of the great historical tradition, and long may it continue. Ideally in 20 years' time all fanciers will enjoy the positive impact of ETS. Thank you all.

FAME AND PERSONAL IMAGE

I am well known in the fancy at large, yet no one knows who I really am. Such is the irony of being in the public eye and self-knowledge. At the end of the day, as long as we know ourselves that is the essence of the beast.

When fanciers do well – and I must mention some of the excellent fanciers in Wales such as the Padfields and Wilf Reed etc – they may receive publicity on the net, in books and through the media. It is exposure to the public eye that makes them fanciers, ie household names. The Massarellas are very famous and although a money-based outfit they really do promote excellence in the hobby. I have a lot of time for them, and they certainly helped me with some of my foundation birds.

Our Western society demands fame and elitism – we thrive on it. Some tragic people, like Marilyn Monroe, are mythological icons and will always be remembered. We know of Einstein, yet he probably was not the brightest – these are good enough to join the nano society, one in a thousand million people. Ronnie Williamson is a great, as was Jim Biss. A great man is Neil Bush of Amcotts, with the most consistent set of 700+ mile NFC results since 1982. I hardly know the man, yet I do admire his independence of the sweet tooth of fame.

Ultimately we must be true to ourselves and I hope you continue to find interest in my articles.

THE ECCENTRIC

Eccentrics forge a unique identity and make unconventionality a convention of their own. The psyche may express novel imagery, perceptions or original thought processes, perceived often in those mad, gifted geniuses who oscillate from one trait to the next or are a fusion of all three personality characteristics. Some exemplars from popular culture are Picasso, Dali, Spike Milligan, Ken Dodd, as well as many others who have had a great influence on mainstream consciousness. Many English people are fascinated by the quirky originality and whimsical charm of these unusual beings. I love them, as all my favourite people are odd, and I would dread to be regarded as anything but eccentric.

BIRDS OF PREY

Birds of prey are rampant in much of the UK and Ireland. More pigeons are killed near the home lofts by female sparrowhawks than any other species and many fanciers are persecuted by these lethal hen birds, especially in the last winter and spring before she nests in April/May. Many of my champions (open loft) were killed and eaten by them, including Mystical Queen, Delta Lady and probably Barcelona Dream. I have seen a bird nailed within three feet of my standing position at Holtby. Yes, sparrowhawks and cats were two factors which contributed to my retirement, along with others. The numbers have increased almost to capacity, due to protection and the banning of the organochlorines, eg DDT, Dieldrin.

A keen hen will walk into your loft and eat a pigeon whilst the others watch; once more Mother Nature's great wheel of life is turned. My solution was to fly open loft and to hell with it – this philosophy served me well. Fewer birds were attacked and/or killed by peregrines and other falcons. They are often used as excuses for non-return birds when we don't know! It is thought that brightly-coloured birds invite attack, yet there are many red champions. It is a fact that thousands of pigeons get past the falcons every year and may outfly them. Some Channel birds race for 10-12 years without damage. Solution – send them and take your chance out to Barcelona.

Arguably the most efficient killer is the goshawk, especially near certain wooded areas. My personal problems were with sparrowhawks. As for the decline in songbirds, today there was a charm of 12 goldfinches in my garden, blue, great and coal tits and lots of songbirds. A balance in nature is maintained with the hawks. My philosophy – keep letting your birds out, they'll get used to it, as mine did over 30 years of open loft. Finally hawks have a place on earth, along with all life!

MR BASKET

Most aspects of racing and breeding are open to debate, from inbreeding to eyesign. We all have our perceptions, ideas and experiences and our thoughts can be based on myths and false beliefs. Look at how many 'old' fanciers favoured an all-bean diet for racers (promulgated by 'Old Hand'). In reality we do what we think is right and if we are relatively successful then we are to a degree right in our judgements. As long as we enjoy and are happy at the end of the day then this is the stuff of life.

Our two International winners, B Sheppard and M Gilbert, got it right, as did the great Biss. In the final analysis and at the end of the rainbow, the one eternal truth is the knowledge that testing your birds in Mr Basket is always right. I would like to encourage fanciers at whatever distance to send their birds and see the results, for this is racing in the purest sense.

A note for my critics on the web and everywhere – most of my birds, like all others, were not up to it. If you send them long enough and hard enough they all fail – no exceptions.

THE AWESOME BARCELONA INTERNATIONAL

In reality many racepoints and races are over-hyped and exaggerated in their significance and importance. However there is one true shining star in the firmament, and this is the Barcelona International race. In this respect I am told and I believe that my promotional writings have made a difference. Yes, the race is gaining acceptance in the minds of the fancy; it is becoming the race to be in.

Brian Riley of Wakefield and myself have been successful pioneers of this race of over 800 miles into the UK, and I am poised waiting for the floodgates to open. I am thrilled to see that the BBC, along with the BICC, may also be having a go at the race of all races. It is reasoned that the extra birdage will improve the UK performances; my intuition tells me that rather than the help of extra numbers, it will be mainly the fact that you are more inclined to find that special and perhaps unique pigeon that it takes another bird or two; my Barcelona Dream was the only bird clocked at over 800 miles in 1995. I like the sense of the individual overcoming great obstacles of stamina and endurance.

To conclude then, I believe that the Barcelona International race is perhaps the only one that ticks all the boxes and whose prestige and quality is beyond question. It is the race for the purists and it is magnificent in its uniqueness, and long may it be so!

BEAUTIFUL IS BEST?

A beautiful pigeon is one that brings you credit at your chosen distance. There are thousands of lovely handling, balanced and aesthetically pleasing birds about, that will never win a race and never breed a winner at any distance.

Now the commercial world of pigeon sales deludes us into thinking and believing that the pictures on the net and in the magazines represent quality racing pigeons. Let me tell you that there have been two top pigeons in the UK and at the Dax International. It is all relative and let us all be happy with what our best can achieve.

One of the most stunningly lovely performance birds I have seen and handled recently is the Marseille cock of Trevor Robinson, nearly perfect in the hand. We have then our own individual perceptions of a good bird; but let the decisive factor be Mr Beautiful Basket and the breeding results. My No 2 stock cock (brother of Dark Destiny) handled and looked like the negative consequence of inbreeding, yet his line is in my strain today. Expert management will yield some nice-looking specimens, and don't pigeons look sad and depressed when half-starved and in poor health? You need to treat your birds to bring out the best as you would yourself – the best of everything. Then you can become a beautiful fancier. Amen.

BANNED SUBSTANCE TESTING

Thanks for the letter from A Walker, Cottingham. Firstly, performance-enhancing pharmacy will always keep ahead of the testing procedure. I believe this statement to apply throughout the world of sporting endeavour. Now the RPRA as yet does not list any banned trade names or chemicals other than in formation referring to steroids, beta agonists etc. Now what are the banned stimulants, as stimulants are advertised widely? I understand that doping tests may become a little more rigorous with feather analysis. So at the moment Mr Walker, you can use all the listed Chevita products and Blitzform (Rohnfried).

To reiterate on my successes, I never knowingly used any banned substances. What I did was to study and learn. Try 'Healthy Pigeons' by Shraag and the Zsolt Talaber books. Work hard and research pigeons if you feel you are an 'ordinary' fancier. There is room at the top for more excellence. Some of the abused drugs etc are steroids, Clenbuterol with EPO and human growth hormone. Many modern designer drugs are now being developed. Keep off these and always stick to the rules (which are due to be revised by the RPRA). Within the 'rules' you are free to do as you wish, as I did, to make your birds fit, healthy and fast and work your way up from Club to International level.

ARE CONTINENTALS BEST?

There is a collective, and mistaken, notion in the UK that Continental fanciers and their pigeons are the best. This, other than at Barcelona International level, is pure illusion and utter nonsense. There are many reasons for this and the primary one is that much of the acquired wisdom and popularity in racing has been disseminated from Belgium. We are besieged by foreign DVDs and sales propaganda kidding us that the Continentals are best. Unfortunately many of us believe this to be true.

However, I do admire the 800-mile second-day Barcelona International birds into Holland, folk like Journa and Brinkman – proper pigeon men and their birds, don't you think? What a belter of a bird The Smaragd ll was for Wim van Leeuwen in Holland – a great gene source still today. Yes, there are some great Continental flyers. As a fancier I like Emiel Denys who, due to good results and the engendered publicity and professionalism, is world famous. He cried when he reflected upon the Tee – a true pro.

Now then, in Ireland Ronnie Williamson is, at sprint to middle, possibly the greatest on Mother Earth. In Yorkshire, and at the sprint, Mark Caudwell is as good as it gets. At 879 miles Barcelona International, my bird is still there to be beaten. Chris Gordon's Tarbes NFC winner is a world great and so why go abroad when some of the best birds and fanciers are in the UK? It is definitely a myth that the Continentals are best. I say think again and buy your stock from genuine men in the UK; or better still exchange some. If you befriend a nice man, he will give you some. I hope I have made you think once more.

THE MYTH OF THE 'CHANNEL'

Fanciers have been brought up with the idea that pigeons which fly the English Channel are good and that it is praiseworthy to win from there. However for people down south it is just a short hop in the early races and some can only get 670 miles from Barcelona. In reality and attempting to see the innermost aspect of things, thousands upon thousands of pigeons negotiate the stretch of sea with ease, especially on good days with a following wind. I suspect that the 60 miles or so of water into Malta can be more fatal, particularly if you time from Yugoslavia as Eddie Newcombe did. Yet we know that in north-east winds with poor visibility the Channel can deter many birds, especially those with a total of more than 700 miles to fly, as 'Odd Ball' did at Pau in 2002 (a bit behind ('Tuff Nut' of Denney). There is one sure and certain thing, and that is that a lone pigeon flying from Barcelona needs to be fit and tuned in to its journey. I do not believe that the Channel is surrounded in the mystique that it used to be. Roll on the next 'hard' National race.

WHAT ARE LATEBREDS?

Traditionally latebreds are hatched after the end of June, although modern thinking may differ. Some people now think April to June hatched birds are latebreds. I prefer the traditional concept of a latebred.

Some people believe they are useless for racing, yet one Barcelona International winner had been hatched late. Personally, having been hard on my racers, I did not like them for this purpose. However, if you are kind and patient and ease them as yearlings into May/June races they may well reward your efforts.

There is a belief in latebreds for stock, and I can assert that I took them from all my good birds. As these were one strain, I paired them together. Today from this philosophy I knew many National winning men (proper Nationals) who are using them in their strains. I am old fashioned in this respect but to create a good strain should be all fanciers ambition. I am dogmatic about this phenomenon.

Final advice – always take latebreds from what you perceive to be your best birds.

THE LURE OF ADVERTISING

Pigeon advertising is the playground of the conman. Don't we love to see pretty colour photos of apparent champions?

Let's start with a simple fact – that the vast majority of pigeons are useless for either breeding or racing at top level. This contrasts with the media, which are full of 'excellent' pigeons for sale. The objectives of advertisements are publicity and money by whatever means. Believe me, there are many manipulative minds and egos behind the structure of adverts to raise as much money as possible. Some people think that a high price equates with quality; it often does, with a LACK of quality. When responding to ads you should ask many questions, eg why are the birds for sale, what does 'many winners' mean, what do 'distance' and 'sprint' mean, are the birds direct, pure or crossed or based on? Many adverts use hyperbole, ie exaggerated claims and adjectives, to describe the fancier or bird; bear in mind that there have only been two winners at International level into the UK.

My advice is to get to know a genuine fancier in the UK who may give you some birds, swap some or sell them from his best for £50-£100. I will advise people to consider adverts that are entire clearance sales, when you may be able to buy the top birds, if there are any. There are honest good men about, but beware of very pricey continental birds which may be bringing exotic diseases into your loft.

Having said all this, we have to make our adverts as attractive as possible, but they should be backed up by facts from actual races, stating the birdage and level of competition. Make enquiries about the 'firsts', distances and age of the birds, and be aware that we can design a pedigree from anything!

SUPPLEMENTS – DO THEY MAKE A DIFFERENCE?

Supplements are substances given in the water and food

additional to the normal food supply of pellets and /or corn. The market is flooded with supplements, some good, some useless.

This year in National and International racing there have been some brilliant if not unique performances. I will wager that in most cases supplementation will have been used, one exception being the Marseille Cock of Trevor Robinson, a bird with outstanding natural constitution, cleverly managed by Trevor, who is known for his plain and simple methods.

In my experience and from the 1980s annuals, certain supplements will trigger the utilisation of fats for energy release to the muscles, stimulate the metabolism and assist in the production of red blood corpuscles (oxygen carriers). Some supplements will produce a physiological and psychological high in the bird. Now in the 1980s I mixed a cocktail of Mycosan 'T' and Chlortetracycline + after experimentation with Chevita products. Today many fanciers use Blitzform and Mycosan 'T' ccs, which contains carnitine, creatine and other things. These metabolically-active agents are often mixed with sugar, amino acids, vitamins and trace elements. I swear by Chevita products; they have been properly researched and all work on pigeons.

The secret is that you can use supplements which are not officially classified as banned doping substances. Some fanciers may have the advantage of esoteric, inside scientific knowledge (I taught science myself) through the vast network of knowledge. Many of the supplements are being used in conjunction with pellets, Hormoform and peanuts to provide main fats for complex energy utilisation by hungry muscles. My advice is to stick to the known rules!

NB Latest on my strain: Chris Gordon clocked a young bird (cross-bred) at St Malo NFC in the dark (after 8pm) to be 4th 700-mile Club. Good luck to all, and remember good birds and management will take you to the top. Chris Gordon's bird was a cross of our two strains!

WHAT IS REAL, WHAT IS ILLUSION? LET'S INVESTIGATE...

First prizes: Usually when we start in pigeons our aims are to win, and to win as many first prizes as possible. We usually want to be the top prizewinner in a club and in the early days this is a sound ambition and a good motivational force. When we develop and mature as a fancier we can look behind the scenes at the real nature of things. There are many questions to be asked such as: How good are our competitors? How big is the club? How many birds? How far was the race? What was the wind direction? I always preferred testing races in north winds with velocities between 700 and 1200ypm. However, there are some obviously good birds with 20-45 individual 1st prizes, usually achieved in sprint or middle distance races. From my area, Geoffrey of the Masons was exceptional. In my judgement a bird with a good performance over 700 miles in National and/or International racing is the one to consider as a key bird in the formation of a strain: it can be a strain maker, not a heart breaker. I prefer first prizes from large birdages like those achieved by Ronnie Williamson in Northern Ireland. He regularly wins with over 20,000 birds, and most of these will be classy wins with quality birds. Unless the bird is exceptional, a win from say three members sending 95 birds should be looked at very carefully and put in perspective. In reality and due to the hypnotic effect of shrewd advertising, a history of first prizes sells pigeons.

To conclude, all fanciers should ask a question of themselves – what have I really won? What is winning all about? Is it at the top level? Just reflect on the fact that the UK has had only two wins, yes two, at the top level, namely Dax International. I openly admit that I would swap all my first prizes for one good bird out of Barcelona International!

SELECTION BY EYESIGN

There is something mysterious and compelling about looking into the eye of a pigeon. We can be moved by the beauty of the colour and pattern and make a judgement on the character and health of the bird. It is also akin to gazing into a crystal ball, in that we can project our individual natures into it. Historically, and in an attempt to control the future through the power of prediction fanciers have imagined that through certain perceived characters in the eye, success in racing and breeding can be seen with foresight. However, in order for this to happen these characteristics would need to be linked with a gene or genes which were required for winning ability. Now prediction by eyesign is based more on faith and belief than empirical, scientific evidence. I have noticed in certain families that certain colours around the pupil become evident and that good breeders and racers can come in all eye colours and types. Yes, there is no distinct eye type, as within top birds they vary. The acid test is whether an eyesign expert can look at just the eye in isolation and predict every time what the bird will do. There are so many other factors to contend with, eg racing hazard and the management of the fancier. I would expect the results not to exceed chance. I feel the need to become an eyesign expert is associated with power, control, fame and prestige, yet so many have been influenced by blown-up pretty pictures of eyes.

In conclusion, I think the eyesign mystery is strongly

linked with personal belief rather than objective and repeatable reality. However, what would we humans be without our myths and beliefs – and of course, science owes its existence to a belief system, doesn't it?

ONE-LOFT RACING

This fairly new concept in pigeon racing has gathered worldwide momentum and prestige. Birds bred by various fanciers are treated as a group by one manager or management team. They are often raced for relatively short distances and verbal hype is used to sell the winners and/or their progeny. I think that in reality these races appeal to those who are hooked on the internet and want to chance their arm at the relatively high hotspot prizes and monetary rewards. In reality, many people come away as losers. However, the one-loft phenomenon is catching on and is here to stay. The truth of the matter, and the core of that truth, is that they test only the breeding acumen and skill of the fancier; they offer no test of his racing and management skill.

We have a Barcelona Challenge in France aiming to compete at Barcelona International. There will be some good performances in this venture, but at only a modest distance of just over 600 miles. In my opinion – and to the real marathon man – this is not far enough, when you consider I clocked at Dax International from 687 miles. I rate the Barcelona birds that have to put in over 800 miles and cross the English Channel. Nevertheless, good luck to all involved.

One-loft racing does have benefits for people who either cannot get 800 miles at Barcelona or are unable to look after their own birds for racing. Remember, the whole essence behind racing and the successful and famous fanciers is that they practised the art and science of breeding and racing that are at the heart and core of pigeons. Long may this continue. You will never become a great fancier by entering a bird in one-loft races. Think about it. What is real?

PERSONAL IMAGE/FRIENDS AND RIVALS

We never know anyone, do we? However, we have our own beliefs and perceptions of a person. In pigeon racing we can make many friends and some rivals – I have a few and one or two I trust. What unites us in principle is the common good of the sport, and with this in mind I do what I can for others – it all oils the cogs of the sport. Some will see me as a know all, yet I am a quiet little man making my mark, that's all. What is true is that I have made a life study of pigeons and as a teacher I like to impart knowledge and experience.

In my early years of racing, competitive rivals were very important and one of the best fanciers to come out of York is Brian Denney. Now I do my own thing and keep myself keen in my retirement, still helping to cultivate my strain, especially in York. I can still claim never to have fallen out with a soul in pigeons since I was three years of age. My advice is to aim high with big targets and become as good as you can be. However, perfection is not attainable, only its journey.

I note that I have neglected the Welsh fanciers. I will correct this failing in my notes, as I have enjoyed travel in Wales, especially Bodnant Gardens and fishing in the Conwy Estuary. Good fanciers like Wilf Reed, the Padfields and many others deserve praise.

THE CLOTH CAP IMAGE

In terms of class consciousness most fanciers can be described as working class, yet different cultural types wear cloth caps. I wear one from the Lake District and made in the Outer Hebrides, and a Barbour hunting cap. It's not just what we wear, it's who we are intrinsically that counts and the values and principles that we represent. Birds are offered for sale at 'working men's' prices, yet many of this type of fancier earn over £25k a year. Believe me there is lots of money available for pigeons. However, sons and daughters of National winners can be obtained out of friendship – it depends on the influence you hold within the fancy. The most I ever paid for my foundation birds was £55. forget money, it is fanciership that counts.

Naturally a recession/depression will tend to hit people on restricted incomes and some 'working men' will be stung. Just think of all those good strags that are champion breeders and racers; remember, if you send 'em long enough and hard enough you lose the lot. Barcelona International at over 800 miles into the UK nails them all. The question of money then pervades the working-class consciousness; this is why I recommend layers' pellets at £6.68/25kg for all your birds, at all times in hoppers. When racing the distance (500-700 miles), cut out road training and send from open loft to the inland races. Pick up your races and the race to be in now (always was) is the Barcelona International. Your birds only need 450 miles as a warm up for this great race.

In other words, if you are a relatively poor working man, reduce your races and training to a minimum. Moreover, some of the top men and women reflect the 'cloth cap' archetype. On the other hand, rich middle and upper class fanciers (using the class stereotypes) can afford loft managers, optimal facilities and supplements. Some of them may even use a chemist – think about it. Wherever we are in society, we normally respect those with great results from small back garden lofts. My pal Trevor Robinson is one of these, as is my old rival Brian Denney. We tend to be suspicious of millionaire fanciers with large commercial ego. In conclusion, greatest respect should go to the creator of a strain from whatever walk of life.

PUTTING THE MATTER STRAIGHT

I do not consider Barcelona Dream to be the best bird I have owned. However, because of the magic of the International, he has become well known. In terms of his record, this stands in the BICC as the longest flying bird at 879 miles. I have never claimed that he had the record velocity at Barcelona in the BICC, only that he was the longest flying bird in the BICC, and of course the result was in 1995. Do not confuse 800 milers and above with those that have flown at Palamos and Barcelona in the BBC – this is a different club. In reality he was the first of three out of six to my loft at Holtby, on the second day. Jim Biss managed Flange at about 778 (approx) miles. My best breeder/racer was Diabolos, whose descendants have scored from 71 to 879 miles for me. I was (I repeat) a better breeder than a racer and I will be delighted for the people who clock in excess of 879 miles in the BICC, and they will.

Thank you all for reading and enjoying my articles which are written to stimulate and inform the fancy. We should be looking to win another International into the UK. Enjoy those birds!

THE HOURS OF DARKNESS

The truth is that certain pigeons will fly home at any time of the day or night, depending on the conditions. We note the two birds (two of five at over 700 miles) that were clocked from 747 and 748 miles at approx 10.05pm in the 'hours of darkness'. From Pau, 735 miles, I clocked Dark Enchantment at 10.08pm with the lights on (her children are producing today). The reality is that hours of darkness rule and a belief in them are a human creation of the mind. A pigeon, as far as I know, is part of, and responds to, nature. There are always debates about birds being favoured by such hours of darkness. To be real, we should cancel such hours altogether to give real chronological time. This will never happen, and I am happy with Derek Cutcliffe's interpretation and model of the hours of darkness (good old captain).

BELIEF IN THE 'SYSTEM'

We tend to think that certain systems, as called widowhood or natural, are the best. The reality is that we each have our own system based on what we think is best. Certainly birds on an excellent widowhood system reach peak form if everything else is right. Systems such as Mark Cauldwell's are poplar, yet you cannot be Mark; he is unique. My advice is to attempt to perfect your methods and if you feel successful, you have won. I still like my open-loft, natural system for 800+ miles in the Internationals into the UK.

HOW A PIGEON HOMES

We do not know in an absolute way how pigeons find their way home. We have done scientific experiments to examine the question, but we are still ignorant and always will be. Humans don't know; they only think they do. The theories are interesting enough, eg extra-sensory perception, landmarks, sense of smell, magnetic field, the sun, etc. These will evolve and change with the scientific model of the day. Most important is the fact that a pigeon does come back home!

USE OF BEANS

Old Hand certainly popularised them and in the context of these they are a good source of leguminous protein and can be part of a balanced mixture for the birds. Beans and layers' pellets would suffice for stock. It is a hard fact that distance/marathon birds need to be on high-fat diets prior to basketing (Hormoform, hemp, peanuts and oils). My father liked tic beans and he is one of the reasons I write today.

WING THEORY

A good bird has two wings, and a 'champion's' wings are always good on the day it becomes one. It is traditional to open a wing and remark. Birds will win in all natural types of wings and flight types. Theories are people trying to be clever! For racing, though, no more than four flights cast, please.

SEVEN

JIM'S RECORD PIGEONS

RECORD PIGEONS

I am now going to talk about some of the best and most remarkable birds. Some of the performances may not be records in the strictest sense. I invite comments and criticisms from the BHW readers.

Woodsider – This mealy cock raced by Jack Paley & Son was of Wescott/Osman bloodlines. He is Britain's long-distance record National winner, being 1st Open BBC Palamos at 861 miles in 1971. Some 788 birds were entered and he beat his nearest rival by 31ypm, flying 163 miles further. Here we have an 861-mile National winner – fantastic, don't you think?

Racing my strain of birds today is using the genes of this cock, since my granddaughter, Generic, was the dam of my No 1 stock hen Daughter of Darkness. I handled this cock at Louella Lofts, where he lived out his retirement – he had a small swelling on his head. He was paired to a daughter of Faith. To beat this cock you need a National winner at over 861 miles into the UK.

BRIAN'S BLUE

Now this blue cock is a proper racing pigeon! In the year 2008 he flew an incredible 748 miles 406 yards on the date of the toss in the NFC Tarbes Grand National race. Of all Brian Denney's good Tarbes performances, this is the one that appeals to me. I hate it when other birds in a race are on a similar velocity; I like the lone individual. Now Brian's Blue was the only bird on the day in Section K and was clocked in the hours of darkness at approx 10.05pm to be the longest-flying bird ever in the NFC on the day.

I am very intuitive and that night I sat at home in anticipation that Brian Denney would clock on the day. This is the performance I will remember in the world-class series of results achieved by Brian. The bird is symbolic of the tough-minded and ruthless dedication of this great York fancier and I expect B Denney to do well in 2010 at Tarbes International.

SYNDALE EXPRESS

This bird is a real champion chequer cock of the Chris Gordon strain and raced with rare distinction by the man himself. In 2005 he came at 725 miles to win the Grand National of the NFC at Tarbes. This is the record distance win for the National Flying Club. We can mention this great result in the same breath as Lancashire Rose at Pau.

Chris Gordon's overall racing results are without equal

in the UK as he is an expert at all levels to Tarbes – a man driven to be the very best there is. A man with a good pigeon brain, as his exemplary work for the RPRA demonstrates. Anyone with marathon aspirations can use Syndale Express as the epitome of racing excellence. The feat of this bird is much greater than my words indicate – the embodiment of excellence. Just imagine winning the NFC at 725 miles!

RILEY'S DUCHESS

It is my pleasure to talk about the best hen that ever flew into Yorkshire. She was a largish blue hen raced by the great individual Brian Riley from the Wakefield area. A most singular man, by all accounts, and an absolute whiz at the extreme distances with a small entry.

The Duchess was 1st Section K Pau, 218th Open 1992 and the 2nd National BICC Barcelona International 1993, covering 863 miles at 694ypm. Before this she had been 21st Section, 567th Open NFC Pau. All these were hard races and her probable flying distance to Barcelona was nearer 1,000 miles, since it was thought that the convoy skirts the Pyrenees. It would have been significant to have paired this hen to my Barcelona cock that I clocked at 879 miles in east and north-east winds. These birds are great lone individuals and set the standards for other dedicated individuals to beat and surpass in the BICC. After 15 years I am waiting for this to happen with an 800-miler out of Barcelona International on the 2nd day into the UK. I emphasise it must be International, as this is as good as you can get in the UK.

Well done Brian, you are a great pioneer of endurance, marathon racing over 800 miles into the UK, and long will you be remembered.

BARCELONA MIRACLE

This magnificent silver mealy cock was raced by A Demaret from Ottignies, Belgium. The bird won the great Barcelona race twice in 1962 from 3,300 birds and 1963 from 3,599 birds. He was rung 2106367/58 and this is an unprecedented and never-repeated performance. Don't performances like this inspire you to improve? Yes, readers, you could become great like this – think it, do it!

UP NORTH COMBINE: BOB DONALDSON & SON

A fast and furious racing organisation with huge birdages, the Donaldsons managed to pull off the incredible performance of 1st NEHU Classic over 36,000 birds. They had the top three positions in the UNC, a feat which was unprecedented in the 104-year history of the organisation. At Folkestone old bird race, 310 miles, they were 1st, 2nd and 3rd on 1737, 1733 and 1732 with 25,466 birds. I would think that they were glowing with pride, and radiant with self-satisfaction, and they should be regarded as heroes in the north-east of England. May I draw your attention to the Sportsman Flying club which are to join the NFC in 2010.

STORM QUEEN AND JUBILEE EXPRESS

These great hens were bred and raced by Ritchie & Whyte of Fraserburgh. When I was a young novice fancier, Storm Queen was a dream and an iconic pigeon for me. She was an inspirational pigeon and held in my mind's eye with a great deal of respect. Jubilee Express was 7th Open SNFC Nantes to record the fastest velocity over 720 miles on the day. She was a double granddaughter of Storm Queen, 2nd

Open, SNFC Nantes, 727 miles in 1966. The bloodlines of these two birds are successful today, making Ritchie & Whyte historic heroes.

There was a bird called Siberian Star that homed from 2,050 miles in the Omsk experimental race in 1993 from Siberia to Ivano-Frankovsk in 21 days, 14 hours, 20 minutes. I find this romantic and compelling and feel the fancier must have been a visionary.

Then there was the great Gorby, 1st National Samara in 1988 and 2nd National in 1989 over approximately 1,187 miles. One has to marvel at the guts and tenacity of all these legendary pigeons and fanciers – heroes all!

What a bird was De Barcelona of Jo Hendricks. It won the Barcelona International in 1980, beating 13,665 birds into N. Holland at 780 miles. I believe this to be a record distance win in the world's greatest race.

The Super Crak Crusson won 3 x 1sts National – from St Vincent in 1972, Barcelona in 1974 and Narbonne. I bet you would like one of these!

A bird of Trenton blood flew into Fort Wayne, 1,005 miles, for C W Oetting on 1122.43ypm in one day in 10 hours 22 minutes 20 seconds. This last pigeon really takes my fancy, although I think a 1,000 miler into the UK is on the cards these days.

I hope you are all inspired to raise the bar of excellence and to push the boundaries of possibility with your birds.

ANNE'S CHOICE

In 1990 this great hen was 2nd Open Pau NFC at 734 miles into York. She remains, arguably, the best performance hen ever to fly into York. She was a 5y and a stunningly beautiful blue pied, 11-flighted bird. Anne's Choice was raced by Jim Wright, wife & daughter to a small loft in Heworth Without. She was so-called because young Anne selected her as a squeaker in a sale at Malten, bred by a Mr Boyes. Of mixed origins, she held some Clanfield Expected lines. When the fastidious and perfectionist Jim retired from the sport he presented me with the famous Champion. He also persuaded me to go into proper National racing. Anne's choice lived out her remaining years (12) in my stock loft a Holtby. On her death her ring went on to a daughter of my Dark Enchantment (02) which should be breeding today. The NFC position has yet to be bettered at York after 20 years of trying. It could be you! Keep at it boys. I will never forget the sporting generosity of Jim Wright.

THE MARSEILLE COCK

This outstanding mealy specimen was raced by Mr & Mrs Trevor Robinson of Patrington. Before Trevor won the BICC Marseille National with this bird; we examined it and his hen in the comfort of my room. He was one of the most beautiful birds, in the hand, I have seen. Now Trevor can claim the longest flying win at 748 miles in the BICC. It really was a seminal performance.

Previously the cock had been warmed up at Tarbes in '07 at NFC, being the 4th bird in the averages up to Tarbes. Interestingly the mealy cock was paired to the '53' bred by myself and 2nd in '07 in the averages of the four NFC races up to Tarbes.

Trevor's friend, Mr Cooper, will be pleased as he bred the bird at his loft from a combination of his own birds and Trevor's. Yes, the bird is of mixed origins (like most birds). We discussed the preparation of the bird prior to Marseille and he was basketed with a big young bird and keen on the '53' hen. Trevor is fairly modest and cool but was more than pleased with the result and will be preserved in history and folklore.

Naturally, all recorded details of apparent 'facts' are open to correction, analysis, update and debate. From a critique by Dave Bycroft of York, I am now inspired to extend my Barcelona Challenge to include the highest velocity of a pigeon on the third day at over 1,000 miles into the UK in the Barcelona International race. The rationale behind this is to set a serious challenge to fancier and bird, which may be possible!

The following list is thanks to Squills and may prove of interest to you. You will perhaps agree that they are all good performances as follows (no absolute accuracy of information is claimed by me):

40 miles – East Croydon race, East Anglia Federation, 1965: A Vidgeon & Son, Wickford, velocity 3229 (110mph).

646 miles (two birds on day) – Lerwick race, Portsmouth NE Federation, 1994: Desmond Coulter, velocities 1348.6 and 1286.4.

751 miles – (on the day) – Lulea race, 1951, liberated 0100hrs, flying time 15 hours 52 minutes to Ystrad, Sweden: Edfelt & Wahlstrom, velocity 1400 approx.

864 miles – Palamos race, British Barcelona club, 1991: R G Wales, Malton, North Yorkshire, velocity 965.

911 miles – All Japan Champion, Kure Federation, 1974: H Oda, velocity 976.

1,013 miles – Palamos race, British Barcelona Club, 1975: A Raeside, Irvine, velocity 675.

1,427 miles – Great Falls race, San Antonio Club, Texas, USA, 1953: E R Shockey, velocity 1125.

KING OF ROME/PRINCE OF ROME

In the 1960s I looked around the museum at Derby and spotted the stuffed 'King of Rome'. It was a blue cock, and it inspired me to contemplate extreme distance racing. Afterwards I would sit in Wardwick Square and catch strays on peanuts including the Revered Violet-Eyed Cock.

In 1909 the Prince of Rome showed promise when he won a race over 202 miles from Oxford. He was bred by Messrs Vester, Scurr Snr and Scurr Jnr of Tudhoe Colliery in the north east. In 1910 he won his first 456-mile race from Rennes in Brittany, and in 1911 was first home from Arlon 475 miles. 1912 saw him win the Rennes race again. Then, in 1913, came the epic Rome race. The birds were liberated at 4.15am on June 29th, 1913, a convoy of 1,653 birds. There were some arduous weather conditions en route. Out of 106 English birds only one appeared to have homed. It was a blue cock of Charlie Hudson of Derby, taking 31 days for the 1,002 miles and crowned 'King of Rome'. Then, out of the blue, on August 18th, a chequer cock raced by Messrs Vester and Scurr homed to Tudhoe colliery, a distance of 1,093 miles and 1,186 yards in 51 days. The bird was dubbed the Prince of Rome.

What a romantic and compelling story, now embedded in history. Thanks to the Northern Echo and George Gaskell.

THE TIPPLER

These lovely small birds are flown in kits of say three or five. They are often blue or grizzle. I recall seeing my first at Alvaston, Derby in the 1960s with one of Gordon Hughes birds. They are the singular most outstanding endurance flying breed in recorded distance. The old bird world record kit flew 22 hrs 5 mins on 21st May 1995 for H Shannon of Ulster. The top young birds were in Germany flying 20hrs 29 mins for Ko Holl, Mudau in 2004.

AGE

My oldest bird was Champion Diabolos at 22 years, 4 months. I can imagine racing pigeons living to about 30 years. The oldest I know was Circus Boy of Jim Donaldson, which was above 26 years. I would like to know the claimed world record. *(note: according to the Pigeons as Pets website www.pigeonsaspets.co.uk, a red chequer cock called Kaiser was born in 1917 and died in 1949 at the age of 32.)*

LARGEST

The largest fancy pigeon is the runt at between 3½ and 5lbs. The largest wild pigeons are the crowned pigeons of New Guinea at 4.4 to 8.8lbs.

SMALLEST

The smallest are thought to be Portuguese Tumblers, even smaller than the Spanish Figuerita. Then we have the diminutive Diamond Dove from the world of doves.

THE DICKIN MEDAL

This medal was initiated in 1943 by Maria Dickin to honour the work of animals in war. It is a large, bronze medallion bearing the words 'For Gallantry' and 'We also Serve' within a laurel wreath, carried on a ribbon of striped green, dark brown, and pale blue. Traditionally, the medal is presented by the Lord Mayor of the City of London. It has become recognised as the animal's 'Victoria Cross'.

From the World War ll era, in 1943 Winkie was the first pigeon to be awarded the medal. It flew 120 miles from a crashed bomber to deliver an SOS.

In 1946 GI Joe, a messenger pigeon, was the only American bird or animal to be awarded the medal in World War ll. The US Air Force was to bomb the city of Calvi Risorta in Italy at 11 am on 18th October, 1943. however, British troops captured the city at 10am and attempts to cancel the raid by radio failed. GI Joe, which had been borrowed from the American airfield earlier and released with a message to stop the raid, arrived as the bombers were about to take off. An estimated 1,000 British troops could have died if the bombing had gone ahead.

In all, 32 pigeons were awarded the medal in World War ll.

EIGHT

THE INNERMOST THOUGHTS OF JIM EMERTON

PLANNING FOR THE FUTURE

One of the essential elements is the fancier's vision of success with the birds in the future. Whether sprinting, middle or ultra-long distance (over 700 miles), it is of categorical importance to formulate a detailed plan in your mind and perhaps on a computer or in writing. A neat way of describing this idea is the self-fulfilling prophecy, where you objectively target the future with the foresight centred on your birds. To plan around individuals or groups of pigeons takes insight into the possible potential of each bird, ie what it may achieve in future racing and/or breeding.

In my Stichelbaut-based strain of birds I set sprint, middle and long-distance targets for myself and all the selected best birds that I could muster. Although I never won a National or International race, I retired content with my racing but delighted with having developed an inbred 'strain' of birds.

Inbreeding planning really does take self-control, since there is a great temptation to bring in fresh birds from other sources at frequent intervals, and this is what most fanciers do. This is the 'other man's grass' syndrome of action and is based on our fascination in the West with externals. Pigeons always vary from individual to individual, and I know of no pure strain due to the diversity of ancestral genes.

In a nutshell, target what you want to achieve with your birds and give exact mental focus to the goals, eg becoming top prizewinner in your Club, Federation, National etc. Good luck to all fanciers who enjoy a pint and their sprinters (up to 250 miles) as I slaved away, waiting for two or more years for my marathon birds to come to themselves. I hope you reap the harvest of your ambition!

BOOKS AND BOOK REVIEWS

My aim is to read every serious book on pigeons as they appear to the fancy at large. As a young man I read my way virtually around the library, with great satisfaction. However, not all can read, so knowledge has to be gained by word of mouth or by practical experience. I recently learnt from reading that the Continental La Sota vaccine can have a performance-inducing effect. If a book yields one good tip, it is worth reading.

Two books I have enjoyed are *Vets' Tips for Fanciers* and *Long Distance Racing* by BHW scribe John Clements. The former is a brilliant work full of scientifically-based fact and insight from five of the world's leading vets. Its international significance is underwritten by the famous Hungarian vet Zsolt Talaber. I recommend this book and I have given mine to Sid Barkel for his perusal. *Long-Distance Racing* shows us all what a profound and passionately analytical commentator John is. Calling upon his relationship with some good distance and marathon fanciers, he well demonstrates his fanaticism with the intricacies of long-distance racing. I was especially impressed by some of the performances of Brinkman from the Barcelona International. Moreover, the penetrative probing of the various fanciers' methods was stimulating to the psyche.

John, why not write your next book on 'marathon' racing, featuring my old chestnut, the Barcelona International? We have some modern pioneers in the UK, including myself and Brian Riley with Riley's duchess, both near to 900-mile clocking. You could also feature the fanciers who have had great success at over 800 miles from Palamos, eg J Paley & Son with Woodsider and Geoff Wales, formerly of Malton – food for thought. In any event, you should illustrate the work of Wim van Leeuwen, who was 1st International Barcelona with the prepotent Smaragd ll and his sister Smaragd l.

Additionally, the life's work of our greatest 700-mile racer, Neil Bush, should be placed in book form for posterity.

DOPING IN PIGEON RACING

We live in a culture where drugs of many types are commonplace. Some of these are legal prescription drugs, eg psychotropic medicines, taken by millions, and alcohol and nicotine. It is, indeed, a drug-fuelled society and many people are enhanced by chemicals in their everyday lives. In racing pigeons, the RPRA has formulated a list of prohibited substances, including anabolic steroids, beta-agonists, stimulants and other physiologically actual substances. However, the list does not specify any common or trade names of these substances, so that many fanciers (including myself) will be ignorant of the nature of certain chemical substances. We have an active testing process and procedure; yet to my knowledge nobody has been caught out. The latter does not imply that banned substances have not been used, although I have no evidence that they have.

Performance-enhancing chemistry is very sophisticated and may well be ahead of the testing procedures in place. It seems paradoxical to me that many fanciers are using what must be deemed legal stimulants. I confess to having used one myself, which I believed to be effective in stimulating the metabolisms of my birds. There is a case to argue the usage of any chemical substance available to the fancy. My personal judgement is to ensure against this position as many substances when abused would be 'cruel' on the birds, and I am in favour of testing procedures to identify any formally banned elements, particularly when practised before racing. I never knowingly used any banned substance, although I am ignorant as to what they all are. I feel I am not alone on this count and remain well aware of actual drug abuse, proven to have taken place in Europe. I conclude by emphasising the need for optimal management of quality birds to maintain health and fitness for racing at any distance.

THE CURRENT STATUS OF THE NATIONAL FLYING CLUB

I have always supported the NFC in its attempt to be the top club in the UK, especially in my earlier days when it was perceived and believed that Pau (735 miles to Holtby) was a racepoint of great distinction for the distance and marathon enthusiast. However, it would appear that the club reached its current historical pinnacle with the magnificent two individual Dax wins. I feel that the club is now in freefall with an approximately 50% decline in membership over 10 years. Naturally the decline reflects the all-pervading general decline in racing participation, which will continue into the future. I think it is very significant that the NFC is no longer particularly distance orientated, with Tarbes being the only racepoint of any long-distance magnitude. The dominant impulse in England is for sprint and middle-distance racing (up to 500 miles). The Committee of the NFC tends to be money and sprint/middle-distance minded and this factor is partly responsible for, in my opinion, a (hopefully temporary) decline in the club.

In writing this I know that many hardened distance and marathon flyers (500 miles plus) will agree with me. I won many sprints (up to 250 miles) yet would sacrifice them all for one good pigeon out of Barcelona (878 miles). I realise that fast, short races are very popular in the UK and for many good reasons, yet I see these as part of a learning process only, both for the pigeons involved and the fanciers concerned.

In reality, and in the present, we have a rival club called the BICC. Now this is as good as it gets in the UK with a top programme of International racepoints at Pau, Barcelona, Tarbes, Marseille and Perpignan. It is simple, if you compete, and only if you compete, in these races you will be racing at the highest level in the UK. I can vouch from experience that it is not too hard to do, since I do not perceive myself to be the greatest racer of a good bird. However, I can tell the bottom from the top, and therefore urge all fanciers to raise their aspirations and go International.

I must conclude by saying that Sid Barkel, warts and all, is a brilliant secretary of the NFC, and would relish the adoption of a proper International programme for the NFC. You know it makes sense. Any comments?

ARE PIGEONS BETTER TODAY?

First of all, I would like to emphasise that birds are as good as the fanciers who fly them, since they will not reach their potential in racing unless they are basketed in optimal condition. I was talking to Frank Kay when he posed the above question. Without any proper statistics or measured criteria, I think the answer lies in opinion and judgement of the situation. For over 100 years writers and fanciers have praised the performances of pigeons, both in speed and endurance races. Some with the appropriate publicity have taken their places in human consciousness.

Fanciers may have read my Hall of Fame column in which I picked out my top ten best pigeons ever. Naturally this was within the limits of my knowledge and of course there are others, one of which is Storm Queen, who was 2nd SNFC Nantes over 720 miles on the day. Compared with some other racing pigeons I would suggest they are at their current limit on about 1,000 miles, for navigation in a reasonable time eg within five days of liberation.

I get the impression that a lot of pigeons are flying faster with modern improvements in health and condition. This is primarily down to management systems, eg widowhood and roundabout as incentives for speed. It would be difficult to actually measure any evolutionary changes that may have taken place in the birds say over 40 years. There will continue to be great fanciers and performance birds, but I think the acid tests for today's birds are the international races into the UK. My Barcelona Challenge, the toughest challenge into the UK, if participated in, will find any birds that can race on the second, third and fourth day at over 800 miles into the UK. I do believe, and this will be tested by the facts, that my challenge is testing the birds to their modern limits of racing into the UK. Any further distance than this will not be easily achieved, although pigeons have homed at far greater distances into the UK, but not on a regular and in-the-clock basis.

In conclusion my basic feeling says that with modern management there are more good birds per level of fancier about than there were 40 years ago. However, what constitutes a 'good' bird?

PIGEON PSYCHOLOGY

There are various scientific papers on the psychology of birds and the excellent articles of Rod Adams, and I will say a little about the observational psychology of pigeons and the psyche of the fancier.

It is true that pigeons may demonstrate changes in behaviour when they come into super condition or form. From personal experience I recall that Diabolos became the most dominant bird in terms of other birds in the whole loft and what a super racer he was, winning the Yorks Middle Route Fed Best Performance Trophy. It was so easy to send and pool him all the way. The bird lived for 22 years and founded a dynasty which is still winning today. Reason? I had the foresight to retire the cock at 2y to stud.

I have noticed that some long-distance good birds (500-700 miles) are very quiet birds (especially hens) which are easily overlooked. These birds tend to travel and rest well in the transporters, and some of them probably have a lower heart rate. Yes, big, bold, dominant cocks are not necessarily the best distance racers.

When racing hens on a type of natural system, I particularly like them when they are reluctant to leave the nest, and when they become very maternal to a small youngster, especially if it is the first one of the year before basketing for a 'big one'.

The widowhood flyers will be able to observe all the behaviours of their birds on their systems and get to know each individual bird's (like humans) characteristics. At the moment my favourite bird is up at Ryhope – he is Dancing Boy, a stunning white pied (from the circus Boy line of Donaldson). His trait was to jump up in the air to me in the loft, I have never observed this behaviour before. I feel that he would have been a racing champion at the distance.

From the fancier's perspective you should be totally dedicated, when you will demonstrate the necessary characteristics of patience, self-criticism, focus, observation, calmness and fanaticism to achieve future goals.

NB – Thanks for all the calls from some tough-nut Barcelona enthusiasts who want to give Barcelona International a crack, especially the diehards at over 800 miles into the UK.

THE UP NORTH COMBINE

On Mother's Day, Jean and I found ourselves at Lindisfarne (Holy Island). I found the remote and rugged beauty to my liking, far away from the teeming masses of humanity. By chance and near to the coach park, we spotted a nice little team of racers flying about, and after careful observation their loft was located. Without trepidation we entered a farmyard and were met by local fancier Jim Patterson, who, with ease and gracious hospitality, showed us around the birds and lofts. Jim has recently restarted with birds from various sources including Helm & Knox of Prudhoe and has already had some federation success. He was proud of a hen which flew Bourges seven times (I believe) at a distance of 620+ miles. We exchanged details and I put him on to my strain for some distance/marathon blood at Sid Barkel's. Now the Up North combine is very competitive with birdages up to around 30,000 and is an organisation to be reckoned with. It saddens me that today with modern feeding and birds the furthest distance flown is usually Bourges, there being no races over 700 miles.

I am hoping that some of the fanciers in the Combine radius will send to racepoints like Saintes, Tarbes and Bergerac. Surely there must be some diehard fanciers who would like to clock around 650-800 miles. The NFC secretary, Sid Barkel, may be able to help and advise on this venture. Believe me it is not too difficult to clock birds from these distances, and with correct management of good birds some notable performances could be achieved which could, with the correct publicity, receive the international recognition they deserve. It all depends on how dedicated and ambitious you are.

This article may have rung the bell with some of you 'distance' men and I make no apologies for attempting to promote marathon racing in the UK. Raising the bar a little more, why not try some International races with the BICC, since standards can always be raised? We have never achieved the ultimate or perfection.

Reminder: the Emerton Barcelona Challenge – The first person/persons with the highest velocity at over 800 miles on the 2nd day at Barcelona International – will receive £1,000 from me. This is a 'one-off' award and is conceived purely to race the bar at marathon racing in the UK. It gives me something to do in my retirement.

CULTIVATING FRIENDSHIPS

As we mature, some of the egocentricity disappears and we realise how dependent on others we are at almost every level of experience in life. I know I greatly appreciate all the people who enjoy my articles and enjoy what I have to say. My aim is purely to tell it as it is to me, and if this is illuminating to others, then so be it. I have enjoyed the friendly contacts from individuals (some tough nuts) who are going to have a go at Barcelona in the near future. In 32 years of racing pigeons, I recall two individuals who temporarily 'fell out' with me and that was two too many, since I like harmony, not discord, in real life. The old cliché is true, you cannot please all the people all of the time and no one is perfect!

It is nice to say that in pigeons I have benefited by my relationships with some good fanciers, eg Trevor Robinson, Jim Donaldson and the Barkels. If you make a bit of a name for yourself you should never need to buy pigeons again, a practice shared by many of the top Continental fanciers too. It is nice to be important but it is more important to be nice.

MY HOPES FOR THE FUTURE

Although the numbers of active fanciers are in decline, I am sure that many will continue to enjoy their birds. Fanciers will always have disagreeable elements, since this is the nature of man.

The ETS furore will gradually die down, as the systems are tightened by RPRA rulings, and many fanciers will happily adjust to the new methods of clocking. I can see some possible compromise solutions if DEFRA moderate their position regarding the avian flu virus.

Many fanciers and some new names will distinguish themselves in the arena of racing. I hope that International racing, particularly the Barcelona International gathers more momentum in the UK and would love to see some good results in the North of England, Scotland and Ireland. I am not expecting my Barcelona Challenge to be won very quickly, although I may be wrong on this!

As long as enthusiasm exists then people will partake in pigeon racing, and one day it may well be classed as a sport. The secret is to make the best of it and the most of it while you can.

SHOWING PIGEONS

There are some absolutely beautiful-looking and handling birds that compete and win in shows, eg the Blackpool specimens. To my eye, the opals of fanciers such as Mr Robilliard seem especially attractive and would grace any oil painting. However, to win or not to win is based on the subjectivity and predilections of the judges, although the physical type of the birds should conform to the modern standard, which has a set of observable criteria.

Some fanciers dedicate their lives to showing pigeons and are masters at producing cleanliness, conformation and condition on the day, and all power to their elbows. The process often involves a degree of added social activity and can be enjoyable in this respect.

When showing racing pigeons, an important factor, the nature of the winning genes or genotype, is not visually apparent to the judge. Experiment tells us that some of the best racing pigeons in terms of actual racing performance never win in a large show. It is amazing, though, how lovely good racing birds appear to the beholder.

I confess to having shown birds on one occasion and scored through the wires, but after that I became a racing purist and never showed again. I see showing more as an art in itself and based on the personal decisions of the judges, yet in racing at any distance the bird is free to home or not to home and the highest velocity wins. Each to his own, and long may the show people enjoy their hobby, or perhaps fanaticism.

I must say that in the development of my strain I loved to see the beauty and two of the most beautiful birds at the moment (yet not in my care) are Dancing Boy and Velvet Perfection. They are lovely feathered, balanced birds of true marathon and distance breeding. My favourite is Dancing Boy, being possessed of great character and vitality.

PREPARING FOR BARCELONA INTERNATIONAL

I can only state the case from my experience of this racepoint. It is important, and probably crucial, that your selected entry birds have some time on the wing over the pond from such racepoints as Cholet, Pau, Tarbes, etc. I feel direct line of flights are not essential, since in my perception of events good races can orientate (by unknown means) from very long and jumped (up to say 500 miles) distances.

It would seem that the health, fitness and qualities of the entries are essential criteria for success to clock from over 800 miles at Barcelona International into the UK. Now when I sent six birds these were those that had manifested the best marathon potential and all had extensive periods away from the loft. It is known that my birds were sent in Amtrak boxes down to the Lyden Bros at Sandwich, Kent, and I trusted these two guys implicitly with my charges.

The three birds I verified were: Barcelona Dream, the great 2y cock who was on his third trip over the Channel, prepared by homing from NFC Nantes at 466 miles a month before Barcelona; Dark Enchantment, my little 4y hen with three previous performances, twice at Pau, 735mls, and Nantes 466mls; and a little dark chequer hen. All the birds had Nantes, 466mls a month before Barcelona and were sent swollen with barley and lined with fat for the 'migration'. My feeding has been well described in previous notes – fat and carbohydrate loaded with plenty of layers' pellets and peanuts. Many methods will lead to Barcelona, yet I like mixtures of Gerry Plus, Superstar Plus, yeast, Hormoform, hemp, oils, peanuts and Red Band. I would use Blitzform and Mycosan 't' CCS in the water, probiotics and also Carbobooster. Conditioning, I believe, is more art than science and what works for you is the right modus operandi.

CLUB POLICY

We believe in a society which many believe to be a democracy. In terms of pigeon clubs and societies we normally have a 'quasi democracy'. What normally happens is that the meetings are dominated by vociferous, noisy or otherwise charismatic or persuasive individuals, who are often running things for their own benefit. It is often very interesting how the votes actually go when the hands go up at meetings and to see who influenced who.

In my opinion, and at 'club' level, the radii should be open to allow all but serious defaulters and miscreants to join in the facilities. North, east, south, west, let the best pigeons and fanciers win. Some members are particularly protective of their loft location and wish to dominate races at the expense of others who should be allowed into the club. In some cities there are lots of 'small' clubs which struggle when a few larger clubs could be made successful and competitive for all.

In relation to the larger clubs in the UK, eg the British International Championship Club, I particularly like the establishment for '08 of a Northern Section (over 620 miles from Pau International point). I am hoping that many people will try and clock for the second day at Barcelona International at over 800 miles. Remember, the highest velocity of the first bird to do so wins the Emerton Barcelona Challenge and £1,000.

I may be banging my head against the wall, but I would like to see the National Flying Club introduce some International races for the future – then we will have a truly International NFC with strong world influence.

I hope you all appreciate my idealism on the above delicate subjects, and good luck to all the club officials who work very hard.

MY BARCELONA CHALLENGE

The Challenge, which I consider to be the toughest in the United Kingdom, is to clock a single bird at over 800 miles on the second day in the Barcelona International race. I am donating £1,000 to the successful person, or partnership, who record the highest velocity in this race challenge. The pure objective is to raise standards of excellence in this type of marathon achievement and it should appeal to other diehard enthusiasts! I am hoping to tempt people like Chris Gordon, Brian Denney and Neil Bush in Section K of the NFC, Section L flyers and anyone in the whole of the UK and Ireland, who wishes to be a pioneer of the future sport. As it stands at the moment, the NFC offers only Tarbes at the marathon distance and we have seen that this has been a relatively easy racepoint to achieve success at. To the dedicated marathon man or woman, all the other points are sprint orientated and too short.

Some of you will know that I rate the late Jim Biss as the greatest marathon and distance man who ever lived and raced in the UK: he managed to clock a bird called Flange to be 2nd National BICC at Barcelona at, think, 778 miles, on a 'hard' day, so it is conceivable that in excess of 800 miles on the second day can be done.

I will also assert in my column that unless you have raced at International level then you have not done the business at the top level of racing. At the moment the BICC offers a full programme of serious racing at International level and makes it affordable and easy for all types of fancier to compete. The Club sets higher aspirational standards than any other club in the UK, and you should join now.

In conclusion, I hope to be delighted to write a feature in my columns on the person (or persons) who equals my challenge.

MY FAVOURITE BIRD

When it comes to my favourite bird, I confess to being a big softie. Over the 32 years of the evolution of my strain some beautiful individual specimens have been developed, some of which have been photographed and seen by readers. This is often done by fanciers for reasons of fame or commerce and for many years – until 1997 – I marketed my birds. Subsequently, primarily for security reasons, I ceased to openly market my birds. I am blessed in that all my foundation birds could be seen as illustrating racing pigeon beauty, although, naturally, my judgement is biased.

One of my old gems was the Iron Hen, bred from two original DVH Stichelbaut-based birds. Not only did she breed my No 1 stock cock in 1979, Dark Destiny, but she used to fly and sit on my head in the garden. This genetic 'tame' factor manifests itself extensively in my birds today. The Iron Hen was 1st Section Clermont and bred an 8th Section Pau winner – over 700 miles – in the early 1980s. When paired to her inbred brother, Iron Man, they bred Dark Destiny, the best DVH-based cock I have ever seen. I could go on forever, but perhaps my favourite famous son of Dark Destiny is Diabolos. He was stopped as a 2y after an incredible string of performances. This was a good piece of foresight on my part as his children have been excellent breeders and key players' in my intensive breeding programme.

For example, the Dark One was responsible for Mystical Queen and others, eg Eric (named after Eric Gibson), the grandsire of Trevor Robinson's The 53, 2nd Average all four NFC races up to Tarbes (722 miles) in 2007; Dark Genes, responsible for the great Barcelona Dream; Dark Dynamo, responsible for the 1st Section K Bordeaux – 578 miles on the day – for Shimwell & Son; as well as The 53 and Demon Seed, that was responsible for 1st Section 1 Nantes for S Wain & Son. All these were cocks, but there was also the daughter of Diabolos. John Clements said it was unusual for an inbred strain to survive for so long (32 years). Remarkably the birds themselves are inbred historically to the 1940s birds of the Master, Alois Stichelbaut.

Perhaps my most famous bird is Barcelona Dream, already mentioned. My current favourite is the white pied, Dancing Boy, as this vital little bird would jump up and down to see me in the loft.

PAIRING UP

In pursuit of my long/extreme distance ambitions, I normally paired the racers together in the first week of March, and the stock on 5th December. Let me explain that the racers would have been separated in January when the cocks started to drive the hens to nest. The short degree of enforced separation increased the desire to mate with the sexes being flown out on alternate days. I would sit outside in January/February and watch them fly (sometimes in the snow). For this purpose I realised that Barbour wildfowling gear is not warm enough.

Since my birds (apart from occasional introductions) are all related, I allowed the racer to form 'love' pairings. Believe me you can never be sure where your good ones are coming from and free pairing in the loft is so easy. It is thought that natural pairing may increase the racing desire back to the loft. Any spare hens or cocks would first form part of the flock, as I liked to play with jealousy when racing.

Having said this, it is good for the ego if you select and match pairs together. I went mainly on the genotype of my birds, yet many fanciers go mainly on their opinion of physical type (phenotype). All roads can lead to distinction yet I know of no one who has been involved with 32 years of inbreeding related birds.

My stock was in a brick-built stable and never separated, with the inducements of Dandy Nests on 5th December. I liked to see nesting activity early in the year, as it pleased me. The birds had access to an open aviary 24/7 and retained beautiful condition at most times. To reiterate, latebreds from my National/International good birds were allowed to pair together. On rare occasions I would match specially bred and selected birds together. Eric is a good example of this, being the highly bred grandsire of The 53 of Trevor Robinson of Patrington.

In conclusion, pairing up is so easy from good birds which are severely tested up to 879 miles. However, I did select small/medium, silky-feathered latebred specimens for stock

PRIZE PRESENTATIONS

I have to confess that the last function I attended was at the Granby Lodge Hotel in York in 1996. This was an annual gathering of the North-East 700-mile Club and I felt like the complete eccentric, having earlier worn my 'Darth Vader' T-shirt. My ideal social gathering of this type would be in a forest, at the side of a mountain or by a stream, since these are the habitats I have enjoyed. However there are many people who thrive on such intense indoor-people gatherings and look forward to speeches and trophy and prize distributions.

In my opinion, and from a psychological perspective,

there is usually an undercurrent of controlled hostility towards the premier prizewinners. The latter can be detected in the conversations of the people attending these social get-togethers. Pigeon racing today is ultra-competitive at all levels and this attribute manifests itself in every way. Many individuals become famous in the sport by using prize presentation functions as self-promotional exercises, since publicity-seeking individuals usually make their presence felt in the relatively insular world of pigeon racing. It should be said that some of the best fanciers in the world do not readily court publicity at meetings, eg the brilliant Neil Bush from the UK.

WHY DISTANCE IS BEST

Like most fanciers I cut my teeth on sprint (to 250 miles) and middle distance racing (250-500 miles). The objective was to be top Club prizewinner in my York area, and on the way I aimed for the first four places every week. I was a determined, cocky, arrogant young man. At the present time I particularly like the achievements of young Ian Willis in the sprint arena, and I recall with affection his father, Freddie, who was a character and a half.

There are some great sprint champions on the world's stage, yet in the UK I especially like the work of Mark Caudwell and Ronnie Williamson. These men have mastered the art and science of pigeon motivation and offer some beautiful specimen pigeons for sale. I expect they engender a lot of negative jealousy in their flying organisations. We have to elevate our spirits above the negative morons. I recall, as a student, being told by Jim Prothero, 'Don't let the morons grind you down'. Like others in the sport I have to confess to some character assassination in my sensitive life. We all have delicate sensibilities and soft spots!

Back to racing, and I can assure you readers that all the sprint wins you can muster pale into insignificance when you clock a little bird around 600 miles on the day or up to 800 miles on the second day. In my mind I can recall my two hens, Dedication and Sister Damien, who came within six minutes of each other at 569 miles Saintes NFC. I had sent five birds from my ancient loft and they were 61st and 80th Open. Of more significance is that these birds are leaving their mark in the UK now.

You can achieve what you like in pigeon racing, but I prefer to be remembered as the creator of a superior strain (family or what you like to call it) of birds. Many will master the art and science of long and marathon racing (500 to 1,000 miles), but few will conquer the technique of forming an inbred gene pool of birds that can take their name into the future. In the UK we have some of the best distance fanciers in the world, and I wish that more had the motivation to conquer the great Barcelona International race. This racepoint is the godhead of racing here in the UK; it cannot be surpassed! I hope you are all inspired by this.

ACQUISITION OF NEW STOCK

I must start by saying that if you cultivate your own inbred family over many years, it is only rarely that you will need to acquire new stock birds. If you have achieved success in racing you may be able to influence others into exchanging birds or cultivate a special relationship where good pigeons are given. In the latter sense I was very fortunate to have made friends and contacts with Trevor Robinson, Chris Gordon, Jim Donaldson and Ian Dixon and my outcross introductions came from these people, in modern times. However, many fanciers spend their money on new introductions from many sources, eg auctions, studs and entire clearance sales.

If you have a keen perceptive eye you may be able to select birds of apparent good pedigree that will enhance your stock loft. It is helpful to gain the confidence of the vendor who, if genuine, may help you with your choice and perhaps racing management. For sprint and middle distance in the UK I would go to Mark Caudwell and Ronnie Williamson. For long distance and marathon birds (700 miles plus) I would go to Chris Gordon, Brian Denney and Jim Donaldson, since these are top men in their chosen spheres of racing and breeding. These birds also have the potential to blend in with my strain.

Whatever you do, be careful with your brass and watch for scurrilous practices, such as trotting up at sales and auctions, since there are many tricksters out there. In the long term good birds will respond to good management!

PEDIGREES

Recently I was looking at a modern pedigree of the great Emiel Denys of Belgium. It was computer-generated, behind a plastic cover, and I contemplated the sheer professionalism of it. Naturally the image of it was linked to fame and commercialism, since it was a slick product. On the reverse were coloured images of the champions, such as Kleine Tee, 5th International Barcelona etc.

Now in my possession is a 1976 hand-written pedigree of my foundation pigeon, Darkness, on a plain piece of paper. How times have changed in pigeon breeding! Pedigrees are good information tools if they are compiled with integrity and accuracy but these two factors cannot be guaranteed. Many fanciers base their expensive purchases on pedigrees and I am suggesting that this may be at risk if the actual origin of the bird is in question, although if you trust the bird and the fancier, then take a risk. Genetic proofing, ie a DNA test, may reveal the truth of the matter.

In my strain I liked to keep records as accurately as possible over 30 years and could compile a pedigree for the birds over time. Usually I could examine the young birds and perceive the parents of them. It rankles me to think that many apparently 'good' pigeon breeders and racers do not know the origins of their own birds or families of birds. This must cause problems in checking the ancestry of the winning lines within the family. I am also used to fanciers having to check ring numbers to identify their birds. On the other hand, some fanciers know every bird in their lofts on sight.

When I sold birds up to 1997 I used Boddy & Ridewood's hand-written pedigrees, yet in modern times we see extensive use of the computer. Remember, pedigrees are as good and as accurate as the compilers, as are all information sources. To conclude then, it is so easy to believe pedigrees, isn't it, when in actual fact they may be wrong!

HAVING A STOCK LOFT

A stock loft is absolutely essential in the formation of a top strain of birds. I regard race management of the birds as being relatively easy and with a master plan you can delegate most of the work to others. Fanciers may know that my birds continue to be inbred after 32 years of their evolution from seven foundation pigeons, some of which can be traced back, assuming the validity of the pedigrees, to Alois Stichelbaut in the 1940s.

In 1979 I recognised my breeding of a prepotent pair ie Dark Destiny and Daughter of Darkness, and having visualised the future I set about concentrating around these birds and their relatives. To keep placing latebreds out of the performance-related birds over many years takes a degree of obsession and compulsive concentrated effort. No matter what families of birds came on the market of temptation, I proved my objective – my own performance family.

I understand that it is modern and trendy to bring in crossbred genes, as did Jim Biss for example. This can be successful, in fact very much so, but Biss did not create a type with many distinguishable characteristics. The early Janssen pigeons, although crossbred to a degree, bear similar characteristics, eg white eyes.

I enjoyed my racing and as a young man like to beat others in the field, later becoming a conceptualist by attempting to reach mental targets of success at International racepoints.

In conclusion then, the stock loft can be a place where serious dedicated thought is practised. My plan was simple. I inbred the latebreds from my best breeders and breeder/racers. Today the fruits of my work are little dark and dark chequers, some of which make excellent birds for cross breeding. An example is Eric (after Gibson of NFC) which is the grandsire of The 53 of Trevor Robinson and in my biased opinion, the best birds racing over five races in the NFC in '07, Tarbes being 722 miles to Trevor.

I could go on and on, but short is sweet. Be lucky.

SPEED OR ENDURANCE?

Ideally I like to see a synthesis of both factors in individual birds. Where velocity counts, egos are gratified by the win, win, win attitude. I have forgotten many of my wins, yet recall and quote the good to great endurance pigeons. I like velocities below 1200ypm, unless over 500 miles. We will never win the race we take part in every year, yet we are obsessed with the racepoint, its grandeur, kudos and awesome status as big picture racing.

Speed races, eg 50 to 70 mph, often depend on wind direction, velocity and geographical location and pack flying pigeons, hyped up on motivational systems, and produced by specialists. There are some ace fanciers in what tend to be races up to 500 miles on the day. The race we fly in, you do well to see one or two in race time; it is a test of endurance for man and bird that generates awe and euphoria.

CHANGE FOR CHANGE'S SAKE

I think the secret of sustained and enduring success is many years of dogged and persistent dedication to developing your own flying system and strain. A few people of note have achieved this arduous task. Why should this be so? There are many influences out there to stimulate and persuade you to obtain fresh birds, ideas from others and other pigeon cultural influences. I feel the lone wolf individual is often best placed to succeed in the long term. I look for oddball and outstanding individual personalities; Nick and I are like purist Barcelona monks in our inner sanctum of devotion. There is a religious fervour to our task which acts like a discipline. We enjoy the spiritual path that we take.

The corollary is that I have inculcated some modern birds and feeding substances/supplements into the overall system of management. Any changes are deeply thought out and reflected upon, and used on an experimental basis. Today's trends and fashions are yesterday's old hat convention. We have a unique system, so any future changes will have to meet selective criteria.

THE INWARD-LOOKING FANCIER

I am well inside this category. Western society tends to be money orientated and outward looking. The main reason why fliers reach the top is that they study and improve on every detail within a system, and this stems from the human brain. Starting on the lowest level, I set out to perfect my system and strain and I'm still hard at it 40 years on. Of course I realise it is but a dream, an ambition, an aspiration and other manifestations of the ego.

In my old age my friends and contacts keep the interest alive in producing another Barcelona International champion. The BICC is the vehicle that makes participation possible. I have looked in on the Irish scene and that is the country that will be highlighted to the world of marathon racing-in time – I promise you. When I look in the mirror of truth, I see that the drive and energy are born of fanaticism and obsession. Look in your own back garden, ask questions of yourself – is my system good enough for purpose? How can I improve it? Have I tested out all the birds to the limit? Do I really need to buy into the latest fashion – and am I good enough?

FEEDING YOUNG BIRDS TO BECOME MARATHON RACERS

The young birds are fed to appetite, as much as they can eat at all times. Flown out all day, if you can, with the old birds in a big colony, they will range for hours and grow and mature very quickly. My Unique Feeding System is on Elimar in print and in my books. The system is simple, as young and old are all on open loft-G10S in the hoppers and in at night with the mix in wooden troughs. You can separate old cocks from hens during racing, if you wish on certain days to gear them up for events. This is the main thrust of how my strain won to Barcelona International level. The essence in any field of life is simplicity, and a bright teenager could execute my system. Send your ybs up to 200 miles to sort them if you wish or a 100-mile toss, private training will suffice. The innate potential of all pigeons is borne out by environmental stimuli and is in the origin and ancestry of the birds. I believe the chief skill of a fancier is in the breeding and cultivation of a personal strain.

ATTEMPTING TO WIN EVERY RACE WITH A SMALL TEAM

This practice usually compromises your flying season, with some success here and there. You are noted for and will recall the good to great results in your career. I would suggest to new starters that they attempt every race in the club and fed programme to gain experience. With this philosophy you and the birds will likely to be past peak before the leading races in June/July. Many people repeat this process year in year out. Great or champion performances are often the result of specialist dedication on particular races. If you have been the premier prize winner in the club or fed, it may be wise to race/rest race/rest and prepare the team for one or two prestigious and famous race points, to really cement your racing career and make it memorable.

On reflection it is the history you make and the legacy you leave that have impact and gravitas. If you are out to beat others with birds, then you may improve by competing against the key players in your area, National or International.

AGE OF PIGEONS FOR BARCELONA INTERNATIONAL

We continue to enter all 2yr old birds to this epic race. With seven timings in four years, success has been reasonable. I reflect on the fact that my cock bird at 879 miles was only 2. Our system is good, and we are trying to produce another champion like Musgrove Addiction. For most people the key is in the race preparation of the birds – I like around 450 miles for all the yearlings, then you have some quality to work on. Really good UK birds are rare in this race, and the Irish one will be seminal, and its fame will radiate around the world, with dramatic consequences. Rapid experience in distance races is key to the maturation of Barcelona candidates.

THE PSYCHOLOGY OF EXTREME DISTANCE

The quintessence of this activity is cerebral, ie a sustained buzz. A chief motivational drive is the need to pit wits against race reality – all the conditions that colour a race of great magnitude. We are talking very long distances for the sophisticated preparation of endurance athletes. It is not something you can do every week, with a degree of rarity and singularity about it. I have to assert the masochistic tendency of it all, yet it makes you feel alive. Good marathon birds will seek food and water en route and have their liberty to do so in France or Spain. Some of the flights mirror migration, if your bird is bonded to you and the loft. Few great birds have lit up the skies with brilliance over the past 25 years, so savour them when they do.

OVERWORKING DISTANCE PIGEONS

When the main races appear in June/July, many distance candidates have had enough. If you race them weekly as sprint birds, and on their regime few will then have the stamina and energy reserves for race points over 500 miles in the same year. There are some notable, versatile exceptions to this. It is hard to maintain motivation on birds that have hit form in April/May in pursuit of first prizes.

The alternative discipline is to race/rest-race/rest. The central philosophy here is to build time on the wing, muscle and fat reserves for a supreme test in July. The bird is brought along steadily, where preservation, not expenditure of energy, is key to the marathon man. When birds have had enough of this racing lark, they tend to go feral in fields and towns – they often indicate this potential in the latter stages of their racing career. Fanciers often approach the long races in a most dedicated and specialist manner, and target a specific racepoint. In race reality one good Barcelona International performance is enough – you can knock at the door too often.

PIGEONS THAT LODGE IN MY CONSCIOUS MEMORY

In the sweet reflection of nostalgia, I reflect on the names of certain birds. The first is Riley's Duchess, which inspired me to Barcelona participation. She was 2nd open BICC over 800 miles for Brian Riley. Tuff Nut was successful for Brian Denney at Pau NFC in 2002 against the wind over 700 miles. In recent years the Marco Wilson cock was 3rd day in a tough Barcelona 844 miles, with nothing near it in the UK. With three Tarbes performances over 700 miles as well , the old dark cock remains a colossus. All the UK International winners are great, yet it is the individual marathon battlers manifesting great navigation and endurance that light my flame. They glow in the minds of men who dabble in history and folklore. Nick and I hope to land a good one this year to raise us out of the teeming mass of mediocrity. To me the sport in its purist state is made profound by the leading lights and their champions.

WHAT DOES A DISTANCE/MARATHON PIGEON LOOK LIKE?

After 64 years observing birds and 40 years involved with racing pigeons, I have learned certain things. A marathon pigeon over 700 miles or distance 5 to 700 miles looks like the ones you clock in race time, from these distances. My two key marathon birds were the biggest cock and one of the smallest hens I raced. There are many shapes and sizes that perform well. We like to examine pretty, balanced, small-medium birds and they are pleasing to behold to the hand/eye. In race reality, the inner qualities and traits of the birds are crucial to performance potential. In part, these are influence by heredity and the genome. Men wax lyrical about the external value of pigeons, yet nice as they appear to the aesthete's eye, the racepoints will show you the reality of each bird.

The philosophy, as a purist, is to race test every single bird in the race team. All ours go to Barcelona International, which in global terms is the premier race and is very difficult. Imagine the task facing Paddy Nolan and the other stalwarts in Ireland when they test their birds in the race of no hiding place.

A REALISTIC APPROACH TO PIGEON RACING

You realise certain truths as time flows by. After 40 years of experiment with racing pigeons, very few pairs in your charge emerge as good producers of quality racers. The potential of a good one is a fusion of nature/nurture – you must master conditioning of the complete bird!

There are many environmental challenges to a flying bird, including predation by cats, hawks and falcons. Many birds just stop coming home again and go feral. Your fellow competitors seldom become real friends behind the personality masks. Interesting how popular the people at the bottom of the result can be!

I doubt that the reason why a bird is a champion can be resolved by knowledge of genetics alone. The true nature of bird navigation/homing is not known by man. Aim to perfect the feeding of your birds, and all aspects of your talents within the sport. Enjoy the game!

SINGLE UP TRAINING

You may think this practice confers an advantage. In reality I have not noticed any ultimate difference using the practice. At the end of the day, all my birds will have to cover many miles of solo flying from marathon race points – a good pigeon will navigate. It needs to be fit, not just shown the way. Birds in great condition will jump hundreds of miles if any good. In the early preparation races I like time on the wing to muscle up and tune the psychology and physiology of the birds, for big performances later in the season. In early training tosses I like the flock that is racing home in a collective group. Many people work too hard in a physical sense, when it is the brain where most of the effort should be placed. We have devised a system where most of the work is done by the birds, which are treated as athletes.

A good bird has great stamina and navigational skills, and may spend some time flying in the hours of darkness – a system devised in an attempt to impose some order and fair play logic on the race for the people concerned, since pigeons can fly any time of the day or night.

SIMPLE APPLIED GENETICS IN PIGEONS

After graduation from the Royal Botanic Gardens Kew, I qualified as a rural studies teacher at Worcester College. During all my studies we hit on Darwin, Mendel and other scientists of luminous intellect. I have probed theoretical genetics, sifted it and applied certain concepts to practical pigeon racing. I attempt to concentrate performance genes and innate potential by close inbreeding to marathon performance birds in my strain over the past 40 years. By the same token I practise inbred/outbreeding to try and produce champions due to the surge in performance of hybrid vigour, as powerful genetic combinants manifest themselves in the offspring in racing progeny testing. I go always towards the empirical evidence concept of science, as the theory side of it is in part an expression of the psyche of the scientific establishment.

At my time of life we look to the quality of the birds, rather than abstract and professorial genetic theory. The most real and evidential thing you can do is to test every single bird bred at your chosen distances and competition levels. This pragmatic, existential approach will reveal all you need to know about the birds and your mind – theory or no theory, ie a personal translation into race reality. My ideas have evolved from the cerebral to the objective, external level.

REAL ENTHUSIASM

Some people dedicate a life to the cultivation and success of their birds. In this case, keenness and enthusiasm may grow with time, along with a belief that you have found the right vocation. In this way specialists and stars are created, in the narrow, insular world of pigeon racing. In over 40 years, I have perceived many short-term enthusiasms that are ephemeral and transient in nature. In modern society, the trend is for instant gratification, with as little hardcore effort as possible. I prefer a more slow-burning and enduring approach to the sport, associated often with the long distance and marathon flier. The concept is compounded by the long-term cultivation of a strain using inbreeding, linebreeding and outbreeding. Enthusiasm feeds on success, which is a consequence of expert management and cultivation of the birds at home. Race reality will dictate if you are up to the mark or not. In my mind's eye, the key to the sport is the human psyche and based in the brain of man and bird.

THE COMPETITIVE SPIRIT

You see it in man, animals and birds. Originating in the brain, it is the source and nucleus of inner motivation to create an identity and prevail. The spirit is the essence of all competitions where individuals seek to prevail, and originates in a similar trait to bullying. The trait may be overt or covert, yet it is there in human society and most social species of animals and birds, and may be an important dynamic in groups. A perceptive person can sense and feel it in others, where a pleasant person may be ruthlessly competitive behind the mask. The politics and business in capitalist cultures are based on it. If possible I keep a little aloof to the main thrust of it in the media and propagandist broadcasting, believing only what I prove to myself to be true.

SOLO FLYING

Solo flying is quite normal for stragglers, latecomers and birds that fly long and marathon distances. Pigeons are gregarious by natural evolution processes in concert with nature. All my marathon birds will have flown and navigated hundreds of miles on their own. The team, sprint man, will be used to birds flying in flocks, and small groups being reliant on breaking, wind speed and direction and trapping, with the accent on first place dominion. We do not train our racers to fly singly, yet distance will dictate that they do so in race reality. I like the great birds that become the only ones in certain geographical sections in National/International events. It is their singular individuality that I covert – the more unusual they are, the more esteem I afford them. In young bird training, I like them to home in singletons.

TOO COLD FOR RACING?

Unfit birds locked in during the winter, especially soft yearlings, may hit the wall in north-east or east winds if the air temperature is below 10 degrees C, ie 50 degrees F. In such conditions they may go missing or return looking hunched up and miserable. Ours are hardened on open loft conditions – out in all weathers – and tend to fly well. We never keep birds home due to weather forecasting. In April I would advise wise caution, as you can knock birds right off form; the air is colder at altitude, yet I have seen birds racing in snow showers. We race with the BICC and rely on their fine decision making regarding liberation. Many ybs will be ready for training in May this year 2016. Cold rain will take the edge off racing birds – give Supersix in the water on return from VYDEX.

DO PIGEONS NEED FLYING EXPERIENCE OF THE ROUTE?

In my experience many individual birds do not need to have seen the sites from the racepoint, although it helps sometimes if they have. I have jumped birds 500 miles and they have done well in racing. At the distance, landmarks are not the sole criteria of homing prowess, nor is the sun and many other factors that are given consideration in homing theories. Over 700 miles for example, we do not know the absolute means or mechanism or ability in navigation. We speculate on the human possibilities of the whole process, not what it is in reality. I do feel that optimal condition in the brain of the bird may assist with orientation and navigation. I like to give ybs some homing experience up to 100 to 200 miles, and some give more. All birds are unique, and you chance your arm if you jump the team say more than 100 miles from one point to another. My partner and I always jump ours.

SPEED OR ENDURANCE?

Ideally I like to see a synthesis of both factors in individual birds. Where velocity counts, egos are gratified by the win, win, win attitude. I have forgotten many of my wins, yet can recall and quote the good to great endurance pigeons. I like velocities below 1200ypm, unless over 500 miles. We will never win the race we take part in every year, yet we are obsessed with the racepoint, its grandeur, kudos and awesome status as big picture racing. Speed races of eg 50 to 70 mph often depend on wind direction, velocity and geographical location and pack flying pigeons, hyped up on motivational systems, and produced by specialists. There are some ace fanciers in what tend to be races up to 500 miles on the day. The race we fly in, you do well to see one or two in race time – it's a test of endurance for man and bird that generates awe and euphoria.

FLYING FROM FRANCE INTO IRELAND

This can be a very arduous task for fancier and bird. To some people out there it is the epitome of difficulty and excellence. The normal limit has not been much beyond 500-plus miles in decent race time. I do feel that with the right dedication, modern systems of conditioning and scientific applications to nutrition we can go much further than this, eg in the BICC. I have two racing partners over there who are adopting and adapting my experience with marathon racing pigeons to have a go. It will be an experiment that keeps us interested and motivated into the future.

I think one really good bird will light the blue touch paper and ignite the fancy at large. It will possibly take some nice big teams of conditioned birds of mixed ancestry. It is all about individual birds, not just fancy names, as one of my best marathon hens was the direct dt of my sprint hen.

People have joined the BICC in Ireland, and with all the costs and marking difficulties some will have a go. The person who times out of Barcelona International in race time will experience cult celebrity status in the pigeon racing world – it will take a pigeon GENIUS!

A THOUSAND MILES?

This was the marathon dream of a few dreamers and purists in say Scotland. There are systems, men and birds capable of such feats today, in these very demanding races of distance measurement. In Poland birds are timed in excess of 1000 miles, and in Eastern Europe there are some rugged marathon individualists who are totally dedicated to the cause and the dream-the long migration post liberation. Men of drive and ambition will attempt Barcelona into Ireland to reach out for International greatness, and become unique marathonists and exemplars of the noble art. At Taunton, we have a breeding son of last year's Polish national winner, located by young Feeney of Dublin. It is an experiment with genes and inherent potential.

KEY CHARACTERISTICS OF A MARATHON PIGEON

A good bird over 700 miles must have the whole package of flying factors. To be able to navigate solo is a gift that few are given. This is assisted by race preparation and conditioning to stimulate the bird's brain. Stamina and muscular power are crucial, and the survival instincts to forage and avoid predation. Sound individual instincts are very special in marathon greats, and the total, being both physical and cerebral, directed towards homing to roost. Some of these birds are proven to fly at night, which challenges many scientific and quasi-scientific hypotheses and theory models. The exact nature of the migration of a marathon bird is nebulous – we can but guess at possibilities in a sea of dogma. I know when we get a good one in race reality that it has what it takes. It is all I know.

A COMMON-SENSE APPROACH TO PIGEON RACING

There are fundamentals to the sport that are simple and obvious. People tend to overcomplicate and theorise about the game. With 64 years around birds, I have learned some realism. Distance birds are those that race well over 500 miles, marathon over 700 miles-if they have not done this, then they are not distance birds, bred or not bred for the job. Good breeders are those that have left lines of good racing pigeons. All so-called strains and breeds of birds are a mixture of bloodlines – good apples may fall a long way from the tree. No person has won the main race into the UK yet, the Barcelona International. A variety of people, systems and locations will produce results with the birds, from the country garden to the millionaire pad. There is one certain way of finding a good bird. I call it RACE REALITY. The end result for all is the satisfaction derived from success, and even making money is ego-based. Always take latebreds for stock from your best racers, and new stock from proven birds if you can. By all means dream large and think big, yet have an eye for realising them. I know of few people who are not touched by fame and recognition in the competitive sphere of pigeon racing.

THE TRUE VALUES OF A MARATHON MAN

These are encapsulated in one race – the Barcelona International. For many a single timing is enough, yet others – a few men – enter every single pigeon every year. The aim is to pit your wits against hardened individualists in the UK, Ireland and Europe. You are on the spot, transparent and out in the open with this race. Only genuine, sound, extreme distance birds will be clocked, whether the wind and conditions are in your favour or not. It is the race of truth, where continuous and repeated results exemplify the qualities of man and bird. With our 8 timings we are building a strain on related Barcelona flying birds. The purist races for the love of the sport and the birds the love of home. These are romantic, traditional, sentimental and idealistic values of the archetypal, traditional marathon sage. Long may they personify what is noble and great about the sport, before the money ethic rears its ugly head.

STARTING A BARCELONA FAMILY

In theory this is so easy to do: the practice of it is so difficult. People praise the race, yet to be able to enter birds that are conditioned for the purpose takes knowledge, skill and expertise, and perhaps years and years. To some it remains their wildest dream, a figment of the imagination. We have bred from our 8 clockings and pair the progeny together to inbreed to Barcelona International performance levels. The concept is translating into practical reality, and it rests on a single criterion: we send every single pigeon to the race. Succeed or fail this is our modus operandi. The 2016 race into the UK was the hardest in my memory, and provided strain-building birds of great quality and genetic potential. The race is open for all who have a real desire and sense of purpose to chance their arm in the race that they will probably never win, but is so exciting.

A CRAZE FOR CERTAIN BIRDS

The desire and want for birds is often generated by others and commercial publicity. To satisfy our cravings, we can make wise choices in the selection process – best as gifts from the top men. I have bought a few over recent years, and trust my selections. However, much depends upon the abilities of the fanciers who were supplied by me. It is the breeding and racing system you need to perfect, since good results are the product of it. 25 years of solid dedication to marathon tasks should see some results with a good bird or two. At Barcelona only good birds will be clocked, as there are no flukes in this, the premier race. We have a great system in place, yet find it a very difficult race into the English West Country. Fortunes come and go, and on a global level to satiate our desires for new birds, as wonder stars of the day. My chaps need to get down now to some serious progeny testing.

IN OUR LOFT TODAY

Our 43 birds are out each day, relishing the September sunshine. Baths assist the moult, which is in full swing, aided by a very rich diet of our own making. We have six special latebreds being treated to offset possible bacteria. The 24 surviving ybs have been harvesting field barley for 2 days and are loving semi-feral life. If they get to Barcelona, the foraging instincts will kick in then. It is a question of maintaining health and maximum growth at all times, and keeping, rugged outdoor condition until breeding and racing time. We got four from the hardest Barcelona International for 25 years in the UK. All birds are being fed plenty of our special creation mixture, and lack nothing. We hope to supply the network with a few birds from our Barcelona family – every bird goes to it.

SPOTTING A FUTURE CHAMPION PIGEON MAN

I mentor a number of different people in the pigeon game. Reading their notes and listening to them, I can form a shrewd perception of their potential. Some may make real marathon men over 700 miles. The key element is not the particular birds, although good ones are rare. They must be dedicated, ambitious, with lots of patience, and a strong sense of purpose and individuality. I favour practical men, with a keen intellect, and great empathy for pigeons. With the choice I would go for a countryman who knows about the weather, nature and the elements, and a desire for perfection and greatness. In the champion profile, there is no room for ordinary. Having said this, I encourage all my mentees and organise supplies of well-bred birds, often of my origin. At Barcelona International the odds are always stacked against us, yet Nick has bred and raced eight good ones at the measured 710 miles. The near impossible challenge is a good one into Ireland, where great management is so crucial.

WHEN THE OLD MASTERS HAVE GONE

Some racing men live to become myths, legends and icons of the sport. This is due to some slick publicity on the back of one or more good to great performance birds. When the sun goes down on a glittering career in the limelight, what becomes of the birds they cultivated from the sweat of their brow? In reality, the birds and the genes are transformed by dispersal, where outbreeding takes place in the hands of other fanciers who may or may not don the mask of fame with generations of the offspring. Some lines are maintained, to a degree, by inbreeding. In the hands of others, and with changing environmental conditions, the appearance and nature of the individual birds change over time in the new lofts and locations, and the type of racing adopted. I have yet to see a pure strain racer – the phenotype always varies, as do the people who breed and sell them.

CAPTAIN DEREK CUTCLIFFE RIP

This great old character died at the end of March 2016. Derek was 93, and in his prime kept a stud of Stichelbaut and Vanhee-based birds at Stile Lofts in Bideford. He was an intellectual, outspoken, and survived a torpedo attack when many perished at sea. A shrewd, sharp and worldly man, he lit up the pigeon press with his extrovert and colourful exchanges with Ken Hanby. For sale at reasonable prices, a few National winners resulted from his breeding. The man remains an outstanding personality in the archives of pigeon racing, and I was glad to know him.

SOME INTERNATIONAL RACING FOR THE NATIONAL FLYING CLUB?

There is a big push, a need and a drive for International racing in the UK. The NFC has declining entries at Tarbes, and there has been a big pull of interest to the BICC with its extensive International race programme. Here we compete against great fliers in Europe and their birds – the radius and birdage are much bigger, and the challenge is great. Our greatest racing man at the moment puts his eggs into the European basket and his rewards are global. To add a modern dimension and fresh incentive to the NFC, why not raise the bar of ambition and excellence and organise an International race with the rest of competing Europe? This will give credibility to fanciers and their birds. The corollary is that it does tend to be more challenging than domestic racing. Think about the concept and discuss it.

WHAT IS A GREAT FANCIER?

A great pigeon fancier is a complex character who has demonstrated many qualities and skills in his understanding of the sport. I like to see evidence of strain building around distances from sprint up to the highest echelon of Barcelona International racing with quality birds over 700 miles and perhaps 800 miles. However I want to see a large feedback, with generous support and mentoring of novices and other people. Values of sportsmanship and generosity to others should be freely manifested, in the form of free or exchanged birds of quality breeding. This person will have esoteric and specialist ideas, and be educated enough to share it with the world of pigeon racing in the form of books or films. He will be well known enough to be a benefactor to others and donate some trophies to leading organisations. It is preferable that this person has bred and raced at least one iconic, racing champion that will be of historical and cultural significance. In my mind's eye I see this person as a real individualist of great moral character and personal charisma. My description is of an archetype, yet certain individuals do meet some of the criteria and one person is Geoff Kirkland.

WHY DO THE SAME PEOPLE CONTINUE TO DO WELL?

These names continue to endure in the results from year to year. We look out for them and notice what they do, as the sport is personality based – the right person will get good results. This is a plain and simple fact of racing. Now all birds are of mixed origins, a right diverse bunch, despite the fact that they take the names of famous fanciers. It is egos, money, fame and publicity that keep them in the mainstream consciousness. All the people at or near the top have developed competitive conditioning methods and overall systems. There is room for other people to have results with time and as the sport evolves, and we are ready for some new birds and folks. Due to the nature of man some will be regarded as giants, icons, legends and charismatic greats in the UK. The irony is that the Barcelona International has yet to be won in the UK. I biased towards old birds over 700 miles, yearlings over 500 miles and ybs over 350 miles, often associated with the North of England.

TIME AWAY IN THE BASKET

Every bird is an individual being, and will have a unique condition level in the transporter. A lot depends on feeding, conditioning and supplementation of the birds prior to basketing. Some birds do not thrive in transportation over many days of incarceration. I will assert that the vehicles require air temperature and humidity control. In the water I would like to see a supplement, eg Vydex, containing probiotics, trace elements, sugars and vitamins and amino acids. This would assist in the rehydration and conditioning of the physiology of the birds. We need to use good applied science and bring racing out of the dark ages. Having said this our 8 timings out of Barcelona International tolerated the conditions of the transporters on the beach at Barcelona. I judge each race on its merits and it is what it is. On liberation the birds are free and beyond our control – it is a tribute to our good system if, and when they return.

THE CRITICAL EYE

I try and filter everything I see and hear as generated by others to see if it smacks of reality or truth, and I include my own thoughts and work in the process. An accurate pedigree is a rare sight indeed. The corollary is, is the bird before me what I am supposed to believe it is? I apply a similar insight to life, until satisfied with some semblance of reality. I remember a pedigree where the ring codes of the parents of the bird were both hens. A bird that is in the clock at Barcelona International is right, yet how high in the results was the performance? Take this to the next logical step and say, where was the UK National winner in the

International echelon? You need to draw the line somewhere and admit that all humans will be at fault, under the close eye of scrutiny. My life has been littered with errors and mistakes, which I try to rectify and compensate for. Wise to do the best you can with the personality you have.

LIST OF THINGS TO BE DONE BEFORE YOU EXPIRE

I think each fancier should aspire to creating a colony of birds with distinct hereditary characteristics, ie a strain of racing pigeons. After 40 years I still play around with this project. Take a walk on the wild side and send birds 700 to 800 miles to see how it feels in race reality. Maybe you can write some books and leave behind a verbal legacy of knowledge and experience. Perhaps a minority will become mentors and benefactors to the collective profile and good of the sport. A must is a 500-mile bird on the day and to be top prize winner in your local club. Make some contacts and associates at home and abroad – you will have few, loyal, genuine friends in life. Be shrewd, wise and enjoy a life in birds, and relish the good ones and times of reflective contentment on your singular journey in life.

SOON FORGOTTEN

When your star is shining, enjoy the moment, as the light for many is transient and ephemeral. Society is a procession of shallow celebrity culture as egos flair and force their way into popular consciousness. For many the light will fade as the sun goes down, on a flirtation with the shallow sting of fame. Make hay whilst the sun shines, as most of the good and great will be occluded by the cold mists of time, soon to be forgotten.

STRESS

The pigeon racing game is laden with stress from top to bottom. We have ours as natural as possible to reduce it for both us and the birds. We aim to build great immunity and condition prior to July when they will face stress. Use the basket as little as possible, and give as much natural freedom in all weathers – contented birds have minimal stress on them. I will not use darkness systems, yet we do separate the old birds from time to time as this brings on condition in the racing season. Our birds are never hungry at home, and the diet is developed using good science and our own intuition. Trying to dominate your club raises the stress hormone levels and involves you in tense situations, resentments and jealousies. It is the most negative, human aspect of the sport, with worry about losses and birds of prey. Some of the top men detach themselves and work from a bubble or an ivory tower with a brass neck and a thick skin.

HUNGER, FIRE, DESIRE

Excellence in the execution of any sport or interest is fuelled by the brain. In my obsessive and fanatical pursuits I am fed by passions loaded with emotion. To be creative it is helpful to tap into and shape the contents of consciousness. The pilot in the process is the self-conscious ego. Some people, especially extroverts, may find it alien to be introspective like this. Mention money, people and external objects and they may tune in. Apparently around two thirds of Mensans tend towards introversion - I can see why. I have been fortunate to maintain a zen-like concentration of my interests over very many years, in an attempt to perfect my exploration of them, thanks to hunger, fire and desire.

SOURCING GOOD OUTBREEDING PIGEONS

With 40 years of inbreeding to the foundation birds, I have sourced some quality inbred birds for experimental outbreeding and progeny testing. These are in different lofts and locations, and I am expecting some success in the course of time. I am a shrewd judge of a fancier and his performance strain. The birds are many darks, but not all, and of tried and tested origins over donkeys' years. We hope to breed and race another champion up to Barcelona International after producing 3. The men who bred my introductions are Marco Wilson, Jim Donaldson, Emiel Denys, Gerhard Schlepphorst, Nick Harvey and Louella Barcelona International family. There are some great genes at large here, so that success will be down to the individual efforts and systems of the people involved – I have invested, as a mentor, in their future.

EMOTIONAL EXPRESSION

In human social exchanges many people appear to be unemotional, yet are inwardly charged with a hypersensitive psyche. The corollary is that demonstrative people may be verbalising rapid and shallow emotions. From a personal perspective, my deepest feelings are expressed in my books – they flow as creative ideas and imagery. I recommend art, music and writing for sensitive souls, as a means of objective expression of the inner man. They have generated euphoria for me.

IF I WERE TO START AGAIN...

I can't beat experience, the highs and lows of the early encounters with the sport and the essential learning process. Life forges an identity from hardship. In retrospect, I would have adopted International racing as the norm some 10 years earlier. Louella looked after me and I would return to them and select five pairs from excellent marathon origins, darks with good looks as well. The rest would be about the personal qualities of sensitivity, tenacity, objectivity and perseverance. I would pursue the goal of marathon racing up to Barcelona International into the North of England over 800 miles. This would be a life challenge, hard enough to stimulate sustained interest over many years. I would aim to raise the bar of excellence, yet everyone I know goes away in the end!

LONG-TERM PROBLEMS THAT ARE HERE TO STAY

For many, many years, certainly the past 30, the fancy has endured some serious and endemic problems. Falcons and hawks continue to eat racing pigeons, and frighten many a bird and fancier. They will reach peak and saturation numbers in the towns, cities and countryside. Racing birds are at risk from wires, weather, obstacles and shooting. In reality, and when free in the air, they make a course home or do not, and at any distance liberated. Most lofts, at times, are invaded by bacterial pathogens and/or viruses. These often run their course with some casualties and may not respond to treatment as new strains and serotypes evolve and mutate. On the human level, jealousy and criticism threaten good sportsmanship. Abuse of power in the political arena is par for the course, since most people work from a personal agenda or motives as they pursue an identity. At the cottage I was plagued by hen sparrowhawks, cats etc, yet we managed to persevere and do well. If it gets too difficult, then contemplate alternative action.

MARATHON MEN ARE RARE

There are reasons why few go over 750 miles, which are easy to understand. The sheer difficulty is rejected by many, the type of patience and preparation of the birds involved, the lack of birds in race time and the rarity of good results. It is not the conventional, popular and competitive thing to do from a back garden loft in town – it will remain so. The vast majority of people go up to 500 miles and many enjoy sprint racing. Influences have come from Belgium and Germany, yet Holland is big on marathon distances over land. It is a lucrative game for the elite. The marathon game demands a great deal of delayed gratification, patience and endurance over protracted time. Have a go – you will live it if you clock one or two good birds. They will sustain you as stock birds in your family lines and be confidence builders.

THE INNER BEING

The essence of a living being fascinates me. If you look with your mind's eye beyond the outer physical form, what do your senses, perceptions and intuitions tell your inner man? I have met some wondrous characters and creatures on my worldly travels. The rewards have been great, from America to Tibet. I try and study the psychological nature of some great artists and poets like Van Gogh and Blake to penetrate the psyche. If you miss the target, it remains an interesting journey into empathy and introspection. The engine of a Ferrari would interest me more than the prancing horse badge on the bonnet. I think the key factor in the life of an introvert is the inner being, its development, knowledge of and survival-often construed as egocentricity.

ATTEMPTING TO FLY BARCELONA INTERNATIONAL

Potentially, the most difficult of all races is a serious proposition for dedicated purists. I recommend you have a dabble, once or twice in a lifetime – you will remember it. It is the premier race for manifold reasons. It is wise to enter all birds over 2 years of age, and then you can evaluate what you can do on the European stage. All your birds in race time will be worth breeding from. Over 800 miles is for dreamers, oddballs, eccentrics, fanatics and specialists or combinations thereof. Develop your system year around one objective and persist until you crack it. It is not for the folk who relish instant gratification, and it is a serious test of the old psyche. Birds that complete the task will be of mixed origins, named or not. In preparation i like around 460 miles for yearlings as a test, and then every bird as it matures to go to the race point, irrespective of colour, looks or breeding. Try and do your research and develop a marathon feeding system for races over 700 miles, and happy flying!

LONG-TERM FOCUS ON OBJECTIVES

If you can muster sustained enthusiasm, you may be able to set goals for future years. It is wise to start with club racing, and learn about all the aspects of the sport. You will meet a rich variety of characters, enjoy some race returns and perhaps win some races. On reflection, a love of birds will help you go beyond the highs and lows of the sport. After a few years you may increase distance levels, acquire more confidence and enjoy the game. After some success a family or strain may start to form, and by this time you may be a fanatic and hooked. Marathon birds come into their own beyond 2 years of age, and some will perform year after year, yet these are rare. With strong progeny testing you never need to cull a fit bird – the basket reveals all the facts you need to know.

FOR THE LOVE OF THE SPORT

With age, sentiment has dawned. I now realise the pleasure many aspects provide and a love of good distance/marathon birds, because of their achievements against the odds. In this I am a purist, a romantic idealist who puts mind over matter and money second and in its place. I am still seeking the next great bird that has flown from the sweat of our brow. A top result gives a glow of euphoria which is priceless. Most of the top, genuine and often old school fanciers do not take the commercial aspect too seriously, yet celebrate great individual performances by man and bird. I did sell birds, yet the true beauty lies in producing birds of endurance, stamina and athleticism. With my lofts long gone, I help my partners develop the old lines, fired by hope and expectation in far-away places, where we keep the dream alive.

TRUTHS OF PIGEON RACING

I raised my first pigeons in 1952. Since then I have come to some conclusions as follows:

Few birds of any breed or origin will make the grade as champion racers or breeders. This applies under any system or management. As race distances increase, fewer and fewer make the grade, until beyond 800 miles they are rare. In the UK at the Barcelona International, anticipate no more than ten percent returnees in the 10 days of race time for the whole convoy into the UK. There are a relatively small number of top fanciers in the UK, and over 750 miles they are scarce. Most marathon birds have a struggle beyond that distance.

Falcons are one of the many hazards under the prevailing conditions of a race, along with shooting, wires, obstacles and climate/weather conditions. Wise to value the survivors at home in your loft at your chosen race distances.

There are no totally pure strains or families of racing pigeons, and being mixed, the apples can fall a long way from the tree.

The way to good results is to try and perfect your system and persist over say 25 years or so in your objectives and tasks to do well and enjoy the sport. Good results put all the theories to practical test.

Many diseases will run their course in your birds, whether you treat or not.

The sport is not an exact art or science, with much individual interpretation by the fancy.

Do your own thing and enjoy it, for you will never be perfect!

GOING BEYOND 500 MILES

Many birds will whizz home, and against the wind, from many origins up to 500 miles on the day. With modern systems and feeding it is frequent. 700 miles on the day of liberation is rare, yet it is often done by the second and third day. These are normally raced by specialist marathon fliers, with years of planning and preparation in the cultivation of the individual candidates. Specialist, esoteric knowledge by the masters make it doable. When you are a novice 700 miles is a daunting and remote task. It remains a distant dream for many and it is talked up, but seldom attempted.

Now 800 miles plus out of Barcelona International into the UK does test the limits of navigation and endurance of all modern racing pigeons, regardless of breeding and condition. Good results within 3 or 4 days of liberation from the beach at Barcelona are very rare, yet you can win one of the four trophies I have donated to the BICC. Few will attempt this degree of difficulty, yet the birds may be proven key pigeons.

ALL RACERS ARE A MIXTURE

Some of the names of the famous people who raced and bred a good bird still survive. There are people who have inbred lines based on some of the key pigeons. It is a myth that the apples never fall far from the tree in terms of performance pigeons. I have bought 28 Schlepphorst Stichelbaut-based birds, a Van Wan Roy based bird and a Van der Wegen based bird. We are breeding from a number of direct Emiel Denys birds. I like the potential in today's racing of all of these. In race reality we anticipate that a small number will hit the mark at Barcelona, when pure, outbred and raced. I like the years of strain building in birds like the Emiel Denys, whom I met in 77. I realise that this process reflects my age and nostalgia, and even after 40 years of concentrated breeding, all my racers are a mixture, just like everyone else's. Naming pigeons is done for commercial reasons, personality and ego and makes nice history and reading. It is other people who create the famous names of the sport that catch the public imagination, and this process continues today in the popular media and the thoughts and minds of men.

HOW FAR TO TRAIN YOUNG BIRDS?

We train ours to about 57 measured miles across Salisbury Plain, against the wind if possible. This is enough at our age, as the birds range on open loft and are out all autumn and winter – some good yearlings will come from these over the water. Times change, as in my day I raced them twice to the coast at around 200 miles, and thought nowt of it. I do like a toss or two, yet would never consider playing around with darkness systems, as I do not see many of those birds flying Barcelona. We have 23 ybs, and one or two more will work back from the fields etc-all our birds will face foraging in their racing career. It is simple, some ybs can find their way home, whereas other cannot in the same liberation conditions. A good yb has what it takes to home in variable wind and weather conditions, no matter how it handles, looks or is bred. The hard fact of reality is when it sits on its perch in the loft. If I were racing, I would give some nice 50-mile tosses to condition them.

CAN YOU MIX SPRINTERS WITH MARATHON PIGEONS?

Pigeon families are not pure for performance potential at any measured distance. Our 700 milers will produce some birds capable of sprint work and vice versa. Believe me, they are all individuals, like the fanciers who race them. They are found out by the methods, approach and system you use at the home end and the prevailing conditions. My best marathon hen was a direct dt of a 4 times first sprint hen. However, some birds will get results only at distances under 500 miles or over 700 miles, for example. It's wise to test each racer in your loft to see what it can do in your chosen races – it is concrete evidence and proof. All the old theories can be given the acid test like this. It's nice to develop a family or strain, yet there are bags of good genes out there to experiment with. The shrewd fancier narrows down the risks on the selection of inmates and new intros. Sensible to breed from your star racers of the year, and pair them together.

WHEN YOU LOOK INTO A PIGEON'S EYE

Apparent vitality and health may be judged in the brightness and depth of colour of the pigeon's iris. The colours will fade with the age of the bird, and go pale before death. On its own the eye is no certain, foolproof indicator of the breeding and racing potential of the bird – it is subjective belief and the speculation of prediction by the person to think it is. We may call it eyewash. Human value judgements reveal a lot about the psychology of the person. Barcelona birds arrive to the loft after sending them to the racepoint. Human iridologists however may explain a lot about the health of the person. In pigeons, eyes do show common hereditary characteristics and we look into them, like crystal ball gazing, when if introspective, we learn much about ourselves, do we not? Certain foods and/or supplements will enrich the brain percept we receive from the external object which is the eye. Pigeon eyes have fascinated man for over 100 years and will continue to do so, since they are mysterious, and I hope to avoid dogma in their interpretation.

INFLUENCE OF THE WIND

This element is key in the life of a racing pigeon. I like good results against the wind with velocities between 3-1200 ypm. Ybs on training will tend to fly with the wind and perhaps turn later eg ours have to fly across Salisbury Plain. The lofts in the west of England have all on in the prevailing southwest/west winds. Good birds are those than can navigate and give speed/endurance results of up to and over 800 miles. All of mixed origins, the ability is expressed in terms of race reality. We concentrate on the returning birds only and the parents of these, irrespective of looks and origins. Many good birds are given or exchanged amongst fellow competitors or friends – keep your cash if you can. I do approve of selling a few birds to perpetuate a family or strain of birds, to help with expenses. The UK is still to stamp its authority on the Barcelona International, which magnifies the importance of the attempt. There may be many wind direction changes during this epic migration. My partner and I accept the near impossibility of us ever winning this race, no matter what strength or direction the wind is. Study the race results and see who emerges at or near the front when the chips are down.

THE RIGHT PERSONALITY FOR MARATHON RACING

A mixture of traits, the people I know show common features. They all have infinite patience and long-term goals and are family or strain builders by nature of what they do. It is a tough old game and the men are hardcase fanciers, yet show sentiment towards proven good birds. The faint-hearted will not survive repeated races over 700 miles and perhaps the magical 800 miles in UK and Irish racing. Where there is a will there is a way. It is always a case of mind over matter, and an effective race system will produce the right birds if you persist and persevere over say 25 years of solid racing. Many of the top men bask in the limelight of the sport, yet some shun publicity – often money is linked to fame! All the top boys think they are, or want to be perceived as, special – the old, individual fame impulse is strong. Each one is an oddball, yet all have hunger, desire and passion to prevail in the sport.

BEYOND THE HORIZON

The sport is safe in the hands of those who reach out to make an impact on the future. Many have realised their dreams, and covered themselves in success or glory. Multiple wins are de rigueur, yet I like to see great individual performances that take some emulating. I maintain that the next really mind-blowing performance will be into Ireland from the Barcelona International. With great dedication this can be achieved, and will shed a new light on the true nature of marathon racing. The cost and organisation of it is somewhat prohibitive, yet an optimistic dreamer can achieve it, with a bird of great endurance and navigational ability. I see it as the final frontier of purist marathon racing, when the thousand-mile goal and tradition of the pioneer seems to be extinct in favour of lesser distances.

DOING WELL WITH BIRDS OF MIXED OR DIFFERENT ORIGINS

A winning system at different distances will develop birds of different distance and performance levels. If you repeat a good, proven system over many years, some success should follow. Each person has their own personalised environment, loft and overall system. Although I still use the genes of my seven foundation birds, they will never be pure in a genetic sense, despite some brother to sister matings over a 40-year time span. Outbreedings are judicious and kept around birds of top bloodlines. In Somerset every bird is sent to Barcelona; if clocked, we rate them as being good and their parents. It is as objective and empirical as we can get, all subsumed by an initial dream. I like direct children of 800 milers if I can get them, yet good ones can come from birds of any racing origin. It is essential to test every racer at your chosen distance.

FINDING THEIR WAY HOME

From the young bird stage right through to marathon distances, we are seeking a certain type of individual pigeon. The most important asset is the ability to find its way home under the prevailing conditions from the racepoint. This can be wind, rain, fog, sun, humidity or combinations of different atmospheres, climates and weather conditions. I want seasoned, rugged individualists with survival and navigational skills. I have dubbed the total conditions race reality. Well-bred, fit and conditioned birds may be fast, yet will fail if they cannot orientate and navigate the required distance. We race in the pursuit of cultivating another champion, with no interest in flock, kit or group birds – the great pigeons are all oddballs. The precise means of homing is still unknown to man or science, as the human psyche is a blunt tool.

KNOWLEDGE OF MEDICATIONS AND SUPPLEMENTS

Beware of so called 'natural' remedies that do not state the chemically active ingredients, as they may be ineffective or perhaps harmful. If you can, read the Zsolt Talaber and Colin Walker books, which are detailed and good science. You will need a basic insight into antibiotics for the control of trichomonads, worms, bacteria, mycoplasma etc. In terms of supplements you can do well to use Hormoform, Tovo eggfood, brewers' yeast, peanuts, hemp, sunflower hearts, oils and liquid feeding of Vydex and Rohnfried products. Experiment, and when you get results replicate your system from year to year. If you can time ybs at 300-plus miles on the day and birds out of Barcelona International then you, the overall system and the breeding and racing of the birds are good to promising. With ordinary mixes and water it is difficult to optimise the health and condition of the birds. In the past I have used Aviform products with success.

THE SIMPLE, EASY SYSTEM

We fly our ybs on open loft from first light and up to dark. They are fed on our marathon feeding system of solid and liquid feeds. A 50-mile first training toss just taps into the great fitness and awareness of the birds. It is far enough to test them, as speed is not what we are looking for – it is long hours on the wing in preparation for later marathon flights of over 700 miles. I like my strain, yet rare good birds may be created from all sorts of birds of many origins – named for ego, personality, reference and commercial reasons. I flew all my birds of different ages together in one colony in one loft. I let them all range around semi-wild in the countryside, mixing with wild birds and avoiding sparrowhawks. If you can, it is a great way to condition free and happy birds. Believe me they will need to forage and fend for themselves in marathon racing later.

For this reason I do like 800-milers in the Internationals, as they have proven their stamina, navigation and desire to get home. I realise this type of racing is not suited to all. It was a logical progression to go from 71 miles to go further and further until my maximum of 879 miles was reached. The hard thing to realise is that few good birds are born and bred from any origin, no matter what you do. Young men pursue hopes and dreams, and then if they persist they will know the meaning of race reality. Suffice it to be aware that results tell the real story of pigeon racing, if genuine, and are all open to value judgements and interpretation. In the last analysis, as long as the birds bring you pleasure, then fair dinkum.

A PROFESSIONAL AND DISCIPLINED APPROACH TO THE SPORT

The top lads and the icons in the game have been meticulous and studious in their total approach to the sport. The primary drive is to perfect the art/science fusion to produce some great results. It's wise to evolve and create a system that works for you and the birds in your local environment, gradually improve it and stick to it over many years, until you realise your dreams. In essence it is brain-based, in your head and that of the birds. A rare few will become champions, and remembered in history, yet there have been some great racemen and birds in the UK over the last 50 years. These have become targets for criticism and praise in the consciousness and popular media of the day. They generate an emotional reaction and excitement which is both tangible and shared in the minds of men. I do like to see records broken and the boundaries of possibility extended in every field of human endeavour, since it is a distinctly human activity. Aim for a system that you can replicate for many years, capable of bringing the best out of each bird.

IN THE RIGHT HANDS

Well-bred birds change hands like sweets, and often at great expense, with associated hype and publicity. In the right hands a minority of these will prove themselves to be good birds with a rare champion. The fancier or man is crucial to any lasting success with the birds at any specialist distances from sprint to marathon racing. It is an illusion to think that some new wonder birds will bring automatic greatness to the loft. The leading men can do well with birds of many origins, which are a mixed bunch anyway. It is wise for a new starter to set about learning how to perfect his management on his own particular system of breeding and racing. The latter takes intellect, creativity and years of dedicated focus, and even then, perfection is a dream. Wise to go to a top man at your chosen distance and learn from him, as there is much more than just the basic quality of the pigeons – they have to be in the right hands.

INSPIRATIONAL PIGEON MEN

I love the Olympics, as it produces the best in global sport. The great personal qualities of people meet the public eye – the talent, skill, dedication and charisma, and the collective humanity of it all. Like Grand Prix since the 50s, I have learned what it takes to do well – the talent, tenacity, focus, desire and sheer obsessive perfectionism. And so it is with the pigeon sport, as each competing country develops its charismatic and iconic personalities who colour history, myth, legend and folklore within their specialist fields. In the UK we have some greats who invite praise and jealousy in the same emotive breath. My conscious life has been stimulated by faster, higher, longer, further and degrees of difficulty. This is the quintessence of the sport and the pulse of its philosophy and psychology.

FORTY YEARS ON

After all this time my strain is still being developed in various lofts in the UK and Ireland. The genes are being preserved and developed by rigorous race testing up to the Barcelona International level of speed/endurance. Nick Harvey is a purist with 8 timings out of Barcelona, the race of truth. Booth and Shipley of York have pure birds along with the experimental matings, and Michael Feeney in Ireland is developing the strain with a small family stud. These men, with some others, will stamp their personality on my 40 years of total dedication and enthusiasm. I must emphasise, as a strain purist I will not accept any money for commercial transactions of pigeons, although my books will be on sale to share my knowledge and enthusiasm with the world at large.

HOW IMPORTANT IS THE ORIGIN OF THE BIRDS?

All racing pigeons are of mixed ancestry from multiple origins. It's great when you hit on a true producer pair, which can create an enduring dynasty. Most pigeons are incapable of greatness, and good ones can come out of many types, names and countries as none of them are pure for any performance trait. I always stress the impact of the fancier in his home environment, as he develops the race condition of the team. I am biased towards the main influence of the fancier, eg Mark Gilbert, for the outstanding condition of the entries. There is more to success than buying a few pretty, well-bred and costly birds. A balance exists, the synthesis of man/bird and environment before the test of race reality.

HUMAN EMOTIONS IN PIGEON RACING

Sadly the emotions we tend to see these days are aggression, resentment, jealousy and mixtures of them. The desire to prevail in competition seems to be the primary motivation, even though it may be disguised behind a subtle personality. It is pleasing to do well and achieve well thought out objectives. The arrival of a champion may induce a heady cocktail of emotions of nervous excitement, joy and euphoria, which we may reflect upon in moments of nostalgia. For many, a long racing season is too much to tolerate and many fanciers have had enough by May or June, due to too much hype in the early season. Racing from a human standpoint is PSYCHOLOGICAL, and it helps the old psyche if you maintain a semblance of patience and calm. We are never satisfied with what we do, and aim to improve towards the impossible perfection. Creating my books is my finest contribution to the sport, and a noble attempt to create some order from chaos.

TOO MANY PIGEONS

It is very simple – if your young and old are not trained or raced far enough, you may well have a surfeit or plethora of birds. I like yearlings to go to around 450 miles, old birds 700 plus, and young birds tossed at over 100 miles or raced to 200-plus miles. If you house too many birds to manage, it will create personal stresses and you will burn out before the season finishes. Ideally, youth and stamina are needed, as age decreases your energy levels for competition, or to fly your birds through from April to September. In the 70s and 80s we club fliers aimed to send to every race, and were caught up in the ethos and mindset of the local working men's clubs. There were some great characters, before I took the lonely route to marathon specialism. With adequate distances sent I did not need to cull and select out any race birds – 735 to 879 miles was good neodarwinism – the personal dimension of natural selection.

HOW TO BE A TOP PIGEON MAN

'Top' is relative to the understanding of the individual. There are certain qualities I look for in my assessment and value judgements, before reaching any decisions on this concept. I like to see the creation and evolution of a strain, rather than persistent buying in to the commercial culture. As a yardstick, 25 years' dedicated focus to the sport is a good indicator of persistence. I like to see an original, detailed and significant contribution to the rich and diverse pigeon racing culture, eg by videos, interviews, articles and books, or charitable contributions to the collective good of the sport. The creation of one or two named racing champions does help in rating the charisma of the fancier, who will be distinct and may transcend the sport in terms of the contribution to it. My percept is a blueprint, ideal or archetype, and no singular person matches it in reality, yet there are some luminous, exemplary individuals and oddballs out there.

AN EXPLANATION FOR LOSSES

Firstly, every bird in a team is a unique individual with peculiarities of fitness, innate potential, navigational ability and motivation to home and many other unknown traits. As the race distances increase up to say 400 miles, fewer and fewer will home in good time. This fact is compounded by ill health, poor management by the fancier, atmosphere or weather conditions, obstacles, shooting, clashing and predation. Losses are expected, and will continue regardless of what we do as racers and breeders. It is said that the clever birds stay away from home. In a pragmatic sense we value the birds that are in the loft after a dose of race reality. Over training triggers the negative impact of young bird sicknesses and will yield burnout as a consequence of your hard work. We like open loft with a few long tosses, when they are left to grow and moult on open loft – out in the sun, wind and rain all day. It works for us in our location and for me at the cottage. We have an eye on Barcelona as soon as the egg is a twinkle in our eye.

PSYCHOLOGY OF A WINNER

Concentration on objectives, targets and certain racepoints will take you a long way if you persist over many years. Competitive racing is a cauldron of emotions, and you will be fortunate to be liked if you do really well, whoever you are. I see the criticism of the champions, and they need the skin of a rhinoceros. On deeper perception, the icons are only human and many suffer for their dedication and devotion to the sport, which has people at its foundation. Pigeons are the means by which we compete, yet the sport is elitist from top to bottom and personality based. Aim to perfect a system that will enable birds to breed and race to their full potential. The annals and archives are made real by the sterling efforts of great men and their prize birds, which were admired, cherished and loved by dreamers, fanatics, chancers and devotees to the humble sport of pigeon racing. My motto is 'think it, do it'.

SALES TRICKS

I recall the sellers and traders in the souks of Syria, markets and bazaars of Turkey, Morocco, India and Tunisia. Every conceivable persuasive trick is used in the bargaining process, and often fed by black market money. The rule of money or 'baksheesh' was all pervasive in the Middle Eastern countries. I enjoyed the colourful people, sights and sounds as cash was exchanged for exotic goods of variable quality and value. I can spot an artist a mile off, and there are some shrewd operators about. In pigeons be careful before you part with your money, and if it bugs you, go for a deal. Good birds are often given and exchanged in a sporting spirit – if you can arrange it. Our top stock hen was a gift from Steve Wain, now retired from the sport. In the teeming mass of humanity there are some genuine folk, if you can spot 'em.

RESTORING THE TRADITIONAL VALUES OF PIGEON RACING

The whole essence of the sport pits man against man with birds as the catalyst. Apart from a few sporting gents who dedicate themselves to long-distance and marathon racing – men of honour and integrity – we see the rise and rise of the mainstream money ethic and rampant commercialism. Attempts by organisations led by certain people are made to straighten out the sport and make it fair. In a total sense this will not happen due to the diversity of people who are in tight competition for the spoils, such as money, fame, power and assorted ego-gratifications. A top man in his field can be the subject of praise and criticism in plenty. In my naive youth I believed in the traditional 500 miles on the day man as a role model; perhaps it was romantic idealism? My partner and I target one racepoint to develop and perpetuate a strain, and this motivates us and to a degree isolates us. In the cold light of day we all plough a lonely furrow in a vast sea of others who pursue their own dreams and desires.

I agree the sport needs a review with the accent on fair play in terms of rules, procedures and their delivery in practice, yet we cannot account for the vagaries and anomalies in human nature which are the beating heart of the personality of the sport. I would like some very positive articles to be dripped into the press and a variety of media after the recent well-publicised negatives. It is an imperfect system, despite our best efforts.

THE LIMITS OF INBREEDING IN OUR PIGEONS

After 40 years we still breed back to my seven foundation birds, with select outbreeding at historical periods. I am interested in the fact that the process has worked, with the progeny testing in place. I know nothing of the actual genes involved, only the results of our testing every race bird out to Barcelona International. This single factor is the test of any theories, be they system, genetic, human or environmental. I have dubbed it race reality, and in five years we have flown two birds of great calibre, both of which were inbred. I like the quasi science and the barking madness of our eccentric approach. We continue to breed around the obvious good ones in blind ignorance of total knowledge of any performance genes involved. The mystery of it all is appealing, as each race is a trip into the darkness of the unknown.

THE CASE FOR GOOD BRITISH PIGEONS

From years of experience I can assert that there are good birds in many countries of the world where good fanciers live and practise the art and science and the love of pigeon racing. With 52 countries and islands, the world can be a wonderful place, if you choose wisely. I have put 40 years into a strain which evolved from birds of mixed countries of origin eg Belgium, Holland, Scotland, England and now Germany and Poland. We do not claim for them to be pure in any respect ie for genes, distance, sprinting or physical type. The truth is that many fly from France and Spain into England, where many of the birds are bred.

I have a global perception of birds and racing, yet I do get inspired by the British greats like Woodsider, Lancashire Rose, Riley's Duchess, Barcelona Dream, Circus Boy, Storm Queen and the Marco Wilson Cock. In my belief, with our crack international birds and fliers of the modern era we are as good as any people and birds on Planet Earth. Why flood to the continent with dreams and hopes when great birds and fanciers fly over the English Channel as far as Northern England, Scotland and Wales? It may be possible for 700-milers into Ireland. Good birds are just that regardless of nationality, patriotism and prejudice, are they not? In my network we swap birds for little or no money under the cloak of human sportsmanship.

NON-COMMERCIAL ASPECTS OF PIGEON RACING

The love of money does tend to leave the sport open to

manipulation and corruption – it is the negative aspect of mainstream capitalism. I sold birds as far as China in my youth, as I enjoyed the buzz of it all. Now after 40 years in the game I pursue purist strain building, and coordinate a network where top bred birds are exchanged for little or no money. The pursuit has an idealistic and moral sporting tone to it which is fairly clean and clinical, despite the ego-gratification behind it. In a perfect world all the birds would be tested in true marathon racing, yet alas this will not happen. It is the rare individual who becomes a Barcelona specialist, is it not? Rampant materialism has got out of hand in the consciousness of the day, and I am still in pursuit of the romance and the dream of producing marathon birds of great stature – we keep plugging away in race reality.

WINNING AND HUMAN NATURE

There are basic needs, drives and instincts that are common to most people. The need for dominion, to prevail and to win motivates people. These traits are often fuelled by aggression which is brain generated. At the heart is the will to power, driven by the ego. It reminds me of widowerhood cocks, motivated and on fire. Birds become living extensions of the human psyche in a system designed to gratify the needs of power, fame and money. My main craving is the continued cultivation of a Barcelona International strain, as it is laden with great difficulty on the western side of England. At the heart of every champion is a pulsating brain, both in man and bird. Most of us try and keep within the boundaries of formal rules and procedures. In the final analysis the personality of the individual is the nature of the beast.

THE WORK ETHIC

It is good to be able to assert that most great birds and fanciers are the result of applied knowledge and dedicated hard work to create great condition in the entries. We race into the far west of England and know the value of low velocities in head winds, ie south west and west. We continue to slug it out against all odds at Barcelona. My friend does not court much publicity, which is a noble trait, yet I write in the media to tell it as I see it. With 40 years put into the objectives and tasks of the sport, I sense some progress. My work is based on the need to promote pigeons, people and the essence of International racing from the British perspective. The legends of the sport today all transcend excellence, and with a few exceptions they deserve what they achieve. Hard work is the sweat of genius.

RADICALISATION OF RULES AND PROCEDURES

Recent and ongoing publicity highlights the fact that reviews and changes in the rules and administration of the sport will evolve attitudes, the politics and the organisation of it. A series of committee meetings will look at the small print and the minutiae applicable to pigeon racing. Politicians, men of words and leaders will debate long and hard. In the final analysis the system will be imperfect, and depend on human interpretation, honesty and integrity. Many people do their utmost to ensure fair play and a level playing field, despite the temptations of money, fame, power and ego-gratification. Where man is concerned it is an imperfect world, and open to negativity and corruption. I hope the circumstances do not tarnish the good and the great in the game and the wonderful birds that have fired our awe and admiration in the past.

THE HUMANISATION OF PIGEONS

However far apart we may be, pigeons can be understood a little, yet the inner being is elusive and mysterious to man. There are people whose senses and perceptions can be tuned into individual birds, particularly for breeding and racing performance qualities. You get a head start by breeding specimen latebreds from the star performers and pairing them together. We name them after the rich and famous, personalise them and give them human-like qualities. The naming of a bird is subjective, and may indicate a quality which we think applies to it. The essence is enriched by the wider pigeon culture and the conscious psyche of the day. My objective behind the accumulation of knowledge has been the development of a performance strain using my brain as a tool. However good you think you are, very few real marathon champions are produced, especially over 800 miles.

OUR YB TRAINING NOW

Team A members were tossed at around 30 miles, whilst 22 of them were flying all night! These will have their first toss around 50 miles. The residue, ie the second toss, will be around 100 miles. We do not need to race them now as results have illustrated that this is not required. After the 100 miles all will be stopped, and left to grow up on open loft. Team B will have one toss around 50 miles in September or October. The whole essence of out tosses is morning liberation to encourage as much time on the wing as possible on the day, ie up to 10 hours. Speed is not important, as all marathon birds are relatively slow from Barcelona International, and every single bird will have nights out in its career. We like our ybs to drink in watercourses, forage if necessary and navigate solo. Late comers are cared for. I very much doubt we will ever win the great race, and we realise the eccentricity of our philosophy and system.

SELFISHNESS AND EGOCENTRICITY

To get to or near to the top in any pursuit, selfishness and egocentricity are essential. In the personality of all the icons and greats in the sport is the beating heart of a huge, individual ego. Many seek fame, personal identity and a feeling of success in the sport. All these factors are psychological and based in the brain, and in direct response to external, environmental stimuli. It is conscious cultural forces that acclaim people as legends, myths, icons and geniuses. These factors are instilled in the popular consciousness by the media. We have to thank the writers who furnish the popular press, as without them and other media star personalities would not exist. The good and the great may balance the psyche as pundits, ambassadors, charitable works as ego-altruistic activities. In the final analysis, ambition and drive are the engine room for personal talent.

INTERNATIONAL RACING IN THE UK TODAY

Mark Gilbert knows the game and where the kudos in Europe lies for his motivation and recognition. To do well up to around 600 miles in these races is the realm of tuned and motivated teams of birds on specialist systems with loft and diet control, and the birds are all of mixed origins and ancestry, where commercialism has its place. The race where the back garden small team man can come to the fore is Barcelona. In 2016 real endurance birds came to the fore, especially on the western side of the UK. We managed to get three eventually. All wise after the experience, we plan them for 2017, along with some new recruits. The first two hens are now in the nesting cycle for the customary latebreds for stock purposes. I would like to see the expansion of this type of racing into Northern England. This is big picture racing and may appeal to people who have high aspirations and ambitions. We send all our birds to Barcelona, and trust them when they arrive. They can all navigate and fly in variable conditions over marathon distances. The total system meets the criteria of selection that we covert. A National win into the west is the ideal result, as it is immersed in great difficulty. Have you noticed the norm, which is lower velocities in Somerset, Devon and Cornwall? I am pleased to report that some of my original stock, now over 12 years of age, are still breeding. I have been concerned about the fate of the Polish 1000-mile men at Barcelona.

RACE PSYCHOLOGY

The secret of a good racing career is the contentment and happiness you derive from it. It is the pursuit of perfection that drives certain people towards the top echelons of the sport. It does not pay to be satisfied with what you have achieved with the birds, since you can always improve your levels pf performance and strain building. The great men of history have been purists, realists and idealists. Not all have coveted the shallow sting of fame and publicity, or bowed to the money god. Central is the excellence of their performances in the most demanding of races. The quality of a bird depends upon the perception and insight of the judge. I like any bird, irrespective of origin, that distinguishes itself over 700 miles, and especially over 800 miles into the UK. The top boys are motivated by dominion and elitism to propel them up the ladder and the personal identity that results give. The whole process pivots on sending the birds to the races that count.

OUR BARCELONA INTERNATIONAL STRAIN

We breed from all the timings which are related and pair the progeny together. Few do this in the UK, and we like the sense of individuality that goes with the labour of love. In time some genetic evolution will take place and some changes in phenotype. These inbred birds are perfect for outbreeding and this is practised from time to time to look for the elusive champion. This dedication is the most purist, conceptual and academic thing we can do in the pigeon sport, when flying birds in the world's greatest race. I do expect some of the birds to respond to a sprinters system though. The strain may increase slightly our chances of clocking each year, yet not by much in race reality. It is all good fun and we enjoy it, from the egg to the clocking.

RESULTS ARE THE THEORY

After 40 years of dedication to racing pigeons, the test of a good bird is very simple in practice. We breed from it, irrespective of looks and handling, if we clock it at Barcelona International. This is the single criterion we use to assess ability and potential and of the parents. The objective is a strain based on empirical, hard results, which have been the fruits of our psyche under the prevailing conditions of racing. Very few birds pass the acid test of race reality, which can be any size shape or colour, since it is the insides of a bird that really count. By all means theorise about the bird after it has achieved, as it is a very human practice, especially about your own inbred strain of birds. With 8 timings from Barcelona we hope to have more, as the strain is the priority.

YOUNG BIRDS THAT FLY ALL NIGHT

This is an interesting phenomenon in England. From our team of 37 birds, 22 decided to whiz around after 10 pm. We encouraged this with our unique feeding system. I have noted this occurrence on warm, bright, sultry evenings, when the birds keep whizzing around all night, as it never gets too dark at this time of year for pigeon flight. The birds returned this morning in dribs and drabs when the energy levels had subsided. All these are destined for marathon racing, so that nights out will help them at this stage. It is thought they are compelled from within to keep flying the form off. We gave the 15 that were in the loft their first toss at approx 30 miles, when they all dropped after 1 hr approx. The second toss needs to be at the 60-mile mark. This is the type of condition that is produced by our system – no rationing for our birds or they won't make Barcelona International.

OUR YOUNG BIRD TRAINING

From open loft conditions, and fed the marathon mix, they

are destined for 3 tosses. Into the baskets they will go for 35, 60 and 100 miles approx, where the residue will be overwintered. Team B will have one 40 to 60 miler in the autumn, as they will have been ranging in the summer living the life of Riley on our unique, marathon feeding regime. I like them up to 10 hrs on the wing after early morning liberation. As yearlings all will prove any potential they may have around 400 miles National racing into the west – often against the prevailing winds. Just note the low velocities of race birds in Somerset, Devon and Cornwall – it is a totally different proposition and concept from Eastern England. My sole arbiter is distance and all my strain must fly over 700 miles in international racing to be valued by us.

NINE

INSIGHTS

THE NORTH-EAST 700-MILE CLUB

This well-organised and prestigious Club was formed in the 1970s to cater for fanciers with long-distance ambitions and aspirations in mind. Long distance for this club means from 500 miles to over 700 miles, which can be classed as marathon racing. The criterion for acceptance into it is 700 miles flying distance from the old National Flying Club distance at Pau. In addition, the club is a duplicate of the premier club in the country, the NFC, and offers the full range of NFC races, e.g. St Malo, St Nazaire, Tarbes and Saintes old birds and a young bird/old hens race, e.g. from St Malo.

The Club can boast in the membership some of the most talented and greatest pigeon-racing people in the United Kingdom, e.g. Chris Gordon, Ken Hanby, Brian Denney and Pete Summers & Partner. These men can hold their heads up high with the world's best, and the primary objective of the club was realised when Chris Gordon set the NFC distance record at Tarbes Grand National, 725 miles to Old Snydale, in winning the race. We must give credit to Mr & Mrs N. Bush for their legendary performances over 700 miles in the club. Other illustrious alumni of the North-East 700-Mile Club include the Wright family, 2nd Open Pau NFC, 734 miles; Brian Henderson, 5th Open Pau; Pete Summers & Partner, 6th Open Pau; Brian Denney, 5th Open Pau, 738 miles, and not forgetting J. Moore's performance at San Sebastian. The history of long-distance excellence is loaded heavily in the results of the 700-Mile Club membership and the NFC Section K is very often won in this club.

On a practical note, each race has 12 places paying out £400, with added pools, assistance is given in taking the birds for marking and there are numerous clock stations dotted about in your area.

MEDICATION AND SUPPLEMENTS

It is fair to say that most fanciers use medication and supplementation to some extent. Some are efficacious, some are not, and there are certain principles that should be adhered to when using them. Make sure that you know what you are giving and why. Do not use fake or quack substances, the origin of which you have no knowledge. Medications, e.g. antibiotics, should always be used at the correct strength, not underdosed or overdosed. If the packaging does not state the active chemical ingredient and the dilution rate, then do not use this product.

Antibiotics should only be used when required and not habitually, at the whim of the fancier, since many disease organisms may show resistance to repeated use, particularly when underdosed. However, prior to pairing up I used Baycox against coccidiosis, Panacur against worms and Metronidizole (Flagyl) against canker. Believe me, most pigeons carry worms, canker and coccidiosis and, these need to be kept under control. In an effort to control respiratory infections before racing I would give Doxy-T (a mixture of Doxycycline and Tylosin Tartrate). From the early 1980s I used a mixture of Mycosan 'T' and Chlorotetracycline+ prior to long-distance racing. These products had a positive tonic effect on the birds and further helped with mycoplasma (respiratory problems).

The Chevita range can be imported direct from Pet Connect, Rue Centrale, Charnosson, Switzerland. These products were my little secret in the 1980s. Against E. coli and salmonella (paratyphus) I would alternate Vetremox, Lincospectin and Baytril. An excellent wormer (a liquid 24-hour treatment) which is harmless is Moxidectin, which also helps to control external parasites. I particularly like this product during moulting, breeding and racing and it can be recommended as a modern, effective product. In the old days I used Levamisole but this has disadvantages in usage. Sourcing the products is easy and I would recommend you contact Nigel Cowood, Gem Supplements or Colin Walker (Australia).

On weaning your young birds, place a drop of 0.8% Ivermectin Solution (Vetrepharm) on the back of the neck. Ivermectin acts in a similar way to Moxidectin. To further combat canker I would alternate Dirnetridazeve (Emtryl) and Ronidazoe (Ridzol) as canker needs to be controlled. I used a range of supplements in an attempt to give that edge to my birds, using Bovril and probiotic in the water on Wednesday (Prolyte) and Aviform on a Thursday. Three days before basketing before big races I used Avimax in the water (Creatine + UCarnitine) and on the Monday I gave Super-Six (Vydex). Other material substances were Hormoform, peanuts and Red Band in the corn mix. I do believe supplements often make you feel better in their bird use and are therefore psychological.

THE FUTURE OF INTERNATIONAL RACING IN THE UK

Some fanciers will know that I have long campaigned for more international racing in the UK. I feel that it gives larger rewards to the BICC and the NFC and their members. There have been some long and testing racepoints for the most dedicated and gifted fanciers, Pau, Perpignan, Marseille and Barcelona, which allows 1,000-mile racing into the UK. There is no greater stage in Europe on which to compete, and the rewards in terms of fame and prestige are great. Note that the record-priced pigeons are usually Barcelona International winners. In 2006 we had Poland competing and a fancier there clocking in excess of 900 miles. Such results are historical and set the standards for the rest of the world.

It saddened me that in 2006 there was no International racing into the UK due to the avian flu crisis. Jan Deacon, the meticulous Secretary of the BICC, must have been perplexed trying to operate an alternative racing programme. For 2007 we need a concerted and concentrated effort by everyone to reinstate international racing. It will require a great deal of legal, scientific and technical prowess to race from northern France and Barcelona. However, unless the avian flu reinstates itself, this can be achieved.

The NFC successfully ran two Internationals and should look at its dates for races in 2007 to embrace International racing, especially as the club is declining in terms of its value and status within the pigeon racing world. I have given a trophy to the SBGDNFC for the first bird over 800 miles in the Barcelona International, and I hope that someone in the UK realises that goal. You don't have to be a genius to clock at Internationals, but you do need to organise yourself and send. My modest performer, Barcelona Dream, was sent down to John Lyden in a single cardboard box one week before liberation.

THE HOURS OF DARKNESS

This is a controversial subject precipitating plenty of argument, debate and discussion throughout the land. This is often a by-product of the success of a good or great pigeons and it would seem particularly relevant as a result of the NFC races, eg Virgo, which won the YB National for Fountainhead Lofts, Nightflight and Syndale Express, the great champion at the Tarbes Grand National sped home for Chris Gordon. Some of the statements and arguments I perceive are motivated by criticism and possibly jealousy by the fanciers concerned. Everyone is entitled to their opinion within the realms of free speech, but what we can say is that the performances were achieved within the rules stipulated by the parent organisation. Derrick Cutcliffe tried to perfect the rule model for the hours of darkness and gained acceptance for this. I feel though that the NFC darkness rules are pretty acceptable, along with the International rules, which are different. Experience tells us though that racing pigeons can and do home at any time of the day or night; surely the nights are never totally black in this country. It would seem that pigeons fly according to nature's dictates, irrespective of man's imposed rules. However the world has room for all our comments.

MY FATHER'S ROLE WITH THE BIRDS

Walter James loved his pigeons, as did his father. I remember him speaking with affection about an old red Tumbler cock which fed eight young birds at a stretch. He also reflected on the value of tic beans and the use of permanganate of potash in the bathing water. Good old Dad introduced me to the pigeons when I was three years old. It was an instant love affair. When we started racing we flew as J. & W. J. Emerton for two years, when he would take the birds to St Lawrence WMC in the back of his sports car. He was well liked at the club but sadly passed away while I was in India in 1979.

QUALITIES FOR THE SPORT

Self-criticism: We are all human beings and mostly capable of improvement. To achieve our goals in pigeons we can be assisted by our attempts at perfection in terms of our racing and breeding results. You may set yourself an objective of winning a National race, and if this is believed the goal could become an International race, although to some it is sufficient to win club races. Yes, some of us find it hard to examine ourselves in the mirror and question ourselves. Were the birds managed correctly in every respect for the race in hand? The birds soon find out the fancier. Some people, because of their inherent predisposition, perhaps cannot or will not blame any fault, but blame the pigeons. There is a complex interaction between fancier and bird. I would blame and criticise myself, although I realise it is easier to blame the birds.

Patience/calmness: These qualities are particularly applicable to the long, hard endurance races at over 500 miles. For my personal races I would virtually camp out at the cottage, some six miles from my home, and indulge in the art of waiting. For this purpose it helps to go into a trance or to keep busy, depending on your personal prediction. I found waiting hard and would normally limit my racing activities in the latter stages to two big races a year, but I am satisfied with my imperfect results. The sprint fanciers, however, enjoy the rapid buzz and triumph of short (under 200 meters) speed racing, and good for them.

Ambition/aspiration: Some fanciers are happy people with the occasional good club result and are often the backbone of the fancy; whatever gives you satisfaction. On the contrary two individuals have won the Dax International into England and it is possible (but unlikely) for the greatest race the Barcelona International, to be won in the UK, in which case the bird would be valued at a world record price.

Sportsmanship: Along with dogged determination, kindness and gentleness with the birds, it seems good practice to reflect kindly upon and to congratulate the winners at all levels of competition in the sport

SELLING YOUR PIGEONS

The International market for the pigeon business is a very lucrative affair with individual birds changing hands for in excess of £100k. The latter usually takes the form of Barcelona International winners, eg Smaragd II, purchased by the Massarella family.

However, the world is your oyster if you want to make a few thousand pounds with pigeons. There are some good contact agents in the UK who will advise you on the export procedure and negotiate deals with foreign agents in places like Japan, China, Taiwan and the USA. When I arranged my own exports from Manchester Airport I would send them in aluminium containers complete with water and the necessary export and veterinary documents. I recall — and how can I forget? — a Mr Norris Wen Chu Wing, who rang me one night to buy birds from me. He said words to the effect of, 'I want Stichelbauts and I want them now!' Later, I duly obliged and subsequently he rang to say, 'Your Stichelbauts no lay any egg!' I sent him a detailed management list.

You can be selling pigeons on your own performances or trade on other people's. It can be better to buy from the winning fanciers themselves; even so there is a lot of money-orientated sharp practice in the game. Other people's results with your birds can be testament to your integrity as a pigeon person and some of the best birds are given or exchanged — and from non-famous lofts.

Selling birds is a way of meeting people and can help establish a reputation in the sport. In practical terms, I used to advertise occasionally in Squills (1990 edition) or sell latebreds from an August half-column ad in the BHW.

I am now glad to say that as a generous gesture to the NFC, Sid Barkel, the NFC Secretary, has my stud of birds.

WITH A LITTLE HELP FROM MY FRIENDS

There is some truth in the saying that every man is an island and that we function as separate, unique individuals in the world. However, in pigeon racing we are only as good as our competitors will allow us to be, and there is normally someone in waiting with ambition to improve upon and surpass our achievements in the sport I would like to see someone aspiring to clock 800 miles into the UK on the second day of liberation, since this would set the new standard for marathon racing 'over here'. Whatever we achieve in pigeon racing is there to be judged in terms of its relative greatness by others in the sport.

In our dependence in other people we should thank our rivals, the club officials, the secretaries and all the support people who have made our achievements possible. I would personally like for the first time to thank Geoff Farmery from York, who arranged for the delivery of my pigeon loft from Tadcaster in 1976. The loft was sold on delivery but housed my birds until 2006, when it was demolished. My old friend Steve Shipley, a cheerful character (never a crossed word in 30 years) also helped to place it and to build the stock loft aviary. I am pretty inept at practical work, so I am very dependent on my craftsmen peers. Eric Gibson, the NFC clock station man. is a genius at design and with wood and has assisted me greatly with the pigeon clocks. I confess to never having set a clock in my life. Eric has an able partner called Duncan Gray and they have vaccinated my birds for me.

On a last note, I would like to thank my fellow scribes for their encouragement and kind words of approval in the BIAW. To conclude I think it is a tribute to my good temperament that I have never fallen out with anyone in 30 years of racing pigeons (although one or two have fallen out with me).

STRAGS

In the United Kingdom there are huge numbers of strays or strags throughout the towns, cities and countryside. It is a fact that not all of these are bad pigeons and there are many champion breeders and racers amongst their numbers. When racing my own birds I realised that if the birds were sent far enough and for long enough they would all fail to return, for whatever reason. There are very few birds which will race 700+ miles more than three times, and it is very easy to weaken or sicken birds off for good. From time to time most of my good birds were strays, i.e. having time out from home, for example Barcelona Dream, Oddball, Mystical Queen. One year my lovely hen, Dedication, sat on a lady's aviary down south at the Nantes National, having spent part of the previous season in Ireland eating maize direct from the hand of an Irishman. 'She will return', I said, and later, having corrected herself, she was 61st Open Saintes National from around 6,000 birds and scored from Pau at 735 miles on the second day. Her bloodline lives in the strain today and she died in the loft.

The management point from this is that persistence and perseverance pay. I found that many of these strays when reconditioned would pull out some good performances. Many sprint men however would have culled these birds early on, although I held other people's strays under suspicion I would feed and water them and try to toss them to help them home. I am only human and sometimes I would try and transfer one into my name. When I donated my birds to Sid Barkel of NFC fame there was a nice blue cock which had flown St Nazaire for me as a yearling. The RPRA has a formal procedure for dealing with strays, and really it is ruthless practice to cull strays when they enter a loft, since some of these may be champion birds belonging to some ardent fancier. In my latter years many of my birds were lost, due to the large jumps I made with my birds and the fact that I was looking to find International pigeons. I must confess, I did not bat an eyelid over this. What use is a loft full of mediocre birds all looking beautiful and eating their heads off?

WINTER MANAGEMENT OF NATURAL PIGEONS

One of my main priorities was to keep the birds as calm and contented as possible through the winter months. I allowed free access in and out of the loft on most days, and it was a delight to watch the birds swirling around in a snow shower or two. Winter exercise seems to sharpen the instincts to cope with predators such as sparrowhawks, and to face the elements; all good experience for later long-distance racing.

I did not separate the birds after racing, since I liked the younger birds to choose their new partners and to be together as a related family flock. It would be in January, when the cocks started to drive the hens to nest, that I could separate hens from cocks and fly them out on alternate days. During this time hens can become skittish and full of fly. I would enjoy dropping these hens out of the sky with my whitish drop birds – all part of the winter fun and enjoyment with the birds. My birds would sit in the fields and on local wires, giving them contentment and awareness of a large home area, which I believed helped the birds to race home from long distances. The loft was dry and cosy with warm deep litter, and the perches and boxes were scraped out daily.

Feeding consisted of layers' pellets (16% protein) in hoppers at all times and a high protein mixture, e.g. Premier Gold, was hand fed in wooden hoppers, as I found that no further additives, e.g. condition seed, yeast, peanuts or Hormoform were necessary in the winter. Science teaches us that all the necessary amino acids, time elements and vitamins are present in good old-fashioned layers' pellets. The feeding was of a high protein nature, as many long-distance pigeons do not complete their moult until January and of course the young birds and yearlings are still growing during the winter. The birds would be treated against cocci (Baycox), worms (Panacur) and canker (Flagyl) before mating in March.

To sum up then, the birds saw the loft as a place of quiet comfort and security from the elements.

JIM'S LIST OF TIPS

1) Your flock of racing pigeons will react positively to white or near-white drop birds. These can be trained to land or release at the loft when nervous birds return, or young birds stray – they are ideal.

2) I believe that a white pigeon acts as a super-stimulus to the racers. Try pairing your top hens to white cocks and see how keen they become. My Dax My Girl raced in July to her first baby of the year, a white young bird, when she had been paired to a near-white cock.

3) In May, with the onset of warm weather, treat the water with Moxidectin to kill red mite, and spray the loft out with Duramitex for control of red mite and northern mite.

4) Gather some thick natural grass stems and twigs for your birds to nest with.

5) Befriend top fanciers throughout the UK who may be willing to exchange top-bred birds with you. I do not believe in the practice of buying pigeons in.

6) To race at the top and to enhance your reputation, consider the option of International racing – it is the best.

7) When you become a little successful, the costs of keeping pigeons can be offset by selling young birds. If you sell July-Sept hatched latebreds, it will not dilute your loft performances,

8) Make friends of the people from whom you can learn and maybe your allies in the future.

9) When racing in the big Nationals or Internationals do not catch your birds on their return from training races – it upsets them.

10) Keep to your targets, do not be deterred by the comments of others!

11) Forget strain or family names, since as soon as you breed birds in your own loft they bear your influence and should take your name.

12) Don't get carried away at auctions; the birds are being hyped up in the 'game' of selling.

13) Think – what is my legacy and how can I leave the sport in a better position?

14) Make sure your birds are exercised around home on every possible occasion.

SELECTING THE RIGHT PIGEON

For racing, this is simplicity itself. Forget all the theories – place your bird in a basket and send it to the appropriate racepoint from say 50 to 900 miles. The equation is simple: if the bird is successful at that distance, then you know it has passed the selection test and was the right bird for the job. It also proves that the present stock birds were right for the job.

If you 'selected' the stock birds, then good for you! However I know of no one in the world fancy who can accurately assess and predict stock birds and successful racers without fail. Although there is a certain amount of intuitive good judgment within the fancy, I do not believe in a selection genius other than the basket. Wing, eyesign, genetic and body type theories are of interest in their own right, but I have yet to see evidence of their 100% accuracy in application to breeding and racing pigeons.

I did find that from a related family of pigeons it helped to breed from latebreds off the best National and International racers. These, usually produced some good performers at the child or grandchild level. In my own strain it was helped further by the selection of well balanced, silky-feathered specimens from the related performance pigeons of the year.

Every fancier likes the look and feel of beautiful pigeons, but let the basket be the judge of beauty. All my birds had to tie the line at the distance, 500-879 miles or fail in the process, be they ugly, beautiful, small, large, fat or thin or of any physical type.

It is amazing how beautiful a good racing pigeon becomes. Having said all this, I did have a penchant for a small medium dark or velvet chequer keeping faithful to the photo of the Bordeaux hen of Alois Stichelbaut in the history of the Belgian Strains Part II.

I believe that there is one exception to the above theories, and that is the human selection of winners in organised shows such as Blackpool – and that is what they are, show pigeons.

YOUNG BIRD RACING

When I raced young bird seriously, I was very keen indeed. Some of my best performances were twice 1st five Open, and twice 1st three Open and the first six from Ashford 210 miles in the club. Later it was my good fortune to clock little Darkie at Sartilly (362 miles) to be the present longest flying young bird in the NFC on the day of liberation. Little Darkie was a May-hatched young bird flown to the perch on natural. After the young bird performances I would place the birds in boxes and just stare at them with admiration in my eyes. They shone with health and condition. The birds were fed at that time on Haith's Widowhood Sprint, with added Red Band, peanuts, Hormoform and yeast. In the hoppers at all times was layer's pellets and the birds were trapped with peanuts, since these restored the energy levels very quickly! Mycosant and chlorotetracycline + were in the water on Thursday/Friday. One of my inducements was to hold the birds overnight in baskets, in the house front room with no food and water and in relative darkness, before basketing the next day. My young birds had the benefit of open-loft flying at all times. The condition of well-fed young birds which free range the skies has to be seen to be believed. With open loft you don't need to train young birds at all, but in my sprint days I would toss them up to 50 miles before the first race.

In later years I looked for young birds which could concentrate over great distances and would send them as trainers the first toss and first time in a basket, being Leicester (95 miles) or Buckingham (138 miles). In 2005 I had nine arrive together at 800+ velocity from Leicester (95 miles) on their first toss from the loft. Believe me, fit young birds do not need to be tossed before racing. Some fanciers do not believe me about the young birds, that is their problem!

For specialist National long distance young bird racing (over 300 miles), fanciers can look to Chris Gordon as he is the best in the United Kingdom, being a specialist in this sphere. Of course most competitive modern young birds are on modified darkness or lightness systems, often with widowhood.

Competitive young bird flying is certainly a pleasurable and skilful job and can be very lucrative.

TIPS FOR THE LONG-DISTANCE FANCIER

By long-distance I mean races between 500 and 700 miles, although some of the Information may be applicable to middle-distance races of 400-500 miles and marathon races in excess of 700 miles.

1. Five days before basketing, quieten and further tame the birds with a mixture of peanuts, Hormoform and condition seed in the boxes. The birds should have free access to this feed with the emphasis on fats. This is like a migratory bird fattening up before the big endurance flight.

2. On the Friday, Saturday and Monday before basketing give the birds Mycosan T in the water. This will stimulate their metabolism. On the Monday you can add Chlortetracycline + from Chevita into the water. The latter Is a product recommended in healthy pigeons by Shraag.

3. On the Sunday before basketing, add Entrobiotic or Vydex Super-Six to the water.

4. In the weeks prior to basketing: Bovril and Aviform 'E' Plus (electrolytes and probiotic) in the water on a Wednesday, Thursday Aviform Ultimate in the water.

5. To restore energy and detoxify the system add Chevita Multivitamin + to the water on race return day.

6. Send all your yearlings to 400 miles plus. I used to jump mine into 466 miles from the coast (about 220 miles). There should be no exceptions, as this will find out the capabilities of the yearlings. The specialists can send their yearlings 500-600 miles.

7. Cultivate the successful yearlings and plan races for them in excess of 500 miles as 2y birds. A good 2y is ready for 800-miles plus racing.

8. To start your own family, breed off your best long-distance racers or producers. Birds from any family of pigeons may be long-distance. The genius of the basket will find them out. A long-distance bird may come from a so-called sprint family, or a so-called distance family.

9. It may be of help to purchase latebreds from a famous long-distance fancier, yet it's probably more important to learn how to fly them.

10. Good widower cocks, managed correctly, will do everything required of them — witness Chris Gordon and Jim Biss. I preferred hens sent on their first eggs or small baby of the year, especially when these birds had been deprived of nest as widowhood hens beforehand. Pair some of your birds to white pigeons for maximum effect!

11. To prepare birds for 700-mile races, send them to a race of 400-500 miles with reserves of body weight, give them a 14-day rest, then a short flight (say 120 miles) followed by the big race.

12. Long-distance candidates will improve with two to three weeks of quiet rest.

13. Many fanciers burn out their potential long-distance birds with too many short tosses and races — it pays to specialise for the long distances, making it your only objective.

14. There are sufficient long-distance birds in the UK without going to the Continent for them, there being more capable birds than there are capable fanciers.

15. Only a small percentage of birds from any origin will perform in excess of 700 miles — Mr Basket solves this problem.

16. Eventually all birds will fail to return if sent: it is just a matter of age and time.

17. Be sure to breed some latebreds off your good ones.

SPECIALISATION

When I first started in pigeon racing I was young, keen and ambitious for success. I tried to win at all distances from the shortest and thought that 500 miles was a really long way. It was my desire to take the first four places in club racing every week. I now realise that this was a ruthless and selfish attitude, yet these are qualities that most good competitors and sportsmen possess.

After a while with a lot of success up to 500 miles I realised that it pays to specialise. By specialisation I mean a focused and concentrated approach to the different disciplines of racing, e.g. sprint racing say up to 250 miles, middle-distance racing from 250 to 500 miles. In my book long-distance racing starts at 500 miles going to 700 miles, with marathon racing in excess of that. These figures are purely arbitrary and reflect my own feelings on racing. However, I never classed Nantes and St Nazaire at 466 miles as long-distance races. These two races always frustrated me, being only middle-distance.

It became evident that to succeed at marathon racing birds should normally not be sprinting in the earlier races, carrying sufficient reserves and body weight for the later endurance tasks.

Racing pigeons and their results are products of the types of management systems under which they are kept. The fancier is paramount — no fancier, no pigeon, no result. For best results up to 250 miles it is probably best to use a very concentrated form of widowhood or roundabout system. Down to management again, there are many tricks that can be used, e.g. jealousy and celibacy. Whatever system that is used, right out to hens on small babies for the marathon races, it is probably true to say that your results will be better by specialising at the different distances. If the system you use is the right one, it will produce pigeons capable of winning on the system. It is not normally necessary to go chasing pigeons that will automatically perform, as it is the fancier who produces the birds with his or her winning methods, both breeding and racing. Once again no fancier, no loft equals no pigeon.

Arguably our greatest exponent of long and marathon racing was Jim Biss. However, it is sad that I have never seen any really detailed systems of his methods which he applied with such genius in the premier International races.

FANCIER OR PIGEON?

This is the old chestnut, a little like the chicken and egg

question. In answering it, your answer depends largely on your psychological type. I strongly believe that the most important aspect in the relationship is the fancier. In simple terms we provide the loft environment in which the pigeon lives, we have a loft with our own feeding and management system of flying the bird — no loft, no fancier equates to no pigeon. Having said this, a racing pigeon must have the potential in itself to be a winner at any given distance from 50 to 1,000 miles. You can have the best management in the world, but without good birds you are doomed. I have noticed though that good pigeon fanciers acquire and/or breed good pigeons with the qualities and skills that they possess — they make sure they produce good pigeons one way or another.

The way to produce good birds is to breed and race them on a winning formula. A good system will produce good birds with a sustained and concentrated effort. This is down to the fancier. It is true to say that a quality bird will not win a National or International unless it is produced for the race in the correct condition. Conditioning the potential champion is the forte of the fancier.

Placing the pigeon first in the 'fancier or pigeon' question is sometimes a device used by fanciers so that they can readily blame the bird when things go wrong and not themselves — the 'it wasn't me' syndrome. The latter is often linked to the fact that many fanciers chase rainbows by often buying in birds from the in-strains of the times. The commercial market for birds is based on this. I feel it is much nicer to take responsibility for your performances and attempt to build up your own family or strain, in which individual birds can reach their potential under your system. To illustrate this, if you race Vandenabeeles, i.e. pigeons bred direct by him, you will become a champion with them only if your way of looking after them is correct. This is down to the fancier who comes first!

YOUNG BIRD SICKNESS

When we speak of young bird sickness, it is an umbrella term that does not necessarily refer to a specific disease or disease syndrome. Young birds are susceptible to a large variety of illnesses, particularly those induced by bacteria and viruses. Some of these may mutate as bacteria and viruses replicate very quickly, so that there may be diseases that we have yet to identify. One particular syndrome manifested itself as holding corn, wet droppings, some emaciation and death. It was thought that this might be caused by a combination of a virus such as adenovirus or circovirus and secondary bacterial infections such as E. coli and paratyphus.

Now in terms of control we have to treat the bacterial infections, not the viruses directly. There may also be complications of many other pests and diseases such as worms or canker. The aim with young birds should be the reduction in stress due to overcrowding and too much basket work and training and having the birds in optimal condition to prevent the onset of young bird sickness.

Health management of the lofts becomes a priority. Some of the products that have aided the recovery of young bird sickness are Adenosan by Chevita and Nifuramycine by Rohnfried. There are many probiotics that are used to aid the growth and multiplication of beneficial gut bacteria (good intestinal flora) and these include Prolyte and Entrobiotic.

It is good practice to stop training and racing when outbreaks occur and to give the birds a period of rest with easily-digested pellets, depurative and multivitamins in the water. In my own case, having flown young birds on the open-loft system, I was not plagued by young bird sickness syndrome and either treated against individual pests and diseases or let nature take its course. I would normally cull severely affected young birds. Two good books for reference purposes are 'Healthy Pigeons' by Shraag and Zsott Talaber's book.

RACING: HENS OR COCKS?

It is probably time to say that most results taken are with cocks. This is in part due to the predominance of widower cock systems of management. Some fanciers race very well in excess of 100 miles on widowhood with cocks, as did Jim Biss with his fabulous International Team, yet many club and Fed fliers also swear by their cock birds to obtain their results.

I see no reason why one sex should be better at racing than the other. However, I preferred hens and in the end was a hen specialist at the distance. I had an affection and a trust in my good hens and knew that if they were prepared in very good condition they could do everything asked of them, even as widowhood hens. Yes, most of my better results came from hens and I would deprive a hen of a nest before sending her to a big race on her first nest or her first small baby of the year. If the hen is of the right quality she can be very motivated in this condition.

My plan was always to pair my hens in March, and often I would send them to the 466-mile mark in June before nesting them and send them on the nest to 600 or 700 miles in the next NFC race. In my latter years with my hens I clocked in two NFC races, not bothering with Saintes at 569 miles as this was too short to be judged an extreme-distance race, being a race for fast day birds. Having said that I enjoyed Saintes when I raced it in the 1990s.

Some of my good hens were Diamond Queen, Mystical Queen, Dedication, Dot's Delight and Oddball, and, of course, Dark Enchantment. The results of these birds have been well documented. Hens at the distance are a specialism and good hens add greatly to the gene pool of your loft as breeding birds. I always bred latebreds out of my good performing hens and paired these together.

Flying on natural and to eggs and babies I sometimes produced good cocks, e.g. Barcelona Dream, Diabolos, Damien and Dark Velvet, and logically I would mate these to the good hens and their daughters to perpetuate the breeding lines in the strain. I feel that my system was better than I was as a flyer of it, and I certainly applied myself more to the breeding side.

I will be most interested to see how the widowhood cocks of Chris Gordon go in the Internationals and will also be watching the progress of Jim Donaldson flying his hens on overdue chipping eggs or small babies in the Scottish Nationals.

RACING AS A PARTNERSHIP

Behind the successful image of a named male fancier, many of the loft chores are being carried out by a woman, or a silent partner. Sometimes they receive recognition and sometimes they don't. Partnerships of two or more people can be successful, especially if the methods employed are labour intensive, or the main partner is handicapped in any way. It is important that the individuals get on and share clearly defined goals and objectives — there should be no compromise on vision and methods. As is known to the fancy my mother, Dorothy, was a great help, especially when I was at work. She helped until she was 91, supporting what I did with a gutsy, competitive and aggressive attitude. In this respect she was a total inspiration and example to all. When asked about her secrets of success she said 'I sing to them'. She used to talk to each individual bird and they responded. Who knows what is in the head of a pigeon? She was like Doctor Doolittle!

Dorothy was an early riser and her first job, in her dressing gown, was to open up the loft, often 5.30-6 am. Young pigeons in particular will fly well early in the morning. She also rang me to let me know of birds returning from Pau etc. One of our finest achievements was to clock Dax My Girl in 2004 at 687 miles in the International from 17,526 birds. It was a lovely day for Jean and ourselves and would have taken some beating. If Dorothy was alive today, she would be very proud of my articles.

PIGEON-RACING CHARACTERS

The world of pigeon racing is, made all the more interesting by the people who occupy it. As a small schoolboy in Derby, I formed the habit of visiting and associating with some of its pigeon people. A man who found a permanent place in my memory was 'Pigeon Percy'. We would sit together on park benches (I sound like a reprobate!) in the riverside gardens, watching and feeding the ferals and strays. Percy was a local celebrity who would spin his head like a performing Birmingham Roller, and he lived to a great age.

Billy Burdett of Alvaston gave me a blue cock from his wheelchair. He said, 'Ays a good 'un, Jim. Look at his eye. Ay'll win Lerwick, ay will'. I took the bird home and settled it to my loft, pairing it to a chequer pied stray I caught. After that I was hooked and trained the bird all over on my motorbike.

Harold Adams lived in Matthew Street. He was a Roller man and gave we his well-known red cock. I enjoyed visiting Harold and lent him my first book, 'Pigeons And How To Keep Them'. It came back with the pages blackened. He also kept show canaries and helped to initiate me into pigeon racing.

Dr Graham Dexter lived near the Blue Peter in Alvaston. I kept a kit of Rollers and so did he. He was a young man then, before his PhD. Today he is a world authority on competition Rollers and has created the definitive work on Rollers called 'Winners With Spinners'. He has judged all over the world and formulated many of the modern rules for competition.

Coming nearer to modern times, from my York area we had the late Ted Booth, who was a delightful gentleman and lived in Melrose Gate. We would all arrive at his house to train OUP birds. He was kindness personified and his wife would cook me bacon and egg. It was Ted who persuaded me to sell pigeons — evidently he could see something in me!

I must mention the late Freddie Willis, who flew in St Lawrence WMC. Fred was larger than life and a colourful local character. He would say 'good ardear' for 'good idea'. His son, Ian Willis, is a top sprint flyer in the area. He really 'struts his stuff' and they call him 'Milky' after the. Milky Bar. Kid. He is cocky and all the better for it!

On a National level we have young Sid Barkel with his managerial and administrative flair, who burns the midnight oil to keep the NFC shipshape and organised. On the phone he projects himself as a quiet introvert, yet there is a tough nut in that skull! The NFC would be worse off without our Sid.

Finally, a mention of Brian Long, who must have a sweet soul to donate so much money to the NFC in the face of serious illness. He is a leading light in the BICC and NFC and a very important man to the sport.

CREDIT WHERE CREDIT'S DUE

How do you think he does it? I don't know. What makes him so good? In the York area at the Tarbes National there was a true genius at work. His name is Brian Denney. At the marathon distance of 748 miles, he made things look ridiculously easy by clocking an almost endless succession of the Denney strain, with most of his 20 birds returning on the second day. These birds had been managed to perfection to achieve this peerless performance in the NFC as they made the race look like a sprinter's job. It makes me wonder what these wonderful birds might achieve in the Barcelona International, since they were saying, 'please send me on'. I would like to see some detailed insights into Brian's methods, as the methods maketh the man and the birds. He has overcome the obstacles in his path with mesmeric grit and determination.

In the same fancier's village we have Gibson & Gray, who are provisional 18th Open Tarbes at 747 Ales. I visit Eric Gibson every week and I am thrilled for him with his hen bred from the Binn's Cock and a direct George Peterson hen (Stichelbaut based). Eric and partner D. Gray have shown great resolve in the face of serious illness to achieve this.

MAKING RACING EASY

I don't believe in being a slave to unnecessary work with the birds and it is lovely to operate within a comfortable system. In my early years I was racing up and down the motorway training birds, so that eventually took the pleasure out of it — it was just not essential for success. One of the simplest ways of racing pigeons, if you are able to do so, is to fly the open loft system. For this you need a loft with a high, safe exit and entrance and not the open door type. I used to fly mine, housing the birds both young and old all together. If you want to practise part or total widowhood you can have two sections to the loft (a dividing door will suffice), with the young birds exercised with the hens.'

My feeding system has been well explained, but young and old were fed the same, hoppers of layers' pellets and my own corn mixture. In concentrating on the greater distances, road training old and young is not required. I used the club programme for training without setting a clock, sending my birds as trainers. It all makes life easy as there is no going to the club on a Saturday and no catching nervous returning birds.

The young birds on this natural, open-loft system reach wonderful condition. With no basket training I would jump their birds into 95 miles or 138 miles with confidence, as they do not need to recognise land marks to orientate home. This means that you save all that stressful basket work, which can induce young bird illnesses.

I did like to see clean nestboxes and perches, but was a great believer in the deep litter system. Scientifically it is thought that natural immunity to disease organisms is induced through deep litter. My deep litter was wood shavings and droppings with some Easibed later on and was never changed, being dry as a bone. People have called me a lazy so-and-so. The essence is that I put the mind, spirit and soul above the material, i.e. subject before object. I see myself as soulful rather than idle.

I hope this article has interested perhaps the disabled or less energetic or more elderly fanciers. Don't forget to use telephone rings on your young birds to save wing stamping. Please send any questions to the editor, when I will take pleasure in answering them. And now it's snooze time!

ALL PIGEONS ARE DIFFERENT

Each individual bird has its own unique qualities, appearance and character. It is nice and useful to the fancier to learn to recognise each bird in his loft. To the perceptive eye this is similar to knowing personal, human friends — we have instant recognition of them on eye contact. Many fanciers have knowledge of the ring numbers of the birds and then refer to the pigeon in a book or on a computer. Now my family of stock and racers were nearly all dark chequers and blue chequers, yet I could identify each bird in the loft by its outward appearance without reference to its ring number. Furthermore I had the added difficulty of being six miles away from my pigeons, so I would sit and think and try and bring an image of each bird into my mind. Once I had done this, I would try and visualise its parents and grandparents. This takes a degree of mental control and focus, but is great fun for the dedicated soul.

Exercise also helps you to focus on your family and strain making and not the fashionable strain of the month. After a while the fancier will have an intimate portrait of each bird in his mind. This is a useful tool when selecting birds for pooling purposes or for stock or for sending to individual races. It is like having an imprint of each bird in the mind, and the degree of concentration involved may yield insights or intuitive knowledge of the birds. A simple way of learning to recognise your birds is not to look at the ring number and just stare at the bird and see what comes to mind. I bred my Dark Destiny in 1979 and his image is still in my mind to this day.

For my Ask a Question column, will all fanciers, wherever you are, please send your questions to the editor of the BHW. I will give my personal answer to your question. We may be able to do something a little refreshing and different

THE TRUE STORY OF BARCELONA DREAM AND DAX MY GIRL

In 1993, at my second attempt, I sent two birds to Pau NFC which were both recorded in the Open result. These two hens, along with two more, secured me top prizewinner with old birds in the NE 700-Mile Club. This result was at my first attempt and went to my head a little. I thought to myself, where do I go from here?

Even at this stage I was most impressed by the endurance capabilities of individual pigeons. Arriving at 1994, Diamond Queen was 72nd Open NFC Pau, 735, miles, with nearly 6,000 pigeons. I had read about the BICC and the Barcelona International race. This race I considered to be the ultimate challenge in Europe, and it still is. In 1995, having joined the BICC, I accepted the challenge and entered my best six birds. John Lyden warned me of the difficulty, as I was the furthest flying member in the BICC. He also generously offered to look after my birds at his home and during marking.

The problem of conveying the birds to Kent was solved

when sent them with Amtrak, five hens to a box and the cock in a single box. The cock was so big that he nearly filled it. Finally, a week later, on the Friday, the liberation took place at Barcelona. At the local club I had asked Brian Denney to strike my clock, since I thought this would be lucky. My words to the Strensall Club were, 'I'm going to clock'. My mother thought it was not possible at 879 miles, being too far. 'It's just a dream', she said. Things were looking ominous as the winds turned east and north-easterly in this country. Now bearing in mind that my home was six miles away, I waited until the big dark cock arrived. When he alighted on the loft I was picking fleas off the back of Freddie the Jack Russell. I named him Barcelona Dream and to this day (12 years later) he holds the record distance in the BICC. Two of the hens were verified. I must admit that camping out waiting at Holtby was hard. With a marking station nearer to home, I would have sent my best birds with the BICC.

There were enquiries from Japan for his children, some of which are with the Barkels and one with Trevor Robinson, and his genes are well spread through the strain. His physical appearance was extraordinary. There were 20,936 birds in the race from Europe. Years ago I campaigned heavily for International racing with the NFC with letters and propositions, and so it was that in 2004 I sent five pigeons to Dax at 687 miles with the International convoy of 17,526 birds. One of my birds caught my eye as she had finished with great speed at St Nazaire, 466 miles. She told me something that day! I nominated her on the entry sheet and in the single bird NFC lib. On the second day of the race my mum, Jean and I sat out at Holtby. It was a pleasant balmy day in July. We waited with confidence and expectation and then she arrived and was duly clocked with no fuss. Dorothy said 'Daxmegel', which is a play on Dax My Girl.

It subsequently transpired that Dax My Girl was the longest-flying pigeon clocked in Europe in the result (top 1/4) and put me on the European International loft rankings. It was her second time at Dax, and Dax II followed on early next morning. I keep campaigning for International racing as I know how it feels. I rate Dax International as a bit harder than Pau NFC. This is what I told Chris Gordon when he asked me. I live in hope of others in the North of England racing at Barcelona and await the first arrival on the second day at over 800 miles in the International. The Barkels have two sons of Dax My Girl, and Ian Dixon has one. Ian has helped me greatly with my house and loft removal and is a human dynamo when it comes to work. He flies as Dixon & Son and has tasted much success with the NFC up to Pau. He is a charming, good-natured fellow.

Dax My Girl was sent on her first large, white youngster of the year with three weeks' rest after 466 miles. She came to be 1st Section B, 4th Open in the single bird NFC. My memories live on — happy days!

THE SQUILLS LIST OF RECORD PERFORMANCES

This is a global list of good performances, which celebrates some of the better performances of pigeons. It is a valuable reference for fanciers past, present and of the future. I have three entries and my aim was to have some of my birds remembered after I was long gone from this earthy sphere.

A famous fancier criticised my performance and I have no axe to grind, other than to clarify that Barcelona Dream is still to this day the record distance flight holder in the BICC. Dax My Girl is the furthest flying bird into the UK to make the result (687 miles) in the Dax International. In 2004 and was the longest flying bird in the result (top quarter) in Europe.

Now Diamond Queen (a beautiful bird, hence the name) is not a record holder. She was, however, the longest flying bird in the top 100 of the Pau NFC, being 72nd Open at 735 miles in V4. In my early days I was proud of her and thus she was included in the list for her performance in 1994.

YOUNG BIRD LOSSES

Mick Rhodes from York has alerted me to the recent young bird losses, particularly on the north road. It is a fact that all birds will eventually fail to home if sent far enough and long enough. There are many factors which contribute to the losses and in some lofts the reasons are many. The quality of many fanciers' methods and their birds is often suspect. It is a hard road to the top and there are many hurdles to be crossed. Many fanciers blame the weather, the transporter and the convoyer first, when it is wise to look in the mirror and do some soul-searching. Was my feeding correct? Is the loft right? Are the young birds bred properly? And if you can face it, am I a good young bird fancier? Many fanciers blame external things, not being prone to such introspection.

In the desire for speed and to win at all costs short young bird races (under 100 miles), birds are often given many short (under 30 miles) consecutive tosses and are trained too hungry to the corn tin. If you have hoppers of pellets in the loft (mine were layers) young pigeons will still trap to the corn mix, since they prefer corn to pellets. However, pellets are better for the birds nutritionally. You should avoid sending starving young birds to the race, as if the weather is hard, i.e. velocities 800-1000ypm, the weaker ones with little reserves being sent too light in the body, will tend to go down. If you race young birds with full bodies, they tend to keep homing days after racing in 'hard' conditions.

Prior to racing, it is best to give a nice toss of 50-60 miles, say on the Wednesday. This, with adequate feed, will help to muscle up the birds and often some of the rubbish will be lost before you pay for race entries. Probably the best way to home young birds is the open loft system, with pellets before them and corn fed at tea time. In 2005 as an example I had nine young birds come together at 800+ velocity from Leicester, 95 miles. These were sent as trainers, with no prior basketing straight to the race point. Now this is condition.

Of course young birds need to be healthy, i.e. free from canker, worms, coccidiosis, respiratory diseases etc. Additionally, if you starve young birds they are not likely to be champions as yearlings!

Two more tips: to put body on your young birds, feed peanuts and also trap with them. Also too much stressful basketing of young birds often induces young bird sickness.

WHO ARE THE GREATEST?

There are some wonderful fliers, both in the UK and abroad. Some of these fall short of our consciousness due to a lack of publicity, which is sometimes associated with commercialism and the need to make money. I regard 'greatness' in terms not just of excellence in results but also the contribution the fanciers have made to the sport. The latter can be in the form of knowledge passed on to the fancy through the media of books, articles, orders, DVDs and other communications.

Perhaps our greatest all-round distance and marathon fancier, in the sense of pure performances, was the late Jim Biss with his results in the NFC, e.g. 1st and 2nd Open Pau and his outstanding results in the BICC at Barcelona, Marseille etc. Alone and in the partnership of Biss & Waite, he had many multi-performance distance birds. However, this legacy of hard facts and knowledge passed onto the fancy is not huge. I feel that he took a lot of intimate and detailed knowledge with him.

In the modern era I rate Chris Gordon as the greatest all-round living fancier in terms of results, with his NFC win at Tarbes 725 miles (a record). His many Section wins in the NFC and BBC and the fact that he is the best long distance NFC fancier in the country (over 350 miles). He appears to reveal all to the fancy through his informative DVD and reports. He also has a good managerial pigeon brain, being the Olympiad team manager and on the council for the RPRA. I regard him as being the complete pigeon man, and with some International results will really emphasise the fact.

If you see International racing as the ultimate, and I do, then no one can compare with the results of Brian Sheppard, who with the Legend was 1st International Dax and followed it up a year later with 2nd International. On the International front we have Mark Gilbert with his 1st International Dax and also 1st National with Night Flight. These two fanciers are of historical importance to the fancy, they are icons.

From other parts of the UK, I notice Ronnie Williamson in Ireland with his many outstanding performances in National and Open competition. His racing methods are a triumph, as can be seen on his videos. Originating in Scotland, and now in Malta, we have the family friend of

Eddie Newcombe with his many SNFC wins. Eddie became world famous in his life and his son at the Macmerry Lofts maintains the tradition of racing excellence with two Rennes SNFC wins.

Staying in Scotland, and from the modern era, we have Jim Donaldson of Peterhead with his record wins at 600-700 miles, including an SNFC win at Sartilly 605 miles, his many North Section wins and a Gold Award with Reims Girl, a distance record. Jim has revealed much about his simple flying system on video with Many Miles with Mott, Vol 12. Jim was a fisherman out of Peterhead and his hard, no-nonsense approach has paid off with his birds. We exchanged birds and my Oddball was bred from a son of Jim's Nantes hen. The above are a few comments about some of our excellent fanciers. The use of the term 'greatness' is purely a value judgement and left for you, the reader to decide. My apologies to all those, some of them largely unknown, who I have not mentioned.

In my local York area, we have some outstanding fliers, particularly at Club and Fed level. I have noticed the excellent results of Cashmore & Miller, Rhodes & Son and Deighton & Lister at Acomb. Over many years, and up to Saintes NFC, but especially at Club and Fed level we have the outstanding partnership of B. & C. Mason. They really go at the job with a vengeance and take an awful lot of beating in both north and south routes, especially up to 500 miles.

I have written before about Brian Denney, but he is a fantastic NFC flier between 573 and 748 miles, a real expert! A famous fancier. I am especially pleased with the recent young bird results of Booth & Shipley. Chris North is the grandson of the late Ted Booth and has inherited some of his quiet, gentlemanly qualities. I feel he has the temperament to be a good distance man later. His partner Steve Shipley is a cheeky charmer and a good support to Chris — nice to see them doing well.

I write this article in memory of Eric Gibson, who with his partner Duncan Gray could clean up in the sprints and enjoyed NFC success up to their recent 20th Open NFC Tarbes 747 miles. Before his death Eric and I studied butterflies on his buddleia bushes. I said to Eric: 'What more could a man want than to gaze up on butterflies?'

HOW DO PIGEONS HOME?

The mystery of how pigeons home is still unsolved in this modem age of rocket science. Pigeons belong to a large group of birds which can migrate over distances in excess of 1,000 miles, although pigeon homing distances are relatively small.

The ability to home apparently varies from one individual to another. As fanciers we try to improve the homing faculty through fitness and training. It is easy to think that pigeons possess a combination of instinct and intelligence, but do they have some sort of mind or self-awareness? How do you perceive what is in the head of a pigeon?

We can observe that pigeons interact with us, but at what type of level of awareness or consciousness? Now science with its methodology attempts to discover or explain reality with its theories and hypotheses. As human consciousness develops and applies science to the homing ability question, it evolves using the theories of the time. Today there have been many experiments to try and solve the riddle such as ESP, the earth's magnetic field, sense of smell, the solar position, and all of these are limited because of their human-based application. We can only know things from a human perspective, and because of this limitation I doubt that we can ever totally answer the question, 'How does a pigeon home?' I am quite happy with the notion that I will never know the answer.

SON OF BARCELONA DREAM MAKES GOOD

For those who are interested in the Emerton and Donaldson strains, Jim Donaldson of Peterhead has kindly sent me some details. In case you don't know Jim is one of the finest fliers of hard, long-distance and marathon pigeons in the world. We first exchanged birds in 1998 with the best of our respective strains. He is a man whose honesty and integrity is beyond reproach.

Readers will know I believe in exchanging and giving good pigeons — there are too many pigeon sharks in the ocean of racing. This principle has borne fruit with the Unique Cock. He is the last remaining son of Barcelona Dream and Dark Enchantment, two of my Barcelona International birds at 879 miles to Holtby, Yorks in the BICC. You will know that I keep urging the fancy in the north of the country to better this in the BICC and, of course, they will do. The Unique Cock represents years of inbreeding to my foundation birds with a trace of Brian Denney — I do not hide from the truth.

Jim Donaldson again did well in the Scottish National Flying Club in 2008 taking 3rd Section, 32nd Open and 8th Section, 53rd Open Alençon, 631 miles, with children or grandchildren of the Unique Cock. Many of his birds live to a great age.

PROFESSIONALISM IN THE SPORT

There are certain standards that you have a right to expect, when, for example, purchasing pigeons. The bird should be what it says on the tin! However a pedigree is only as good and as accurate as the pedigree maker and even with DNA certification there is room for exploitation. ft is sad that many fanciers are tricked out of their money by over-hyped advertising. There are relatively few champion pigeons about and most birds from any strain will not make the grade between 700 and 800 miles in hard racing. A lot of fanciers are carried away by feelings of over optimism and seek to buy pigeons from a humble strain which has been made famous by the giant egos behind the word of advertising. Now there are many dubious National win claims: the only three Nationals in England are the NFC, the BICC and the BBC, all the others, in my opinion, being hyped up by word power.

When buying pigeons, I would always judge the honesty and integrity of the dealer or fancier first, before judging any individual pigeon. Of course there are fanciers out there who can be trusted, but believe me the waters are infested with sharks!

For many years I sold pigeons at £60 each or £290 for six, which I consider reasonable money. The exception was Barcelona Dream's children, which were £250 each. You don't always get what you pay for and I quote the dictum of Jack Ross: 'Good pigeons are given, Jim.'

GOOD SPORTSMANSHIP

An injection of this would certainly make the racing world a better place. In striving ruthlessly to be No. 1 in their clubs etc., many fanciers forget to use good gentlemanly qualities of sportsmanship. If you can shake the hand of the winner and mean it, it says a lot. There are so many winners who are hungry for a good pat on the back! One way of sharing it could be to buy a round of drinks with your pool money. The lack of good sportsmanship is possibly the fundamental illness of the fancy today. Another good example is when a good flier gives good pigeons away to the novice or less fortunate. A lack of sportsmanship is also linked to the political manipulation of rules to gain advantage.

REVITALISING THE NATIONAL FLYING CLUB

Surely the NFC has reduced both prestige and membership during recent criticism and counter propaganda. Although I long been a devoted fan of the club, I feel it requires a radical shake-up to restore it to its former glory, in both the National and International spheres.

At the committee level we need united and progressive leadership to progress the NFC as
England's premier club. I know of much in-fighting within the Committee which is having a negative impact on the running of the NFC. The sole collective idea and principle should be sustained improvement in the club. I know that Sid Barkel, who has my birds, is an administrative whizz, with his heart and soul behind the club, and this invites loyal support.

Some practical possibilities to improve the club are to: a) Increase the subs to say £30. b) Sell young birds off the current year's winners to the fancy, advertising them in the fancy press. c) Come on you millionaire fanciers, donate to the NFC. d) Allow YBs ringed with other than NFC rings to compete in the YB National, and encourage fanciers from other organisations such as the MNFC to do so. e) Appoint some young/progressive men or women to the Committee – by young shall we say those under 50 years of age. f) Incorporate the Barcelona International and Paul International races into the NFC programme, since we live in the world, not just in England. Our winners, both fanciers and pigeons, could then be recognised throughout the world. There are many more suggestions – these are just a few points.

STEVE WAIN, A CUSTODIAN OF THE EMERTON STRAIN

Steve Wain, from Foston in Derbyshire and the Steffan Club, is an emerging force in the National Flying Club. He tends to be a rather quiet, small team fancier who chooses his few entries with great care and enjoys a flutter. Fanciers will be impressed with his Section I wins and positions.

What I like about Steve is that he cultivates my family of birds, taking great care in the preparation and pairing of his candidates. He recently sent me some sample pedigrees and enlarged photos for my perusal. They are true to type, with names like Tuppence, Ha'penny, Birthday Bird etc. Luckily he has established a no. 1 breeding pair (so far) and is concentrating around all my key birds like Dark Enchantment, Dark Velvet, Barcelona Dream, Mystical Queen, Oddball etc.

Steve, I feel that you are ready to take on the Internationals in the BICC, so go for it. He's a man who has no great desire for lots of fame, yet likes the idea of being known for flying a good pigeon. You certainly do that and the big guns are taking note!

A LITTLE VISIT TO MICK SWALLOW OF YORK

On my way for a country walk I took a detour to Mick's house in York. Let me state that when I started out with racers in 1976 he was at the top of the tree and in many people's minds this is a position he retains to this day. We sat down and enjoyed bringing the great, lost days of the characters in the St Lawrence WMC to mind. Mick recalled the pleasure of those times, the halcyon days when you could enjoy the race, some banter and 'one of each' on the way home. Now, Mick was more of an inspiration to me than he realises!

Clocking a chequer pied cock for Brian Shipley, I eventually acquired it. It was from Mick's Albert Witty-based birds from Blow Home and The Boy. Now Casanova took over my loft, so I gave it to Wayne Aldous of York. The old cock bred to a great age and sired many winners. At the moment Mick has a beautiful collection of Roland Janssen-based birds direct from Louella Pigeon World. These looked stunning, in great condition and will breed many, many winners for others. Mick generates a buzz from selling quality birds at reasonable rates to others. The birds are from the best lines available and unlike most people's birds (have a look at yours!) were free of quill mite. Mick really cares for his birds and their condition is an outward expression of his management skill.

That was the day in 1995 when Mick stopped to congratulate me in the street on the efforts of Barcelona Dream. At that time he had chalked up 11 firsts in a season. You are a dedicated man, and long may you enjoy your birds.

A JOURNEY OF THE SOUL

In my perception, both birds and humans have an inner or spiritual nature. A fancier in a heightened state of consciousness can know the 'oneness' of man and pigeon. This is racing at its very best and most rewarding state. It is a spiritual experience, a journey of the soul.

Writers give credence to the mystical and, for example, if you clock at Barcelona International, the fact should elevate the ego. When we start at say club level, if we are ambitious we want to win and win, irrespective of the quality of races, I may add. We then set out to be top prizewinner at club level, beating the local 'experts'.

Now to the initiated and on an esoteric level, racing is a larger playing field than this. We can see the wisdom in testing and building a strain, we can test the outer limits of endurance of our birds. I can say that I did this as a modern pioneer at 687 miles, Dax International into Yorkshire, and to verify three out of six birds at Barcelona International, 879 miles. Now ponder the actual flying distance of those endurance athletes that would dogleg around the Pyrenees.

My strain of birds is fit and well after 34 years and this is true testament to the spirit of racing.

DOES A PIGEON THINK?

This question is posed by Steve Wain, the well-known National (NFC) man. Due to the limitations of human consciousness, the collective knowledge of science and any other human endeavour probably falls short of absolute knowledge of anything. In other words, we can probably never answer the question in a total way. However, we can use the human mind to gain biased judgements when answering questions. To think, a pigeon must have *a priori* a mind. If so, does it have any sense of self-awareness — a normal human trait?

From my perception as a human a pigeon can react, communicate with and respond instinctively to its world. We perceive it to have senses and we know that some individual birds can navigate and race up to say 1,000 miles in three days. The distances pigeons 'navigate' in terms of the Arctic tern are relatively short. If a pigeon does or does not think, what impact on 'homing' does this have? There is a correlation between possible thinking and homing. Current scientific thought process attempts with empirical experiments to determine the means of navigation aided or not aided by any thinking process. In my opinion we as humans will never know!

Yet, from my inner self on an intuitive/mystical level I believe a good bird 'knows' its way from Pau or Barcelona in the basket in the 'dark'.

THE EMERTON STRAIN

There have been a few comments from fanciers regarding the strain of pigeons that I raced, so here are a few details of the original stock that I brought in and based my family on many years ago.

My strain was formed after 1976 from seven birds, being four from the stock of Descamps van Hasten origin, these being inbred to Alois, the Stichelbaut original of the 1940s, one cock being Darkness, the same genes as The Tee direct from Emiel Denys. There was also a grandson of the famous van Wanroy Kleine Donkere, which has a legacy of winners at the distance, plus a granddaughter of Woodsider, and

Claire is also in the family. Then there was a daughter from the origin of Faith, the 1,000-mile bloodlines.

My number one pair was Dark Destiny, inbred to the Descamp van Hasten Stichelbauts and paired to a daughter of Darkness.

My best racer/producer from the number one pair was the great Diabolos and thanks to Louella and the Ponderosa UK, they are still winning races today.

CARING FOR PRISONER STOCK BIRDS

It is often believed that prisoner stock birds are not fit and breed inferior youngsters. On my travels I have seen that in many cases this is true; birds are dirty, depressed, flea ridden and just not healthy. Apart from any inborn congenital weakness the answer lies with the fancier. For the health of any stock bird the No 1 priority is an aviary exposed to the sun, snow, wind and rain, i.e. all the elements that nature offers. A bath with salts can be placed in the aviary. Now watch for condition and contentment, the beautiful glossy feather of the birds.

Feeding is as follows: layers' pellets, peanuts, high protein corn mix, brewers' yeast, mixed oils, Hormoform and some small seed. The supplement should be Gem's Matrix. Now watch those babies grow to their full potential. Human treatment of the birds should be gentle and kind, time to be ruthless at racing time! I am writing this having seen the cruel and pitiless plight of some stock birds in the UK. In contrast note the stock birds of Jim Donaldson, which live in contentment to a great age.

FACING DIFFICULTIES

In our pigeon lives we will all have difficulties to face and overcome. Some of us are handicapped and have family and work pressures and responsibilities. We must try and overcome all these problems and keep clear in our focus on doing our best with the birds. One of the most famous triumphs over adverse conditions was Jed Jackson with Genista, a Pau NFC winner. Ably assisted by his splendid wife, he knew by handling with his inner sight each bird in his possession. This is the stuff of lasting folklore.

I am pleased that ETS systems make things easier for many fanciers. You want to forget the few seconds' potential advantage and offset this against the benefits to man. I recall the two birds I missed from Pau 735 miles due to sleeping in. ETS is here to stay and good stuff.

My personal racing from 1979 onwards involved travelling six miles each way to the loft from York to Holtby. Dorothy and I put the birds at the top of the agenda – we left no stone unturned in our quest! In 1996 I retired from active work and spent years tending to my gradually ailing mother, Freddie the dog and the birds. My birds bred the natural life as many marathon birds do, and I would sit out in the snow and happily watch them fly about, sit on wires and be like wild ones. These take some beating in the Internationals.

In October '04 I stopped Dorothy going to the loft because with her frailty (osteoporosis and a bad heart) she nearly blew over in the wind. Yes, she was as hard as a bag of nails and indomitable (it takes a good woman, you men!)

I admit I am obsessed with birds and enjoy my pigeons again today. At the end of the day my lasting memory is of Dax My Girl, who I rate as good, if not better than the

Dream. Her result was 4th Open Single Bird NFC (All England) and longest flying bird in Europe to be clocked in a Dax International in England in the top quarter of the result, 17,526 birds 687 miles. She was a lovely hen and expected on that lovely day in July when Jean, Dorothy and myself sat with expectation and anticipation. Since I was three, pigeons have nurtured my spirit. I hope you gain inspiration from this.

OUTBREEDING MY STRAIN

Most fanciers by now will be aware that I am a confirmed inbreeder around my seven foundation birds with good results from 71 to 879 miles with the same Stichelbaut-based pigeons, all acquired for a song. I am so pleased that my stock birds have been distributed around the UK and Ireland. One of the key birds of the present is Velvet Destiny; now this little hen had 21 times the No.1 stock pair (Dark Destiny and daughter of Darkness) in her blood. I know of no one who has gone closer. Some of her offspring when outcrossed (outbreeding) are special.

I can report that I am again involved in racing — it interests me in my retirement. Now Brian Denney and I have been rivals, yet I recommend his strain as a related outbreed into my own. This recommendation is catching on big time. Some special birds will come out of this philosophy and perhaps a really good Barcelona International bird.

I do not know what Brian really thinks of me, although I rate his Tarbes NFC as world-class and somewhat unique, certainly in the UK. Good will come out of this article, as it will benefit the fancy in general.

Reminder, don't forget your distance and marathon men

— have a go at the Internationals into the UK with the BICC, BBC and one day (I hope) the NFC. All the best.

A VISIT BY REMBRANDT AND PICASSO

Fanciers may know that when I donated the Emerton strain to the Barkel Bros, Sunderland, we moved from Holtby to a bungalow. I am very happy with hardly any things and my writing pens. Jean decided it was decoration time, so we employed the services of a local pigeon master decorator, Chris Booth of CJB Decorators, York. Chris duly turned up with his comedic, artistic partner David, and the chaos started, punctuated by hilarity and good-natured banter which lasted for nearly five days. Chris decided to obtain some more of my birds (he has a small stud of four pairs) and David acquired a black and gold MENSA mug for keeps. We bored the hat off David with pigeon talk and David entertained us with his loves. I was so impressed with the quality of the workmanship that I christened them Rembrandt and Picasso (not Monet and Manet). Goodness knows what they really think of me!

ABHORRENT BAD PRACTICE

Young Chris Booth from York informs me that one of his cocks returned minus metal ring and ETS ring. Various types of people can perpetrate this crime; it may be young lads wanting to keep a strag, or people resentful of the ETS system. Often 'fanciers' take a fancy to a strag and try and conceal its identity by removing all trace of ownership. Aren't there some rogues in pigeon racing? Chris was upset, and sometimes strags reared to be champions. Many a champion is a strag in someone's loft at some stage. Nearly all of my top distance and marathon birds had time out!

On a kinder note, it is nice to see some recent success from up and coming Brian Shipley (brother of Cheeky Charmer) and good luck to all York fanciers.

OBTAINING PIGEONS FOR LONG-DISTANCE STOCK

Pigeons that will perform well in races between 500 and 800 miles are very hard to come by, even from the best of families and strains. It is wise to remember that the best pigeons in the world will only respond under the influence of good sound management techniques. However we do have some excellent long-distance fanciers in the UK, such as Jim Donaldson in Scotland, who may be willing to part with some birds. Jim is a hard and honest taskmaster who keeps a strain of 500 to 700 mile performers. Another fancier is Chris Gordon, who in my opinion, after the sad demise of Jim Biss, qualifies as the best all-round fancier in the UK. He is also highly regarded and gives much to the sport of pigeon racing. There are also excellent fanciers in the north of Holland who clock 800 miles plus on the second day from the Barcelona International.

Commercially in England there is Louella Pigeon World, without doubt the origin and source of some good home-produced strains of birds. In 1976 I was fortunate enough to have the personal attention of both John and Michael Massarella. We spent a long time debating the merits of a large number of direct Vanhees and Emiel Denys. We eventually narrowed the choice down to a blue Vanhee cock and a dark chequer Emiel Denys, very similar to the Tee. The cock was the most expensive, £55, and sired my No 1 stock hen Daughter of Darkness. I will always be grateful to John and Michael for this.

The following pedigree illustrates the progeny produced by this No 1 stock pair. Diabolos GB83S35305, whose best performances included the Yorkshire Middle Route Trophy, 1st Section; 6th Open Nevers, 516 miles, 2,516 birds; 2nd Section, 5th Open Beauvais 3,500 birds; 2nd Section Melun 408 miles approximately 2,000 birds; 1st Open YB Rievely Cup Race. Diabolos' bloodline produced birds to score from 70 to 900 miles, and from club to Barcelona International level. The sire was GB78S6321 Dark Destiny, No 1 stock cock; the grandsire GB77S34778 Iron Man, D. V. H. Stichelbaut from a brother/sister pairing won 4th Section Clermont; the sires granddam was Iron Hen GB77S34776 1st Section Clermont, 350 miles. Diabolos' dam was GB79S09349, the No 1 stock hen Daughter of Darkness; grandsire Darkness Belg76-4415080 Emiel Denys; grandam GB76J83650, a granddaughter of Woodsider, Claire, Rossall King.

Once I had found my golden pair I religiously linebred and inbred to this pair and the relatives Dreadnought and Delilah (D. V. H. Stichelbaut-based) which I bought from Louella Lofts. Incidentally the Iron Hen would fly down the garden and land on my head. To this day a lot of my birds are quiet and tame, which is a good quality in long-distance birds. By the way, Diabolos lived to 22 years of age.

A NOSTALGIC TRIP TO RYHOPE

On the misty morning of 21st October, Chris Booth set the satnav on the Jeep Cherokee and performed his Lewis Hamilton impression as Steve Shipley and I set off to meet the Barkels. Dorothy Barkel, our secretary's mother, met us and directed us to the pigeon lofts, where we were met by Sid senior and his sons David and Sid junior. The extensive lofts, bathed in sunshine, looked out over a series of well-made terraces, dominated centrally by two lions. What a lovely place to sit and look at a perfect, panoramic view of Ryhope.

Then it was down to business, as David, who has a good brain for a bird, helped me to look through my old stock birds and racers. I immediately recognised these as my little hard, dark diamonds, the results of 30 years of intensive racing and breeding around my foundation pigeons. We divided them between the out-and-out breeding birds and those that had been in the race loft.

An important discovery was made when we found a key bird in Eric, a little dark cock which I had bred especially for stock for Gibson & Gray. However he was raced (Brian Denney thought he looked like a blackie) and was Eric's and Duncan's sole surviving latebred. Later, being injured, he was returned to me, where due to his fabulous breeding he was put into stock. Eric is a son of the Dark Velvet Hen, Mystical Queen and a grandson of Dark Velvet and Dedication. Mystical Queen was an inbred granddaughter of the great Diabolos and a daughter of Sister Damien. Now all these birds were inbred and line bred to my foundation birds – concentrated breeding at its best. Eric has a sister and she bred my best performance long-distance hen before I retired. Stressing the value of a brother x sister mating, David is to mate Eric to his sister for stock. It transpires that Eric is the grandsire of the second best NFC bird calculated from the computer over the first four NFC races in '07 for Trevor Robinson of Patrington. Eric is also the sire of two of the Barkels' top yearlings when paired to a daughter of Dax II.

I wish the Barkels well in their 500-mile plus ambitions and to clock in an International at Ryhope would make them world-famous, it takes dedication with Mr Basket, that's all.

Sid, the NFC Secretary, took us to the nerve centre of the NEC in his house and showed us all the sophisticated technology used in the execution of his office, a nightmare for me. He is a brainy lad our Sid, and without him the NFC would fall apart at the seams. A very dedicated man indeed, his mind trained in the right direction.

Towards the end we enjoyed a traditionally large Sunday lunch prepared by Dorothy, and met young Sid's three beautiful children, his lovely wife Karen, and David's beautiful wife. It was nice to see the extended family and let's hope for more pigeon greatness.

This is the last in this series of 'Insights'. I hope you have been stimulated by my articles and the truth as I see it. Fame in pigeon racing is relatively easy to achieve with hard work and dedication. We live in a society where the culture of the celebrity is paramount. Ironically, I have a great admiration for those who are happy with themselves and do not seek fame, it being an illusion of the ego. Fame is not to be confused with greatness, which is affirmed by others' perceptions of you. However, to reach the public eye as a fancier you need good management, good birds and publicity — beware the trickster and con-men who will take your money.

Thank you readers, and 'bye for now.

TEN

Features and interviews

JOHN GHENT INTERVIEWS JIM EMERTON
British Homing World, October 5 2012

Jim, there have been many articles, interviews and forum threads about your work and life. What I want to know is, what kept you striving towards your goals, and what mindset did you need to accomplish what you have done in life and the sport of pigeon racing?

I have a relentless and obsessive drive and aim to reach perfection, to taste life on the edge of possibility, to feel excellence in my life and to teach other people. In the search for the end of my aspirations, truth is found. It is a spiritual/existential truth to unify all the aspects of my personality. In my life passions I immersed myself in love, travel, MENSA, science, mysticism, the arts, high culture etc. My one real dream and master is total immersion in pigeons. The mindset is total preoccupation 24/7, sleeping and waking. It embraces my entire universe. Persevere. Persist. Endure in life's epic odyssey.

Where did you develop this mindset? Who, if anyone, were your role models and how was the young Jim formed?

As a child I was a gifted, hypersensitive boy with an intense inner life. At grammar school I was slow to mature, yet had a profound love of nature, especially birds, with which I share a Taoist-like feeling of empathy. I have felt at one with the elements, especially wild winds on the Wash foreshore where I was a wildfowler with the great Kenzie, the wild goose man. I felt wild, free, liberated. My old friend from 1960 is John Shinn, an expert shot, big game hunter and hard case. We lived the boy's adventure dream. My parents and sister inspired, bullied and motivated me to push forward to fulfil myself. Think it, do it, mind above the material.

Is there a single event that comes to mind that changed your thought processes in the early days? If not, what succession of events (education, work, relationships) made you the person that you are today?

As a withdrawn, aloof teenager, my sister Pat fired my inner imagination with the proclamation that she had six O-levels to my four, which woke me up to desire, to ambition, to become. The consequence was 11 years in formal/academic education, with degree level studies in the sciences and later the arts. My finest hour was passing the MENSA test with an IQ score of 154. I now write for six interest groups and love that!

Jim, you have travelled the world, met many people and immersed yourself in different cultures, which place or culture has had the biggest impact on you?

My travels have taken me to Africa, Asia and the Americas. I went right into Afghanistan to the Bamiyan Valley. The Himalayan people, the Nepalese and Tibetans were lovely, happy people. Spiritual folk in the majestic Everest and Annapurna ranges. Lake Dahl in Kashmir was enchanting, while the Golden Temple in Amritsar, India is the finest building on earth. Travelling into remote Turkey, to Odessa in Russia, I met happy-go-lucky folk, generous with honest smiles. An American academic, Joe Lemak, a giant of a human being, and I shared wonderful times from London to Nepal in 1979. I miss him.

As you have previously said to me, it took 30 years of dedication to get your strain right to tackle Barcelona, and I am aware of your dedication towards MENSA and the arts. Is there anything close to your heart that we do not know about, or have you always opened up everything in the public domain?

I have great compassion for the needy, troubled souls who yearn for spiritual guidance and approaching the age of the sage I like to guide them through relationship difficulties. Sadly my youthful euphoria is tinged now by cynicism as the truth is realised – oh, I still have the old travel passports! In reality we are little grains of sand in the cosmic hour glass of time.

Do you believe in luck? Whatever the answer, why do you/don't you, and do you believe the building of your strain had anything to do with luck at all?

We are all at the mercy of the cosmic influences and elements that we know exist or perhaps via human limits of consciousness do not know exist. The extroverted psychological type tends to concentrate on the external phenomena referred to as reality. Without going deep into abstract metaphysical issues, I intuit that luck could be a human way of compartmentalising certain life conditions. I had a dream, a vision, to eventually build my own strain progressing a club level and with singularity of purpose to be as good as I could become with as much actual personal control as possible. The aim is to be tenacious and manage a researched system of sending birds in any weather forecast to any distance in pursuit of actual results facing real environmental race conditions. In an absolute sense I know nothing, a philosophical issue. Good fortune to those who believe in luck, may your beliefs go with you.

Did you set out with the mindset to create an ultimate marathon strain or did the realisation of this come to light after the first years? What led you to invest in the birds that you did in the beginning?

I wanted to assert myself in all races from 1977. Seeing an advert for Louella DVH Stichelbauts I said to my father, they are the ones for me. I picked a pair on handling/pedigree and judgement. These bred the great Iron

Hen and Iron Man, parents of Dark Destiny, my no 1 foundation stock hen, when paired to a granddaughter of Woodsider. The rest is history, with rare introductions from Denney/Donaldson/Robinson, all great marathon men with inbred birds. I had great belief in my birds and myself.

Did you always feel different to the club mates that were club clocking and average chasing year after year, and did you ever feel any resentment from them?

I always felt individual/different, full stop. Yet until 1992 I raced in club/fed and opens. It is difficult to be popular and a good racer; I have sensed human emotions from others and for many many years I trained only in organisations before National/International races. Thank you to all the good people who helped me from 1976. I have a UK network of friends exchanging and cultivating birds of my strain origin, good men all. We are on this earth to help one another.

When was the first time you realised you had struck gold with the strain of pigeons that you created? Was it the offspring of a particular pair that hit the nail on the head, a single bird that made the penny drop?

In the late 70s I struck gold, breeding the fabulous No 1 pair, parents of my greatest bird, Diabolos. Descendants of these birds are scoring at Barcelona International and relatives have won and scored from 35 to 879 miles into the UK. The insight is close family breeding to performance racers and breeders on winning methods. Tip: test your birds in Internationals.

Did you ever make any bad introductions that just did not work? We have heard before about the good introductions, but was there a bad apple anywhere in the history of the Emerton strain? If so, did it put you back at all?

Not being perfect (and neither are birds), I have introduced/bred and raced more low-quality than good-quality birds, always taking stock latebreds off the perceived best and using old Darwinian principles of selection. Always persist. In the past I have sent to marathons with zero results. Tip: Empty the loft as a real tester in the big races.

So, we know about your methods Jim, and they contradict most of what many fanciers do. How did you develop the ideas, the system, the selection process to allow you to clock from Barcelona in 1995?

As a child roaming the countryside at Skendleby in the Lincolnshire Wolds I tasted real freedom. Bird-nesting, exploring and being a boy of Mother Nature, my poetry reflects my passion for the elements today, sharp and perceptive. I observed and empathised with the instinctual and survival behaviours of wild doves and pigeons and marvelled at their speed and acceleration in fog, wind and rain. Later I would graduate in rural studies, sciences, horticulture and the arts. What a bookish introvert I became. Moving to Sycamore Cottage in Holtby in 1976, with an old loft at 60 pounds, cried out loudly for a free/open loft system in real nature. My academic/scientific training fuelled my psyche into formulating my unique system. It consists of liquid feeding/supplementation and almost optimal firing and fuelling up to maximise endurance levels, using the analogy of the migrating swallow. Selection is simple, yearlings, and all of them, at 466 miles in the NFC, then all 2ys between 735 to 879 miles at Barcelona International. The distances produce the right birds in a total sense eg stamina/ speed/endurance and orientation which are genome based. Years and years of study, my friends.

Following on from that, how confident were you when you sent to Barcelona that year and how did you select which birds would go?

The clock was struck at Strensall PRS by Brian Denney of York, England. In a dramatic and prophetic moment I said I was going to clock; it was predictive and seminal, as it transpired there were east and north-east winds during the flight in England. It was harder than hell! Verifying three, I had sent the only remaining six birds in the loft, would have been great if I had 20 available. These were 2 and 3ys, ie Diamond Queen/Barcelona/Dream/Dark Enchantment etc. These were sent in boxes via Amtrak to John Lyden in Kent for marking, thanks again John. Now Nic Harvey of Taunton and I send all 2ys to Barcelona International at 710 miles to form a strain based on the Emertons.

JIM EMERTON AND THE SPORT OF
MARATHON PIGEON RACING

British Homing World, August 1st, 2008

Although no longer actively involved in the breeding and the racing of our flying thoroughbreds, Jim Emerton of England, based upon earlier participation, has left his mark in the realm of marathon racing in Europe. And although not actively involved as a pigeoner, our subject contributes to the sport through his involvement in pigeon racing journalism. He is a person who reveals who he is and what he knows because of his lifetime love of marathon pigeon racing, an undying love that may again open the door to his participation.

Jim is a person of high intelligence and advocates that the gift or faculty of the latter should be applied in the breeding, racing and all aspects of the sport of the gods. Thus, as one who values the knowledge and the experience of others from the top level of our sport, I decided to interview Jim on the back of an earlier insight.

In this introduction I must add that Jim's late mother Dorothy played an important part in the sport during his years of success, and to her I dedicate this article.

The following in essence is Jim's answers to 20 questions which I put to him and which outline a marathonist of the highest level, a person who possessed a unique insight into the art and the science of long-distance pigeon racing. Via his father, Jim senior, our subject has been in contact with pigeons since the age of three. He realised early on his earthly journey that pigeons made him happy, including the non-racing varieties.

As a family the Emertons lived in various parts of their native land, a nomadic experience by which Jim came into contact with a number of pigeoners during his early years. These encounters deepened Jim's love for our flying athletes and indeed this deepening attachment developed a mystical relationship with the racing dove, an association which heightened the imagination of an intellectual who in his school years wrote an essay concerning the clocking of a long-distance candidate from Marennes in France. Perhaps an example of dreaming dreams and asking 'Why not?'

Arising from the family's nomadic lifestyle, the Emertons eventually settled at Sycamore Cottage, Holtby, York, in 1976, where Jim made friends with a pigeoner called Jack Russ. This fancier gifted our subject with some squeakers and via his new friend Jim became a member of the St. Lawrence W.M.C. in York. Through the gifted squeakers our subject experienced his first win in the sport, which fired him so much that in due course a few Stichelbauts were purchased from

Louella Lofts, coupled by a grandson of the great ' Kleine Donkere' from the Ponderosa Lofts, UK. Thus the foundation of the Emerton strain was very soundly laid. Also I must add that Jack Russ was the person through whom Jim met Jean, his partner of 30 years.

Thus at this time Jim Emerton reached for the stars, and in due course he had them in his grasp. It was a journey which saw his birds fly marathon distances against the odds across the English Channel from the European mainland, brave feathered warriors that had to break off from thousands of equally brave Continental thoroughbreds on their journey to the land of the rose. Yes, it took courage as well as intelligence to branch off from the security of thousands and face a lonely journey into the Western Isles, a journey which he shortly hopes to see with an arrival from the Spanish race point on the 2nd day into the UK as part of what has become known as the 'Emerton 800 Miles Barcelona Challenge'; for Jim has promised £1,000 to the owner of the bird which accomplishes this act of endurance and intelligent orientation.

Jim contended that genetic quality was more important than looks or handling qualities, stating that a good pigeon, genetics-wise, will endure hard conditions over 700 miles and that the internal factors, allied with the basket, differentiates between the champions and the also rans. Such pedigreed stock must dwell in hygienic conditions, preferably a litter of wood shavings and Easibed; he opines that such a system ensures immunity from most diseases. In relation to disease, Jim doctored for worms and canker but holds the opinion that the sport has taken a wrong turn through over-dosing, especially the increasing use of antibiotics.

His breeding methodology involved all aspects – in, line and cross. Once he had discovered a golden pair, 'Dark Destiny' and 'Daughter of Darkness', Jim line bred and inbred to those great producers for 30 years without many introductions. Some of the latter were stock from Brian Denney, Jim Donaldson and Trevor Robinson.

Our subject admits to making managerial mistakes, but is of the opinion that the implied wrong decisions are the materials by which the potential to achieve greatness or genius arises, being of the opinion that the essence of genius is simplicity itself, thus keeping management simple, allied with a well-thought-out plan that took account of and accommodated failure. Yes, Jim sent birds in terrible weather conditions and too early on in the season and rued it, but being a thinking pigeoner he learnt from his mistakes. Would that others would do the same. Then there would be fewer strays dotting the landscape from over-producing pigeon lofts that bring the sport into disrepute.

His advice for the novice is to read all that the experts of the sport put to paper. Befriend top pigeoners and seek their advice. Test young birds and yearlings hard, the latter up to 400-470 miles, and if possible from an open loft with plenty of air, space and light. Then as two-year-olds, if off the right pedigreed stock, they are ready for marathon tasks of 600-plus miles. He states that candidates for such long distances should not be rationed, foodwise. His feeding was the same for both old and young birds. In the hoppers at all times layers' pellets were available, but they also received Gerryplus and Superplus with peanuts, Red Band and Hormoform.

In his later years of participation in the sport Jim did not train his young birds but lifted them from the loft into races of 95 and 138 miles, and they flew well. In his younger years he would toss midweek at 90 miles from all areas of the compass, and they did equally well. He usually started training a fortnight before racing began. The old birds for national and international racing were trained by entering shorter races of the programme. Here Jim reminds us that old birds do not need to be taught the way home and that good, fit birds will orientate very well.

When he was actively participating in the sport, what epitomised Jim, to those who know him, was that his personality was dedicated to breeding, racing and all-round management of the sport. Yes, he was involved at Club and Fed levels of management as well. Such dedication and commitment were bound to bear fruit of immense proportions, such as many wins in club and above.

Perhaps of his many successes in the sport, the outstanding achievement of 'Barcelona Dream' in the

Barcelona Marathon International of 1995 was the greatest reward for his commitment and genius. Jim's great athlete finished 13th Open in the British International Championship Club section at the distance of 879 soul-destroying miles. What an act of endurance; what an act of intelligent orientation; what a display of managerial ability. Of course our subject has other great successes, such as 'Dax My Girl', who arrived on the second day after covering 687 miles to score 4th place in all of England, and a one bird nomination at that. Then 'Mystical Queen', who was 10th Open Single Bird N.F.C. from San Sebastian at 737 miles and the first arrival over 700 miles. Jim also bred good birds for others, including 'The 53' which won for Trevor Robinson 2nd Average National Flying Club 4 races up to Tarbes (France), 722 miles in 2007. Yes, many more could be referred to, but as I recall I made reference to the concept of 'genius' above and now in conclusion may the reader bear with me, for it is the best advice I have ever heard from a member of our sport. Jim contends that genius is 10% inspiration and 90% perspiration. Thus the key to his success lay in the latter percentages. Therefore dedication and perseverance are the ingredients required today, especially by those pigeoners who reach for the stars and ask 'Why not?' Of course a bit of humour won't go amiss, for as Jim confessed: 'I think that the sparrowhawks chasing my birds helped to keep them fit'. What a character – what a pigeoner!

LIAM O'COMAIN

THE 'OLD PIED' REPORTS ON JIM EMERTON OF HOLTBY

From The Gazette, January 1986

The subject of this report is one of our younger 'stars' who was born in January 1949 into a background of Tumblers and Fancy Pigeons. His father kept Tumblers and fancy breeds such as Priests, Jacobins and Magpies, and when only three years of age Jim became involved with their management.

It is interesting to relate that before getting down to pigeon racing Jim had a go at other less fashionable sports, and I was intrigued to learn that he had broken two records shooting wildfowl on the Wash, as a friend of the Wild Goose Man, Mackenzie Thorpe. He is also unbeaten as an arm wrestler and has broken an athletic record. Quite a sportsman is Jim.

He got down to pigeon racing in 1977 and obviously decided that he was going to go about it in the right way by getting good basic stock. He selected two D.V.H. Stichelbauts, one direct Emiel Denys cock and a hen of Extreme Distance Family from the Louella Lofts and actually chose the first three from over 300 birds. John and Michael Massarella assisted Jim in the selection of the Denys cock from some 200 Vanhees and Denys birds and a local fancier, Jack Russ, gave him some birds and introduced him to the club.

The first fanciers who drew Jim's attention by virtue of their performances were Michael Descamps, Van Hasten and Emiel Denys of Belgium, the Newcombe Bros of Scotland and J. O. Warren of England. A really impressive group of fanciers, and I would not like to estimate how many big wins they have achieved between them.

The Jack Russ birds were mainly related to his Warren

pair, the hen being a J. O. Warren family and the Stichelbauts. Jim says he has won with representatives of all the families he has tried since starting in 1977.

In the early days Jim made the usual mistakes and in particular lists such things as pairing up too early, rearing too many YBs off racers, lacking a breeding and racing plan, sending birds to races on a 'willy-nilly' basis in the hope of winning something, listening to too many old wives' tales and training old birds too early and in terrible weather conditions. There are not too many of us who have not trod that path in the early days, the product of perhaps too much enthusiasm, coupled with impatience to go places.

He has always had the same loft, which he describes as a 22ft long aviary with door and air vents top and bottom. The birds are comfortable in it and have 'V' Perches, Box Perches and plenty of dark corners to rest and nest in. Jim is certain that the two most important factors fin loft design for natural pigeons are air space and light.

When asked to name the reason why some fanciers race for years and years and never visit the prize table, Jim said they are not dedicated enough, do not apply their total personality to the sport and lack direction.

Jim maintains a reasonably-sized team of birds, numbering some 15 pairs of stock birds and 30-35 racing birds and rears between 40 and 60 young birds each year. The stock birds are mated at any time from December onwards and the racers between the last week in February and the third week in March. Jim believes in keeping as near to nature as possible and says that although 1sts can be gained by widowhood birds he prefers to select and pool pigeons for individual events. Further, he is always looking for first-class racing hens to advance the stock team.

The birds have a semi-open loft and both young and old

birds are trained mainly by racing them. The birds are hopper-fed as well as hand-fed which, coupled with maximum exercise, helps the birds to develop, muscle up and reach condition. As individuals, the natural birds vary according to the nest-cycle, although pairing has the effect of increasing the desire at times.

Jim races in the Strensall PRS and the Yorkshire Middle Route Federation which is very large and has three sections, of which the Western is very tough to top.

The present birds are Busschaerts from the 'speed king,' Glyn Machin, and the Stichelbauts, which are Jim's own family originating from Van Esten, Emiel Denys, Claude Hetru and Roger Vereeke. He finds the Busschaerts are best up to 340 miles but the Stichelbauts are very versatile and win at any distance.

Some of his OB performances achieved over the past three seasons are well worth recording and these include 37 x 1sts, 31 x 2nds, 26 x 3rds, 28 x 4ths, 23 x 5ths and 25 x 6ths at club level. In the strong Yorkshire Middle Route Fed he has won 1st West Sect and 1st Open from Melun, 408 mls, 1,931 birds and, from the same racepoint, 7th, 13th & 19th Sect; 2nd Sect & 11th Open and 5th Sect & 8th Sect. From Nevers, 516 mls, he has been 1st Sect (604 birds) & 6th Open, 2,516 birds and 14th Sect. From Beauvais, 341 mls, he has won 2nd Sect (533 birds) & 5th Open, 3,083 birds, also 10th Sect & 15th Open, 2,972 birds. At Lillers, 277 mls, he has a 3rd Sect, 416 birds. From Fareham, 217 mls, the tally is 4th & 7th Sect & 4th & 7th Open, 5,223 birds. From Hatfield, 156 mls, he has won 3rd Sect & 3rd Open.

I must mention the performances of 'Diabolos', a 2y cock which has already won 5th Grantham, 1,000+ birds; 3rd Stevenage; 4th Grantham Open, 330 birds; 2nd Sect & 11th

Open Fed Melun, 1,931 birds; 3rd Club & 3rd Sect Fed Lillers, 416 birds; 2nd Club, 2nd Sect & 5th Open Fed Beauvais, 3,083 birds; 1st Club, 1st Sect & 6th Open Nevers, 2,516 birds – all this and still only a 2y.

'Dot's Delight' is now a 4y but has won 1st Yearling Trophy in Club in Vaux Oudenaarde; 1st West Sect & 1st Open YMR Fed Melun, 1,931 birds, the first time the race had been won in that Section since 1956.

The two birds highlighted above are both from Jim's Stichelbaut family and the details of positions won were all achieved in old bird racing. Young birds have also done well with perhaps the best results with these being a 1st, 2nd, 3rd, 4th & 5th Imperial Open from Grantham in 1983 and a 1st, 2nd, 3rd, 4th, 5th, 6th & 8th Ashford, 210 mls.

Jim found it difficult to recall his most thrilling experience in pigeon racing but, on reflection, he thought it must have been the performances of 'Diabolos' and, in particular, when that bird won from Nevers in 1985. On the other side of the coin he thought the most disappointing experience was the discovery that the 1984 Young Bird team was not up to scratch. But, as he said, the successes help to ease the pains of the disappointments.

We always ask if other members of the family take an interest in the birds and in this instance we were informed that both Jim's mother and his wife, Jean, take an interest. In fact, he described his mother's interest as almost obsessive and related how this good lady once caught a male kestrel in the loft, thereby saving the birds from a lot of fear. It is always refreshing to find such instances of the ladies taking an interest in the sport.

Jim was asked if we had any ideas on how to get the best out of your birds and back came the answer, 'Yes, read every book/publication ever published, consult the vets, nutrition experts and experienced pigeon fanciers and anyone and anything which will help you to devise and record a detailed management plan.

He races youngsters up to Ashford, 210 miles, but only selected birds go to the longest racepoint. As yearlings they are expected to fly Melun, 408 mls and after that to Nevers, 516 mls.

Jim did admit to using tit-bits and specifics, naming 'Red Band', 'Hormoform', 'Aquasan', `Aviform' and 'Old Hand' products.

As stated earlier, Jim's birds have the Open Hole and although it varies, the training schedules are fairly light i.e. OBs – one toss at 15 mls then the races; Yearlings – one toss at 35 mls then race and YBs – 4 x 5 mls, 2 x 15m1s, 1 x 35 mls and 1 x 50 mls.

When asked about favourite conditions for birds going to the long races, Jim said that the favourite one was that at which the birds perform the best and, thinking about it, this was a very sensible reply. However, he did add that he found the best were Old Hens with a big YB and Old Cocks sitting about 10-17 days.

Jim is a committee member and also a delegate to the Yorkshire Middle Route Federation and says the objective is to properly represent the club and give an accurate report to his members on what had taken place at the Fed meetings. In other words, Jim believes in doing his job properly and we all know there are not too many who do this. A lot of delegates, usually pushed into a job they don't really want, go to their Fed meetings, say nothing, come back to club and still say nothing and have not even made notes.

I was interested in his answer to the question, 'If you had the power, what law would you pass for the benefit of the sport?' It was different from the usual, i.e. 'I would like to see an honest and fair interpretation and application of rules and regulations to develop more integrity in the sport for all'.

His advice to new starters is also very concise, i.e. 'acquire five pairs of August-hatched squeakers from a fancier who is famous for his performances'. He also thought the most important factor required by a fancier before he or she can achieve success is 'the new fancier should eat, breath and sleep racing pigeons – if he or she wakes up in the night then they should be thinking or dreaming pigeons'. In other words, total dedication.

Jim considered that the best flyer in his area is Brian Denney of the Strensall PRS, because he puts up good performance from all distances year after year. He thought that the reason why so many fanciers make mistakes is through lack of dedication and because they are too quick to try and follow influential trends such as Widowhood without adequate research.

As always, one of the questions was if he could account for the reason why so many fanciers experience 'flyaways'. He thought the answer would have to be hypothetical but mentioned such things as 'overcrowding', 'wildness' and 'unsuitable loft location'. He suggested that fanciers who did suffer 'flyaways' should compensate by breeding two or three teams of young birds at different times.

PIGEON RACING – ONE MAN'S DESTINY

From The Homing World Stud Book, 2009

I love writing. There are some beautiful minds who have left lasting imprints in books. It makes me happy that my work has been read in different parts of the world as a result of study and dedication and any inbuilt talents that I may have. When my body turns to dust particles and atoms I believe some of my work will still be a source of interest, somewhere in the world.

I was born in the Nightingale Home in Derby before moving to Skegness, Lincs, at an early age. My father, a cool, kind and gentle man, introduced me to pigeons at the age of three years. Although a quiet, socially inept and deeply sensitive boy, I was instantly hooked and fascinated by the gentle beauty of Charlie Fantail and other lovely fancy pigeons and cross-bred birds.

Before long we had bought some brightly-coloured tumblers, and my formative years were spent gazing into the sky at the acrobats of the pigeon world. Soon, at Skegness, I became aware of stray racing pigeons, and with stealth and cunning caught many a one. The first stray I saw, at around the age of five, was a pencil-blue young bird, complete with race rubber. In the early years I developed a love of all things natural and was later to graduate from The Royal Botanic Gardens, Kew, and qualify to teach Rural Studies at the University of Birmingham's Worcester College.

Some time after my sixth birthday we moved to run the post office at Skendleby in the Lincolnshire Wolds. We had three acres of grass paddock and orchard and I spent five happy years gazing at my roller pigeons and walking the woods and hedgerows. From this time on, everywhere we travelled I caught stray racers and kept them in the house loft. I was always out and disappearing, serving my apprenticeship in nature. Having said that, I was also a cruel, ruthless boy who, like many other country boys, took up shooting, and later became a good rough shot and wildfowler.

Although quiet and polite, I was cheeky enough to knock at people's doors and charm my way to catch roosting strays on their windowsills. (I still call on people today to see their birds and I am normally welcomed due to my cheeky self-confidence.)

At the age of eleven we moved back to Derbyshire, settling in Alvaston, and managed to settle the good red roller cock and some other chosen birds. My teenage years were spent cultivating my Birmingham Roller team, whilst enduring the strict teaching regime at Spondon Park Grammar School. I would rush home from school to watch my rollers perform, a habit which developed in me intense observational skills, although it got a little out of hand because I would not do the homework the academics demanded. I got to know the roller men, the tippler men and the racing men of Derby. Jack Whitehouse, now in his 80s, is still a big name today. Also developing fast was my competitive and perfectionist attitude and I always tried to do my best, an attitude which was cultivated by my strict and no-nonsense upbringing. My father had been an army sergeant, but I could beat him at arm-wrestling at 12 years of age.

In Derby city centre were the riverside gardens, and there I would sit like an old recidivist and catch strays with peanuts. I recall good old Pigeon Percy, a colourful and well-known character. Catching the most wily of old racer strays, I would put them in a battered fishing creel and return home to Alvaston — an electric ride on a trolley bus. Soon, since I excelled in my chosen horticulture, I was sent to Askham Bryan College for two years for advanced study, and had to part with some newly-acquired racing pigeons.

I confess to having become an institutionalised and professional student, spending a further three years at the

Royal Botanics, Kew, and a further year at Teacher Training College, studying for 11 years in total. What an incredible amount of hard work it was. You see, I had a very greedy intellect and thirst for knowledge. All this has been worthwhile, since I am able to express my inner core in print. My study years were punctuated by pigeons, like the time I hand-reared a baby woodpigeon taken from the trees at Askham Bryan College at night. Then there was the racing pigeon I kept as a pet in my wardrobe in my digs (out of sight of my landlord).

In 1976 1 started with racing birds at Sycamore Cottage, Holtby, York. The development of my strain and my racing activities have been well documented on websites and in magazines. I enjoy my life today where the sweat of my brow has borne fruit.

JIM'S FLIGHTS OF FANCY

From Mensa Magazine, December 2008

Renowned racing pigeon expert Jim Emerton
reveals how he applied a Mensa mind to the
task of achieving sporting success

Jim Emerton was just three years old when he met his first racing bird. "My late father introduced me to pigeons when we lived in Skegness. I have a photo taken from slightly later, when I was five, and you could see from the broad smile on my face how happy the pigeons made me. I had a very strong affinity with nature when I was a boy. It's a love of nature that I have had all my life, a strong, overwhelming emotion for nature."

That introduction was to be the start of a life-long love of pigeons and of nature, one which was to lead him to become one of the best-known 'pigeoners' in the country, a reputation cemented when one of his birds, Barcelona Dream, clocked up a record 879 miles flying from Barcelona to Jim's home loft at Holtby, near York, in 1995. It is a record, ratified by the British International Championship Club, that still stands today.

At the height of his fame as a marathon pigeon racer, Jim also achieved a little bit of immortality — by creating his own string of progeny now known as the Emerton Strain. "I am really proud of that," Jim says. "They are known all over the world. They will live on when I am dust, and that gives me a nice feeling."

Jim began racing pigeons when he moved to Holtby in 1976. It was, Jim says, his competitive nature which led him into racing. And the use of his Mensa-level IQ... "I have always in my life had an ambition or dream and I have always been determined to follow it to the limit. When I was studying I had a need to excel in something logical. That was why I took the Mensa test, it was asking a question of myself. It was one of the highlights of my life when I passed because I had answered that question."

Jim applied this marriage of intelligent logic and his competitive determination to pigeon breeding, training and racing, with almost immediate success. "My first race was into York from Grantham and I had first, second and fourth. It just went on from there and soon I found I was winning a lot of races.

"I like to think that applied knowledge and intelligence in planning is important as a natural talent. I visualised all my targets, I have the ability to see the end result of something and then go for it. I believe if you visualise your goals then it helps you to realise your inner target. It's about using the mind.

"Of course I had a lot of help. My father loved pigeons and my mother, Dorothy, helped me with the birds until she was 91 years of age."

Jim, now a household name in marathon pigeon racing circles, is retired from competition. Logical as ever, he can remember the exact date he gave up the sport. "It was the 22nd of May '06. I passed on the birds to the national flying club organisation at Ryhope near Sunderland. I had about 140 birds then. Their progeny will be worth a lot of money now, I expect. Do you know, I once had a Chinaman ringing me up at two in the morning because he wanted to buy some of my birds."

Sadly, Jim says, the great traditional sport of the working man is now in decline. "There are fewer members, fewer people in the sport. But then the cream will always rise to the surface, so those still competing are good."

Jim freely admits he misses life with the birds. "I miss them, yes but I have friends I can always go and visit and I can handle their birds."

While he may now be retired from competition, Jim is becoming increasingly well known as an expert writer and commentator on the sport.

THE JIM EMERTON STRAIN

by Liam O'Comain

from Racing Pigeon Pictorial International, no 501

Jim Emerton was introduced to the sport by his father at a very early age, but the resulting strain's foundations were laid in York from about 1976. They were mainly Descamps Van Hasten Stichelbauts with a direct cock from Emiel Denys (closely related to the 'Tee') plus some 'Woodsider' bloodlines. Jim Donaldson of Peterhead's family and Brian Denney's Stichelbauts were later added to the loft. He also used a cock bird presented to him by Trevor Robinson from the latter's great 9th Open Pau over 700 miles.

In his first young bird race into York he was 1st, 2nd & 4th — surely an omen of things to come. However, he was not alone, for his mother Dorothy helped with the birds until she was in her early 90s. Under his planning and guidance Mrs Emerton willingly and capably carried out most of the tasks in the loft.

Emerton's astute mind knew that in order to race marathon distances he needed the right goods, and it was a spark of genius when he decided to base his dreams of success on the historical Stichelbaut dynasty and the golden bloodlines of the 'Tee' etc. For from this base in due course came such outstanding thoroughbred athletes as 'Barcelona Dream', who was 13th Open British International Championship Club Barcelona at a record distance of 879 miles (an outstanding racer which succeeded against both east and north east winds); 'Dax My Girl', 31st National Flying Club Dax 687 miles, longest flying bird out of 17,526 birds in Europe; 'Odd Ball', 3rd & 66th Pau (735 miles); 'Diamond Queen', 72nd Open NFC Pau; 'Dedication' and 'Sister Damien', 61st & 80th Open NFC Saintes 569 miles on the day; 'Mystical Queen', 10th Open SBNFC San Sebastian 737 miles, winning the Denney Shield for first bird over 700 miles into England; 'My Girl', 1st Section B, 4th Open Dax 687 miles; 'Dark Enchantment', 9th & 30th Section K Pau.

The loft has had the only bird in the clock station on the winning day at Sartilly YB 362 miles, Dax 687 miles and Barcelona 879 miles. Other good results have been obtained by others racing the Emertons in the BICC and the NFC. At least four NFC Section winners have been reported and other good performances from Marseille and Barcelona for others. In 2011, Trevor Robinson's two Barcelona birds at 853 miles were down from Jim's 'Dark Enchantment', inbred to Jim's No 1 pair.

The birds were line and inbred for over 30 years. They were accommodated in a brick-built stock loft with an aviary and a small back garden loft made from wood and asbestos with plastic skylights. The ventilation was derived from an opening at the top and there were no floor grilles, not even in the nest boxes. Deep litter was used and it was estimated as being 15 years old on one occasion.

The racers were paired in the first week of March each year and without training the hens were lifted into racing between 90-110 miles and the cock birds between 110-140 miles. Our subject has been known to lift birds 500 miles into races, seeking to discover their orientation ability. He placed a strong emphasis upon the pigeon's instincts at all times. Yearlings flew 466 miles and old birds 700 miles. Jim would normally have 20/30 birds and all would be entered into races over 700 miles once they reached two years old, always bearing in mind that pigeons are individuals and there are good and bad in all strains. When sending birds to Pau for example, Emerton liked his candidates to have had at least a 10 hour fly in a prior race. For International racing, 2-3 weeks' complete rest was required with no road training and the internal organs were lined with fat.

So there you are, a strain moulder who did not adhere to many theories apart from no more than four flights cast on racing. A man who reached for the stars and touched them. A man who now sadly is bereft of his outstanding strain, because he called it a day, and in doing so presented gems of the fancy into the care of secretary of the National Flying Club Sid Barkel. Jim is surely a unique individual who was an artist of the sport and one of the best Britain has produced in long distance and marathon racing.

Printed in Great Britain
by Amazon